Ethnography and Education Policy Across the Americas

Ethnography and Education Policy Across the Americas

EDITED BY
Bradley A.U. Levinson,
Sandra L. Cade, Ana Padawer,
AND Ana Patricia Elvir

Education Policy in Practice: Critical Cultural Studies
Bradley A.U. Levinson and Margaret Sutton, Series Editors

PRAEGER

Westport, Connecticut
London

Library of Congress Cataloging-in-Publication Data

Ethnography and education policy across the Americas / edited by Bradley A.U.
Levinson . . . [et al.].
    p. cm.—(Education policy in practice : Critical cultural studies)
  Papers from the Eighth Interamerican Symposium on Ethnographic Educational
Research, held Oct. 1999 in Bloomington, Ind.
  Includes bibliographical references and index.
  ISBN 1-56750-673-9 (alk. paper)
  1. Educational anthropology—America—Congresses. 2. Educational
anthropology—Cross-cultural studies—Congresses. I. Levinson, Bradley A., 1963–
II. Interamerican Symposium on Ethnographic Educational Research (8th : 1999
Bloomington, Ind.) III. Series.
LB45.E838 2002
306.43—dc21   2002016339

British Library Cataloguing in Publication Data is available.

Library of Congress Catalog Card Number: 2002016339
ISBN: 1-56750-673-9

First published in 2002

Praeger Publishers, 88 Post Road West, Westport, CT 06881
An imprint of Greenwood Publishing Group, Inc.
www.praeger.com

Printed in the United States of America

The paper used in this book complies with the
Permanent Paper Standard issued by the National
Information Standards Organization (Z39.48–1984).

10 9 8 7 6 5 4 3 2 1

Contents

Acknowledgments

This book emerged out of the Eighth Interamerican Symposium on Ethnographic Educational Research, which was hosted by Indiana University in October of 1999. There are many individuals and organizations at Indiana University to thank for making this event possible. First and foremost, our greatest support came from the School of Education's Fund for the Advancement of Peace and Education. Our thanks to University Dean Donald Warren, Associate Dean for Research and Development Catherine Brown, and especially the anonymous donor for making this remarkably generous grant possible. We also received substantial support from Research and the University Graduate School (RUGS) and the Office of International Programs, and we gratefully acknowledge assistance from a variety of units across campus, including the Center for the Study of Global Change, the Office of the Chancellor, the Office of the Dean of Faculties, the Center for Latin American and Caribbean Studies, the Department of Sociology, and the Department of Anthropology. The Beatrice S. and David I. Miller Education Seminar Series made possible the keynote addresses by Elsie Rockwell and Frederick Erickson. Finally, a hearty thanks to the faculty, and especially the students, of the Department of Educational Leadership and Policy Studies, without whose dedication and hard work the symposium would not have been possible.

For their work on the preparation of the manuscript, we would like to thank Sandy Strain, Cindy Wedemeyer, Edward J. Brantmeier, Jane Garry, Marcia Goldstein, Shara Korn, and John Donohue. A special thanks to Lysa Salsbury for her translation of several Spanish essays in this volume. We also thank our families for their understanding as we labored to put this book together.

Introduction

Ethnography and Education Policy Across the Americas

Bradley A.U. Levinson and Sandra L. Cade

For over 10 years now, qualitative educational researchers across the Americas have gathered almost every year to exchange research findings and share ideas about the process of doing educational research. Convened initially by a small cadre of colleagues and friends across the U.S.-Mexico border, especially at the University of New Mexico and the National Autonomous University of Mexico (UNAM),[1] what began as the Inter-American Symposium on Ethnographic Classroom Research has now grown to encompass more participants from a greater range of countries and institutions. At the time of this writing, the group has met nine times, with the tenth meeting in planning for Albuquerque, New Mexico.[2] The name has changed slightly to reflect broadened interests and shifting debates. The exclusive focus on "classroom" (*salón de clases*) research has been eclipsed by questions of social context and policy, while the presumptive focus on "ethnography" has often been broadened to include various qualitative traditions (see below). In any case, the ongoing dialogue and collaborative network created by the symposium has enriched research agendas on both sides of the border, assisted in the training of graduate students in qualitative research methods for education, provided valuable comparative perspective on the educational processes under examination, and clarified the roles and commitments of the educational ethnographer. Scholars have learned to think and theorize across national and disciplinary boundaries, including sociology, anthropology, psychology, philosophy, history, political science, pedagogy, and curriculum.

In October 1999, the Eighth Interamerican Symposium on Ethnographic Educational Research was hosted by the School of Education at Indiana University, in Bloomington. Some 45 core symposium participants were roughly divided between Latin American and U.S. citizens.[3] Latin Americans came from such diverse places as Chile, Argentina, Colombia, Brazil, Nicaragua, and Mexico. For perhaps the first time, symposium organizers proposed an organizing theme: "The Relation between Ethnography and Education Policy." In the past, the symposium had explicitly broached questions of the "social commitment," or the political/practical relevance, of qualitative educational research. At the Bloomington Symposium, such themes were specifically reframed around the notion of education policy. Participants were given two distinct but interrelated sets of questions to ponder in advance: (1) How do we make our work more powerful and accessible to those empowered to make education policy? What risks and promises does this movement entail for our activities and identities as ethnographers? How does research change when it tries to be "policy-relevant?" And (2) What forms would an ethnography of education policy take? What are the many ways we can define and study such policy? Following what had by then become a symposium tradition, a public plenary session (see Chapter 1 in this volume) was followed by a full day of public paper sessions and discussions. Then, for the next day and a half, the core symposium participants "retreated" to a more intimate setting at Bradford Woods Outdoor Leadership and Education Center. There, participants divided themselves into two distinct workshop groups, which were given the charge of discussing the following questions:

Ethnography and Policy: State of the Art

- How should we define or understand education policy in terms that make it amenable to ethnographic study?
- How can we conduct ethnography (as research process), and how can we produce ethnography (as research product) in ways that help formulate and/or influence education policy?
- How can we best study education policy ethnographically, and to what ends?

Teaching the Ethnographic Vision: A Way into Policy?

- How can we best train teachers and policymakers to "see" and think ethnographically?
- How can schools study themselves ethnographically? What are the promises and perils of encouraging such study?
- Should everyone become an ethnographer of his or her own institution? Why or why not?

Several scholars in each group responded to such questions by delivering brief "position statements" and thereby initiating discussion.

The contents of this book reflect the proceedings of the Eighth Symposium. Several authors chose to submit full papers for consideration, and we have included most of them here. Several others re-worked their original position statements into brief papers in their own right. About half the contributions are from Latin American scholars, with Spanish papers translated into English.[4] We have organized the book roughly as the symposium unfolded. Following Elsie Rockwell's revised keynote address, we present five chapters that address the relation between ethnography and education policy through sustained empirical attention to specific research sites and projects. The next section of the book presents the shorter position statements, interspersed with a transcript of selected exchanges at one of the workshops. We hope and trust that this innovative format, while it eliminates certain contextual referents, will nevertheless be illuminating to readers. Finally, Frederick Erickson, who also delivered a paper at the Symposium, provides a closing commentary on the book.

Before moving on to a summary of the chapters in this book, we think it important to briefly address some of the creative tensions and dynamics that have emerged in the symposium. Over the course of the 12 years that the symposium has been in existence, contrasts and differences in Latin American and U.S. educational realities, and corresponding research approaches, have become apparent. One key difference that bears mention is the level and scale at which education policy typically gets formulated. The U.S. educational system is famously decentralized. Local school districts and boards have a great deal of authorization to create policy within general parameters set by the states and the federal government. The federal level plays more of a coordinating role. In Latin America, by contrast, most nations follow some variation of the Spanish or French educational systems, in which policy making is highly centralized in the educational ministry of the nation-state. Policies and reforms are typically formulated in federal education ministries, then "implemented" in schools throughout the country (However, see Ávila and Camargo, this volume, for an interesting account of a decentralization reform in Colombia.) Therefore, even more than in the United States, the nation-state itself becomes a key interlocutor, and a space of struggle, in the development of research programs to influence policy.

Another notable difference is the stronger Latin American tradition of public intellectuals and the often greater permeability and exchange between research and policymaking bodies. While U.S. academics have in recent years decried the increased professionalization of research for its tendency to insulate scholars from their vital roles as public intellectuals, Latin American scholars typically enjoy a much higher public profile, writing and speaking in venues outside the academic circuit. Moreover, Latin American researchers are more likely to take on policy formation roles when they are recognized by governments and invited to participate. Unlike the relatively strict divide between "career academics" and "career policymakers" in the United States, Latin American scholars often move more freely into consulting and policymaking roles for months or years at a time. They may retain an active research agenda even as they take on more policy work.

A running debate of the Interamerican Symposium has involved the definition of ethnography. Some meetings of the symposium have broadened the title to qualitative research, and at least one publication (Calvo et al., 1998) has chosen to use that term instead of ethnography. By now, most scholars involved with the symposium have adopted an ecumenical stance. They have accepted a broad-minded definition of ethnographic research that preserves the distinctiveness of its focus on contextualized observation and interviewing, along with the interpretive reconstruction of social action, while relaxing imperatives of, say, long-term participation or an explicit theorization of culture. In fact, in his essay in this volume, the well-known educational ethnographer Geoffrey Walford lays out seven criteria for work to be considered ethnographic. One of these criteria is "long-term engagement," yet in his own recent work he goes so far as to suggest that a "compressed ethnography," consisting of repeated short-term visits stretched over a long period of time, might produce newer and richer kinds of knowledge than a long, continuous immersion.

Another aspect of the debate about ethnography and qualitative research has involved the question of self-study, especially in the case of the teacher as researcher movement. As evidenced by the discussion questions for the second workshop theme above ("Teaching the Ethnographic Vision: A Way into Policy?"), the symposium has a long history of reflection around these questions. Some symposium participants have played leadership roles in developing qualitative methods for "studying your own school" (Anderson, et al., 1994), and Barbara Greybeck provides a nice illustration of the benefits of self-study in this volume. Others are less sanguine about the prospects for teachers, given the other demands of their work, to carry out substantive qualitative research. They prefer to maintain a special role for the ethnographer in producing special and surprising knowledge about educational processes (e.g., Bertely, 2000).

A word may be in order about different styles of ethnographic writing and representation in the United States and Latin America. Over the last 20 to 30 years in the United States, debates about representation and "ethnographic authority" have produced styles of ethnographic writing that privilege both the use of the first-person voice and the abundance of what anthropologist Clifford Geertz has called "thick description." Typically, analytic and theoretical points are substantiated through long expositions of observational and interview material. At the risk of generalizing, one could say that in the reporting of ethnographic research in Latin America, detailed description need not always be presented as an evidentiary base for the theoretical analysis. Rather, Latin American ethnographers tend to develop rich, suggestive, evocative analyses without systematic or extensive descriptive reporting. Moreover, the Latin American authors in this volume may have chosen to highlight certain conceptual aspects of their work because of the rare occasion provided by English publication. In other words, the contingency of this particular publication outlet has probably conditioned a certain style of writing. In order to let this style show through, we have tried to edit with a light hand.

Finally, the problem of translation has often vexed the proper communication of ideas across English-speaking and Spanish/Portuguese-speaking traditions. Yet at least with regard to the term "policy," the problem of translation has proven illuminating as well. As noted in the workshop transcript included in this volume, Spanish does not have different terms for "policy" and "politics." Both of these concepts are indexed by the Spanish term "*la política*." In Spanish writing and speech, then, the reader/listener must be attuned to contextual clues to know whether *la política* refers to a body of codified, normative guidelines—policy—or the power-laden process of making decisions—politics. Yet this potential for ambiguity also suggests a recognition of the inextricability of policy formation from the process of politics. In Spanish, it would seem, policy is always a part of politics: the exercise of power in the distribution of rewards and resources. The English linguistic distinction, on the other hand, allows and perhaps even encourages a rather more innocent conception of policy as distinct from the political process—there is politics, and then there is policy. Given emerging social scientific studies of policy as political-cultural practice (Halpin and Troyna, 1994; Shore and Wright, 1997; Sutton and Levinson, 2001; Walford, 1994), however, the analytic divorce of policy from politics would seem naive, if not misguided.

OVERVIEW OF THE CHAPTERS

In her essay regarding the social construction of difference and its influence on the way educational ethnography has been variously conducted in Latin America and the United States, Elsie Rockwell (Chapter 1) draws attention to the mutually formative, and yet often unrecognized and implicit, relationship between ethnography and education policy. Her deconstruction of the taken-for-granted power of the categories of race, ethnicity, and gender within a framework of minorities in the United States, contrasted with the various ways that difference has been configured in Latin American countries, illuminates the power of social categories to influence research and foregrounds the articles that follow.

Acknowledging the existence of various subcategories of voluntary and involuntary minorities, Rockwell correctly identifies a U.S. research focus on disparities that are perceived as locked within a racially defined minority concept. This agenda looms larger as racial groups, which by virtue of their numbers and their exclusion from political power have been constructed as *minority* in the United States, move to positions of numerical majority. In Latin America, on the other hand, Rockwell notes, "*majority* exclusion from schooling, *majority* cultural difference in relation to elite patterns of schooling, and above all, *majority* poverty" focused education policy on socioeconomic class. As their U.S. colleagues study educational disparities bound up in distinctions of race as defined by perceptions of color, Latin American researchers concentrate on social class distinctions. Additionally, in contrast to the United States' relative silence on indigenous education, Rockwell notes a Latin American preoccupation with policies profoundly influenced by language as well as the tension of indigenous and cosmopolitan cultures.

Questioning the existence of national cultures within the hemisphere, Rockwell calls our attention to the need to research *civility*, "the possibility of living together in diversity." She contrasts a Latin American focus on *interculturalism* with the U.S. attention to *multiculturalism*, calling for "research on how we construct diversity, both socially and academically, and how we may overcome some of the discriminatory and destructive effects of our categories of difference."

In his essay on the dilemmas of doing ethnography—a typically "slow" process—when policy "moves fast," Geoffrey Walford (Chapter 2) speaks perhaps most directly to the themes of this book. Using his own recent work as an example, Walford discusses how to design and conduct educational ethnography in ways that can make impacts on policy but also question what policy is and how it operates. Walford makes a crucial point when he says that the "idea that some people are 'policymakers' while others implement 'policy' simply does not hold." Drawing on Stephen Ball's distinction between "policy as discourse" and "policy as text," Walford argues for a kind of "compressed ethnography," perhaps best conducted by experienced ethnographers with more political clout, which can make progressive contributions to the policy process. "Policy as discourse" refers to the languages and ideologies circulating in society that are also embedded in policies; discourse sets certain parameters on what can be thought, imagined, and done. "Policy as text," on the other hand, refers to the multiple local readings and appropriations that can always be made of discourse-based policies, even within the parameters and constraints such discourse establishes. Policy-oriented ethnography, Walford contends, must examine contributions that could be made to either one of these senses of policy. Walford briefly relates his experience with two separate ethnographic projects, one on the "City Technology Colleges" in Britain, a new kind of science and technology school created in the 1990s, the other a comparative study of state involvement with funding faith-based schools in Britain and the Netherlands. In both cases, Walford suggests ways that ethnographic work can positively influence both policy as discourse and policy as text.

Graciela Batallán (Chapter 3) contributes a novel ethnographic approach to studying policy in Argentina by focusing on the institutional life of a particularly important school document, the *Cuaderno de Actuación Profesional* (Notebook of Professional Performance). As she puts it, the Notebook is an important artifact that serves as an intense space of negotiation between teachers and the policymakers who establish the conditions of teachers' work. The Notebook is a product of policy, to be sure, and its role in school life, as well as in defining the teaching profession, changes over the course of 60 years of political change in Argentina. Indeed, the Notebook is anything but inert. Rather, it serves as an illuminating diagnostic of the "microphysics of power" (Foucault). Through a fascinating historical-ethnographic analysis of the ways the Notebooks get inscribed, and then used in teachers' professional careers, Batallán is able to show how teachers are at once workers of the state—recipients of state policy— and professional "subverters" of state intentionality. Unless the "contradictory logic" of professional evaluation is seriously examined and addressed, Batallán suggests, Argentine teachers will forever remain stuck between the "bureaucratic structure" of state education policy and the full professional status that recognition of their actual day-to-day work might enable.

Stanton Wortham and Margaret Contreras (Chapter 4) describe the appropriation of culturally relevant pedagogy within an ESL (English as a Second Language) setting in a rural New England high school. They ground this pedagogy in an effort to use students' home cultures as a resource, both to teach the standard curriculum more effectively and to develop students' pride in those home cultures. Contreras designed and ran her ESL room to match the more fluid spatiotemporal boundaries around activities that she had observed in many Latino homes. These culturally relevant innovations succeeded in making Latino students feel more at home, but she only sometimes managed also to help them master the standard curriculum. Other school personnel, and some of the Latino students themselves, often perceived these as mutually exclusive options: either the Latino students would learn the standard curriculum in standard ways, or they would participate in the "less academic" culturally relevant practices. The chapter draws two conclusions: first, in some cases teachers, students, and policymakers may be faced with hard choices between the conflicting values embedded in mainstream schooling and in the students' home cultures; second, education policy gets appropriated in varied ways in practice. Their paper deftly illustrates how an increasingly popular "policy option"—that of providing "culturally relevant pedagogy"—may occasion new kinds of resistance.

Using a literary style common among many Latin American intellectuals, Rafael Ávila Peñagos and Marina Camargo Abello (Chapter 5) describe their research in Colombia on primary school culture, and more specifically the conceptions and practices of teachers in relation to the Proyectos Educativos Institucionales (PEI), state-mandated local "institutional education projects." One of the most remarkable aspects of Ávila and Camargo's study is the way that the term "social construction" has entered into Colombian policymaking discourse. Upon passage of a new law for educational decentralization, which mandates that each school "socially construct" a PEI, Ávila, Camargo, and their colleagues chose five elementary schools for intensive study. In studying these schools, the authors show that an official policy designed to facilitate greater autonomy for schools and greater professional authority for teachers is constantly challenged and undermined by older, established school routines. The PEIs become mere documents that can be interpreted and appropriated in a great variety of ways by those involved in the schools. Ironically, a policy designed to facilitate greater autonomy and flexibility in schools' self-definition gets played out as yet one more bureaucratic requirement. The possibilities for policy coherence, and the potential for full teacher solidarity and participation envisioned by the PEI, must also reckon with the many contradictory programs and interests that converge at the school, and with an older culture of "subordination" that suppresses an emerging culture of "coordination." Based on their research, Ávila and Camargo venture to suggest ways that the PEI, as a progressive policy meant to encourage schools to "socially construct" their own "projects" (read: mission), be accompanied by other concrete policies and initiatives designed to strengthen emerging horizontal relationships over the hierarchical authority relationships of old.

As described earlier in this introduction, Ávila and Camargo's research traversed what in the United States would be a divide between research and governmental policy work. In the latter area their project sought to "test a method of teacher assessment designed to add dynamism to the construction of the PEI." Initially, the authors encountered the same sort of resistance from potential participants reported by Demerath (this volume); that is, to involve themselves in projects from which they perceived little future benefits. Once signed on, however, teachers in each of the five participating schools provided the sort of heterogeneity in data common to ethnographic research. The metaphorical reporting of the data as an "invasion of underground energy . . . the boiling up of rigid attitudes which unfreeze with the effect of cultural wounds," provides powerful images of local issues long ignored by a centralized power. This history, according to Ávila and Camargo, goes far in explaining the construction of the PEI as yet one more "sort of floating project" that fails in its goal of producing schools that are organic wholes capable of fruitful growth. Thus, Ávila and Camargo provide a model for doing ethnographic research about an important reform of education policy, while providing their own policy intervention based on ethnographic findings.

While providing us with a fascinating history of "nongraded" schools in

Argentina, Ana Padawer (Chapter 6) also shows us how teachers at one contemporary nongraded school in the province of Buenos Aires draw on their own professional ideas and "pre-theoretical" notions of education and society to develop an "oppositional identity" to official education reform policies that are designed to endorse only a certain view of nongraded schools. It is crucial to understand, says Padawer, that the development of contemporary nongraded schools takes place against the backdrop of a powerful policy context. After eight years of military rule in Argentina, new democratically elected governments "introduced a far-reaching policy focusing on the dissolution of authoritarian practices in all institutions, including schools." This new political space created an opening for the development of "nongraded schools" as an "alternative project" to mainstream schools. Nonetheless, by comparing two different nongraded schools, Padawer shows us that oppositional identities, informed by a history of alternative education "recovered" by teachers from the past, only come to fruition in certain schools. As she herself says in conclusion, "The emergence of the nongraded school system may be viewed as the manifestation of a political practice, which opposes regional educational policies, expressed at the local level in several different ways. Even if these innovative projects, in terms of their objectives, are aimed at overcoming students' academic failure, teachers and principals alike are forced into situations of both alliance and confrontation with educational authorities and prevailing educational policies in the district."

Drawing on her initial findings from a study of rural teacher-training colleges in Mexico for her position statement, Etelvina Sandoval Flores (Chapter 7) encourages us to examine how ethnographic research can problematize the logic informing education policy. Sandoval demonstrates that new Mexican educational policies for rural teacher-training colleges plainly misunderstand and misrepresent the kinds of complex actors and intentionalities that exist in the colleges themselves. Failing to attend to the situated realities of schooling in rural, urban, and indigenous communities, centralized teacher-training policy often results in graduates "ill-prepared" to serve diverse populations. While arguing that most ethnographers are motivated "by a political interest in the transformation and improvement of public education," Sandoval describes the potential role of ethnographic analysis in capturing "the heterogeneity of actions in, and the multiple interpretations of, the settings that comprise today's educational exchanges." She suggests that ethnography's attention to such diversity can lead to education policy regulations conceived not "at the very margin" of real-life situations, but linking policymakers and the people whose lives are impacted by governmental regulations.

Like Sandoval, Patricia Medina Melgarejo (Chapter 8) is concerned with the needs of the research subjects "within the school environments themselves, as well as certain key figures within the decision levels of the policies to be developed." Her powerful discussion of the links between ethnography and politics points out the dangers of research bearing a priori needs for change and alerts us to its potential to disrupt existing structures without carefully considering local social concerns. While the relationship between political agencies and researchers is often more apparent in Latin America, Medina's warning must not go unheeded in other areas of the world.

In his position statement, Peter Demerath (Chapter 9) suggests that ethnographers who wish to have more of a policy impact with their research need to more deliberately apply the "perspective taking" inherent in the ethnographic sensibility itself to the relationship between ethnographer and practitioner-policymaker. Demerath suggests ways to navigate the "tension" between producing research to enable forceful policy impacts and maintaining the complexities and contingencies of our research findings. Noting the need for ethnographers in particular to understand informants' epistemology, local needs, and perceptions of the utility of research, he enlivens his discussion by referring to data from a comparative study of student culture and academic engagement in a suburban and an urban school. A major issue among informant gatekeepers was the past history of university-sponsored research in the schools, a relationship that one principal graphically described as fostering a resolve not to "pimp" the people entrusted to his care.

Demerath reasons that anthropological fieldwork, carried out "in the stream of daily life, and anchored in the notion of *participation*," naturally demands a "problem-based methodology" (Robinson, 1998). He argues that researchers should not only "partner with local schools to help them achieve their improvement goals," but be willing to take on roles such as advocating in policy arenas. Not denying the need for researchers to identify issues in need of study, he suggests that multifocal research, which aligns research questions with local concerns, will benefit from the focus of a new lens on identified problems in educational practice and policy.

During the second workshop discussion, Barbara Greybeck (Chapter 11) shared a wonderful example of reflexive research and teaching, as she reframed the question of "How can we best train teachers and policymakers to 'see' and 'think' ethnographically?" Here we include her expanded statement. Describing the investigation of her own teaching practices and policies in the classroom through systematic ethnographic attention, she proposes the value of such action research for the transformation of "prior beliefs about human development, learning, and social interaction." Her reflective study of teaching and learning in a community college remedial reading course reveals the power of initial assumptions to hold back the success of some students, particularly English as a Second Language learners. Greybeck ends with a call for practicing teachers to explicitly examine whether practices based upon "good intentions" tied to faulty assumptions are holding back student success. She also shows us how it is possible to enact new kinds of teaching practices and policies in the classroom after systematic ethnographic attention.

Finally, the Brazilian educator Isabela Cabral Félix de Sousa (Chapter 12) brought to the second workshop discussion responses to each of the questions posed for the Interamerican Symposium. Among her responses is a proposal to use ethnography "as a device for understanding culture with the objective to exert social control and influence policy." Such use has long been a part of teacher training in Latin America and echoes developments in the United States such as Luís Moll's (1992) *funds of knowledge* work, and Ann Nihlen's (1992) use of ethnography in teacher education at the University of New Mexico (see also Anderson et al., 1994). After providing a brief review of the literature on the development and reduction of prejudice, Cabral suggests a teacher-training course to introduce potential educators to the dynamics of social class and minority status reproduction, and then to turn to an examination of self. She also proposes some ways that ethnographic research can serve to raise the consciousness of education policymakers.

NOTES

1. The core group of initial participants included Juan Fidel Zorrilla, Mario Rueda, Miguel Angel Campos, Gabriela Delgado, and Beatriz Calvo in Mexico; Gary Anderson, Kathryn Herr, Guillermina Engelbrecht, and Ann Nihlen in New Mexico.

2. The first two meetings in Mexico City, in 1989 and 1991, resulted in substantial edited volumes published mostly in Spanish, with some English contributions (Rueda, Delgado, and Campos, 1991; Rueda and Campos, 1992). Then, in 1992, the meeting was held for the first time in the United States—in Albuquerque, New Mexico. Subsequent meetings were convened in Costa Rica, again in Mexico City, Ciudad Juárez, Mexico, and Guadalajara, Mexico. Another bilingual edited volume appeared in 1994 (Rueda, Delgado, and Jacobo, 1994), while the most recent symposium volume was published through agreement between the University of New Mexico Press and the press of the Universidad Autónoma de Ciudad Juárez (Calvo, Delgado, and Rueda, 1998). Yet another edited volume, in English, mainly grew out of the network of researchers initially brought together through the symposium (Anderson and Montero-Sieburth, 1997).

3. The participants included a "non-American," the well-known British ethnographer, Geoffrey Walford, who we affectionately came to consider the welcome intruder from the Old Empire.

4. Lysa Salsbury was the translator of the essays by Batallán, Sandoval, and Medina; she also revised previous translations of papers by Padawer, and Ávila and Camargo.

REFERENCES

Anderson, G., Herr, K., and Nihlen, A. (1994). *Studying your own school: An educator's guide to qualitative practitioner research*. Thousand Oaks, CA: Corwin.

Anderson, G., and Montero-Sieburth, M. (Eds.). (1997). *Qualitative educational research in Latin America: The struggle for a new paradigm*. New York: Garland.

Bertely Busquets, María. (2000). *Conociendo nuestras escuelas: Un acercamiento etnográfico a la cultura escolar*. Mexico City: Paidós.

Calvo, B., Delgado, G., and Rueda, M. (Eds.). (1998). *Nuevos paradigmas, compromisos renovados: Experiencias cualitativas en el estudio de la educación*. Ciudad Juárez, Chihuahua: Universidad Autónoma de Ciudad Juárez and University of New Mexico Press.

Halpin, D., and Troyna, B. (Eds.). (1994). *Researching education policy: Ethical and methodological issues*. London: Falmer.

Moll, Luís M. (1992). Funds of knowledge for teaching: Using a qualitative approach to connect homes and classrooms. *Theory-into-Practice* 31(1), 132–141.

Nihlen, Ann S. (1992). Schools as centers for reflection and inquiry: Research for teacher empowerment. Paper presented at the Annual Meeting of the American Educational Research Association, San Francisco, CA, April 20–24.

Robinson, V. (1998). Methodology and the research-practice gap. *Educational Researcher* 28(7), 4–14.

Rueda, M., and Campos, M.A. (Eds.). (1992). *Investigación etnográfica en educación*. Mexico City: UNAM.

Rueda, M., Delgado, G., and Campos, M.A. (Eds.). (1991). *El aula universitaria: Aproximaciones metodológicas*. Mexico City: UNAM.

Rueda, M., Delgado, G., and Jacobo, Z. (Eds.). (1994). *La etnografía en educación: Panorama, práctica, y problemas*. Mexico City: CISE/UNAM.

Shore, C., and Wright, S. (Eds.). (1997). *Anthropology of policy: Critical perspectives on governance and power*. London: Routledge.

Sutton, M., and Levinson, B.A.U. (Eds.). (2001). *Policy as practice: Toward a comparative sociocultural analysis of educational policy*. Stamford, CT: Ablex.

Walford, G. (ed.). (1994). *Researching the powerful in education*. London: University College of London Press.

Part I

Looking Across Borders

Chapter 1

Constructing Diversity and Civility in the United States and Latin America: Implications for Ethnographic Educational Research

Elsie Rockwell

SOCIAL CATEGORIES AND RESEARCH ON DIFFERENCE

I will begin by recalling a few things that by now are evident in our trade as educational ethnographers. Difference is not inherent to the social order, it is socially constructed. Difference has a history, just as sameness has a history. Difference changes with changing circumstances. It is now well known that the category "white" has not always included the same "coloring" (no one is actually white, in fact);[1] likewise, being Indian, or being an immigrant, or being a citizen, have not always meant the same thing.

Social categories, once constructed, render certain differences *visible*, while others remain *invisible*, as Rosaldo (1989) so clearly argued. Collectivities—from gangs to social classes to ethnic groups—are not given facts of society; their identities are not essential cultural traits, but rather products of social construction. Their emergence is a process, an achievement. Collectivities are made visible, or kept invisible, by many sorts of public discourses and everyday practices. However, categories made visible through policy and discourse often mask alternative identities and conceal internal differences.

Social categories influence research. The analytic categories used to construct ethnographic texts are not autonomous; they are rooted in the societies in which they are first used, and they reflect actual ways of constructing difference in those societies. Thus, research categories favored in each country tend to reflect the social history of these countries and do not always bear the same meaning in other lands. These categories also hide some of the underlying dimensions of those very societies in which they emerge. In this vein, I will trace some of the ways of constructing difference—particularly in educational research—in Latin America and in the United States. My aim is to bring our mutual understanding closer without losing sight of the particular histories that separate these regions (Rockwell, 1998).

CONSTRUCTING THE DISCOURSE AND REALITY OF MINORITIES

When we—as educational researchers in Latin America—began reading ethnographies of education produced in the United States during the 1970s and 1980s, we were struck by certain themes. One of the basic categories in this research was "minorities." Minorities were defined through evident social boundaries: in the case of "blacks" and "Indians," internal boundaries surrounded ghettos and reservations; in the case of immigrants, highly controlled national borders rendered certain groups illegal or problematic. Educational processes, particularly school failure, were often explained in the literature on the basis of this construct. "Minority cultures" were seen to be incompatible with the "mainstream" cultural patterns that presumably characterized public schools, and this conflict was considered a cause of low achievement. The theory of minority difference evolved, and over the years ethnographic research in the United States has developed a clearer view of what exactly happens with "minorities" in schools and, moreover, how such minorities are produced in the first place.

Two relatively early voices were significant in this history. After closely examining interactions in educational settings, Fred Erickson (1987) concluded that it was not cultural difference per se that caused poor achievement, but rather it was the micropolitical uses of difference that led to failure in schools. Such uses included, on the one hand, discriminatory practices linked to labeling children as different and, on the other hand, resistance expressed through the self-assertion of cultural differences. From another angle, John Ogbu (1987) distinguished *voluntary immigrants*, who had come to the country with a view to upward mobility, from *involuntary minorities*, who were well aware that their history of oppression had condemned them to a position in society that could not be overcome through schooling alone. Each group, he posited, would react to schooling in a radically different manner, one seeking assimilation and the other resisting the false promise of advancement.

Recent texts have elaborated this distinction, though the overriding concept continues to be that of *minorities* (Ogbu and Simmons, 1998). Margaret Gibson (1997) offered a finer classification that includes economic immigrants, political refugees, illegal aliens, guest workers, and immigrants from former colonies, and has extended the discussion to analogous processes occurring in European states. She has further examined internal variability, in terms of gender and generation, and above all urged us to ponder the overriding force of asymmetrical power relationship between the different groups and majority sectors and institutions in order to explain the destiny of the young in schools in the United States. Two points may be noted here, however. At a local level—Los Angeles, for example—Hispanic minorities are fast becoming demographic *majorities*, as Genevieve Patthey-Chavez (1993) and others have pointed out, though Hispanics are still a clear minority in the broader national purview. Second, studies of migration have begun to challenge the concept of national borders in defining relevant populations, and thus one might also view some *minorities* as part of larger transnational *majorities*.

The recent discussion of the different types of minorities in the United States has curiously tended to leave out Native Americans. Treated as a case apart, circumscribed to reservation life, these groups are hardly considered in the scheme centered on the problems of inner city schooling. This absence is particularly significant, as we shall see, from the viewpoint of the rest of the hemisphere.

The notion of *minorities*, the very term, seemed foreign to a Latin American perspective.[2] First of all, the region was witnessing massive school failure, rather than problems with minorities. We were observing *majority* exclusion from schooling, *majority* cultural difference in relation to elite patterns of schooling, and above all, *majority* poverty and oppression. This perception forced upon us the central issue of *class difference*, initially precluding other issues, such as those of race, ethnicity, and gender.

Second, the political heritage of the French notion of *laicité* was very strong in Latin American educational systems. The doctrine stressed *equal* education for all, based on merit alone, and mandated neutrality; educators were to be blind to all distinctions among students. This tradition made educational researchers in Latin America reluctant to single out populations on the basis of ethnic and racial characteristics. Its effects on the cultures of schooling can be clearly seen in ethnographic research done in Mexico (see, for example, Czarny, 1997; Levinson, 2001). The only exceptions, as we shall see, were certain indigenous populations. Schooling, of course, was never actually blind to cultural and racial difference; however, the distinctions were generally not openly institutionalized, but rather played out in covert ways.

Third, the construction of difference in terms of *racial and cultural minorities* ran counter to the tendency to view Latin America as the land of *mestizaje* ("racial mixing"). The biological and cultural mixture—the new "cosmic race," as the Mexican educator Vasconcelos named it—was deemed capable of overcoming the limitations of the antecedent races and cultures. Extensive intermarriage in many regions of Latin America was practiced among European colonists, the indigenous population, and the population of African descent.[3] In contrast, in the United States, populations considered "colored" were generally kept separate by strong social

and legal constraints on mixed marriages. In most Latin American countries, all official ethnic and racial distinctions were abolished at the time of
independence. This history worked against the use of ethnic or racial categories for organizing the population, as was the pattern in the United
States, and made credible the ideology of *mestizaje*.

In Latin America, other concepts were available to study social difference. Some of these matched our perceptions of what occurred in schools.
Of course, any scheme risks overgeneralizing across regions, in what is an
extremely varied part of the world, yet some features seemed constant. I
will begin with an early typology, proposed by the Brazilian anthropologist
Darcy Ribeiro, to mark the contrast with the U.S. emphasis on minorities.
Ribeiro (1972) identified three groups for all of America:

- *Pueblos testimonio*, or testimonial peoples, the indigenous or native Americans,
  that mark particularly Mexico, Central America, and the Andean countries—
  Ecuador, Peru, and Bolivia.
- *Pueblos trasplantados*, or transplanted peoples, including Anglo-Americans, on
  the one hand, and the majority populations of Uruguay, Argentina, and Chile.
- *Pueblos nuevos*, or the new peoples, formed in America through the intermarriage
  of Native, European, and African peoples, and forming the majority populations
  of the Caribbean, Cuba, Colombia, and Brazil.

First it may be noted that Ribeiro's category of *transplanted peoples* is
different from the category of *immigrants*, as now used in the United States.
It refers to the *descendants* of the original colonial rulers and subsequent
waves of European immigrants, who became the dominant minorities in
Latin American countries. For the United States, this category would include the majority "white" population, although in the past many of those
now included were at one time segregated as minorities—for example, as
Jews or Italians (Jacobson, 1998). In Latin America, many of the "transplanted peoples" had arrived during the economic boom of the late nineteenth and early twentieth centuries and were recruited and welcomed by
ruling elites proposing to "better the race" in the official project of *mestizaje*.

The last group set apart by Ribeiro, the "new peoples," were seen as the
product of this *mestizaje*. In Latin America, they are generally considered
the core population that led the struggle for independence in the early nineteenth century. The cultures resulting from the mixture of indigenous and
Iberian roots were claimed as the foundation of the imagined communities
called nations, as Benedict Anderson (1983) has so well documented. Ribeiro and others stressed the "third root"—the oft-neglected African heritage—of these groups, predominant in the Caribbean nations and Brazil,
yet also present in the majority populations of many other countries, notably Mexico. A few groups in Latin America during the post-colonial years

had at times been treated as unwelcome aliens. For example, early in the twentieth century Chinese immigrants were persecuted in Northern Mexico. However, the category of *minority*—with reference to diverse immigrant groups, particularly Orientals and Africans—did not become ingrained in the very organization of society, as was the case in the United States.[4]

Beneath the broad category of "mestizos," there are numerous local and regional realities. In Mexico, the different ancestral origins in any particular place are impressive. In Altar, a small town in northwestern Mexico, for example, settlers in the late nineteenth to early twentieth century included Mexicans from further south, an Irishman, two Germans, a dozen Chinese, six Japanese, six Frenchmen, many Spaniards, several Americans from Arizona, an Iranian, a few Papagos, and perhaps some people of African descent. Each family is identified with particular economic niches and cultural resources: the Japanese and the Iranians were famous for cultivating vegetables and spices; the Chinese led early trade—some of an illegal sort—with Californians; the Papago legacy was a wealth of botanical knowledge; the Irishman contributed a certain style of farmhouse construction; the Americans were noted miners; the French and Spaniards were large-scale ranchers and owned the local store; and so on. Social distance and wealth had a distinct racial tone at the time, favoring settlers from the United States and Europe. The descendents of these settlers have fully intermarried by now except for the Chinese, who were expelled from the town.[5] Though Indian origins are acknowledged, at times with pride, the African legacy is ignored, betraying a particular form of racism that is still prevalent in the region. Toward the end of the twentieth century, the town became a port of "illegal" entry to the United States, and people from as far as Korea, Bolivia, and Russia have been known to travel through there. However, the real "others" are now Mexicans from the southern states, generically classed as "oaxaguitas,"[6] who arrive seeking ways to cross the border in search of work.[7] Similar stories can be found in the novels of Jorge Amado (for Brazil), Isabel Allende (for Chile), or García Márquez (for Colombia). These histories betray the limits of the ideology of *mestizaje*, since despite the mixed biological and cultural heritage, internal categories are created anew to legitimize the growing inequality in power and wealth.

Finally, I shall focus on the first group, *the testimonial people*. Ribeiro saw these as the foundational population in Mexico, Central America, and the Andean regions, where their biological and cultural heritage is strongest. What is striking in their history is that colonial societies, and thereafter the newly independent nations, progressively transformed the native peoples, who were collectively the majority at the time of the conquest, into *minorities* (Gruzinki and Wachtel, 2001). The process was accomplished, in part, through physical extermination, particularly with the spread of diseases and the use of forced labor. Most of those who survived were congregated to live under the vigilance of friars and royal authorities, who exacted tribute and labor for the construction of the colonial cities and convents. Other groups fled to the mountains and rain forests, learned to live off the land in extreme conditions, and are even now being subjected to continual exploitation and warfare. During the twentieth century, the policy of *indigenismo*, with a significant input from anthropology, marked the institutional relationship with indigenous groups and was eventually denounced by the Indian movements in Latin America.

Over 500 years, the different regimes of colonization and national domination, together with native strategies, have produced very different patterns of ethnicity in the present. The nineteenth century witnessed various processes of "reindianization," as native populations reclaimed ethnic identities and collective rights (Reina, 1997). There are groups in the Amazon region whose trajectory may be closer to that of native peoples in the United States and Canada than to the patterns in Mexico or Central America. Other groups have gained a central role in the formation of society and state, as in Ecuador and Bolivia. In Guatemala, the Maya people are still counted as majority, though even in this case educational policies, particularly when directed through world financing institutions, treat them as linguistic minorities.

I will illustrate the process with the case of Mexico. During 300 years of colonial reign, the Native American population remained the majority and preserved a degree of autonomous rule. During this period, linguistic and cultural differences among the native groups were accentuated and at times even created, as particular peoples were restricted to certain regions and activities and even obliged to wear distinctive clothing. On the eve of independence, native Indian language speakers still outnumbered Spanish speakers. Mexico's founding constitution (1824) abolished all colonial privileges based on race. Reform laws, theoretically aimed at achieving equality, destroyed native governments and privatized communal lands, affecting the very basis of Indian livelihood and culture. Yet racial distinctions continued to be used, for example in the census data. Centralized governments of the nineteenth century curtailed Church control over Indian populations, yet they also waged wars and sent colonists in order to gain control of indigenous territories, resources, and labor. The indigenous population was slowly transformed, either assimilated into the ongoing process of *mestizaje*, controlled on haciendas and in communities, or isolated and forced to retreat. During these years, many Indian groups developed strategies of survival and resistance while creating new cultural resources and appropriating whatever external elements served their purpose.[8]

After the Mexican Revolution of 1910–1920, the government finally abandoned the category of race, yet marked differences on linguistic grounds. This change reduced the proportion of population considered Indian and increased the ideological prominence of the *mestizo* category. In the state of Tlaxcala, for example, the 1900 census reported over 50% as "pure" Indians; by 1930, the category, constructed along linguistic lines, included only 18% as speakers of the Mexicano language. By mid-century, the Mexican population was divided into a majority of Spanish speakers, and 56 official groups, totaling over 10% of the population—the surviving speakers of native indigenous languages. Census data systematically under-estimated the indigenous population in Mexico, by excluding children under five years old, and counting only those who acknowledged use of the native languages.[9] This accounting contributed to the certainty of the eventual extinction of indigenous peoples.

The linguistic category for marking ethnicity has taken hold in Mexican society so that no one would claim Indian identity on the basis of having one-sixteenth Indian "blood," as occurs in the United States, for instance. However, underneath the official versions, at the regional level, other distinctions were reproduced, modified, or constructed that combined linguistic, racial, and cultural dimensions. While official distinctions referred to native languages, and "*mestizos*" continued to use racial marks in labeling others as "*indios*," actual indigenous identity was established primarily through bonding to a community and acceptance of local obligations and rights, and might well include persons of "mixed race" and of diverse linguistic competencies who accepted communal life.

By the middle of the twentieth century, Indians were considered a thing of the past, soon to be forgotten, as official education policy strove to further integrate the remaining groups into mainstream culture. Then changes began to occur, prompted largely by the growing Indian movements in other parts of America. One of the most important academic voices was Guillermo Bonfil, a Mexican anthropologist. Bonfil (1987) radically challenged the image of Mexico as a nation composed of a majority *mestizo*, "mixed blood and mixed culture," population, plus a number of residual, fragmented, native indigenous minorities. On the contrary, he claimed, an "elite minority" ruled the country, constantly imitating and fostering alien cultural and economic models, and attempting to impose "Western civilization" upon the rest of the population. Bonfil dubbed this elite minority group the "imaginary Mexico." The *majority* population, he argued, was still deeply indebted to the Mesoamerican civilization. He claimed that most Mexicans shared this deeper cultural matrix, which continued to shape everything from habits of everyday life to ecological niches and concepts of time and space, and a sense of solidarity and celebration, all of which characterized the "*deep Mexico*" (*México profundo*).

For Bonfil, the majority population included not only the speakers of indigenous languages but also most rural peoples and many urban dwellers, whose lifestyles continued to bear witness to underlying, albeit changing, cultural patterns. Surviving in a situation of domination that wrested from them the right to fully decide their own cultural destiny, they engaged in an ongoing process of resisting the imposition of an alien culture partly by appropriating and adapting elements of other cultures. The heterogeneous urban populations, Bonfil claimed, included many recent migrants from the rural regions who effectively "indianize the cities," marking out their own spaces, creating rituals of identity and networks of solidarity, and maintaining links with the rural homeland. In the process, they create new, autonomous, popular cultures, rather than melding into a nonexistent, homogenous national culture.[10]

Bonfil's concept of the *deep Mexico* defied previous positions, both left and right, that had regarded Indians as a residual category in the lineal evolution toward modernity. It also provoked immediate controversy. Some scholars argued that Bonfil had forgotten the *ranchero culture*, the nonindigenous rural people who had populated the Northern states during the nineteenth century and who had played a crucial role in the Mexican Revolution. Anthropologists everywhere stressed the extreme diversity among the indigenous groups in the country, suggesting that perhaps Bonfil's scheme worked for central Mexico, but not for the northern tribes, nor for the Maya people of the south. Lomnitz (1992) objected that the "imaginary" Mexico was not so imaginary. He and other scholars, such as Vaughan (1997), saw the postrevolutionary state as contributing to the formation of a national culture that effectively permeated and interacted with local cultures. They built up the notion of *regional cultures*, which serve to articulate the specific and extremely varied cultural configurations in Mexico and in other Latin American countries. However, whatever the objections and arguments, Bonfil's book had laid bare the deep rifts between the indigenous Mesoamerican heritage and the dominant groups in Mexican society, making it increasingly difficult to use either the category of indigenous *minorities* or the notion of a uniform *mestizo* national culture without reflecting upon the long-term history of the region.

In recent years, the notion of a *mestizo* or hybrid culture has been severely questioned by anthropologists on several grounds. On the one hand, it may hide deep differences underlying a group's apparent compliance with a dominant "mixed" culture. On the other hand, it often assumes preexisting "pure" cultures, as distinct from mixed cultures (Ohnuki-Tierney, 2001). In contrast, recent theory considers all cultural configurations to be the product of the thousands of years of border crossings that have marked human life. Hybridization and creolization are seen as continuous processes, yet they have rarely led to the creation of homogenous national or ethnic cultures.[11] Hannerz (1992) offers a detailed account of ways in which the free flow of culture in situations of encounter among groups is constrained by the institutions of power and commerce, resulting in both creolization and new internal distinctions. Thus, differences of class and power often override or shape cultural difference.[12] By taking a long-term view, attention is turned to the multiple ways in which migration through the ages has gone into the building up and breaking down of nations. In the long run, we are all transplanted peoples, we are all migrants or descendants of migrants.[13] This perspective serves to rethink the complexity behind the formation of cultural minorities, on both sides of the border.

OTHER DIFFERENCES IN MARKING SOCIAL DIFFERENCES IN EDUCATIONAL ETHNOGRAPHY

The above discussion on minorities, I believe, shows ways in which our basic categories are socially, as well as academically, constructed. Other distinctions that emerge in research have similar histories. I will not be able to develop these themes but I would like to set them on record.

In U.S. ethnography of education and the corresponding debates, the categories that have been most visible to an outsider, particularly during the last three decades, are *race, ethnicity* and *gender*. When critical theory gained sway, social class entered the scene, primarily through the influence of British research. However, in the United States it was soon overshadowed by the claims of racial, ethnic, and gendered identities. The force of these three categories emerged from particular social movements: the struggles of African Americans, the Chicano or Latino movements, the high visibility of other immigrant groups, and the feminist movement. Later were added the concerns of the handicapped and of gay/lesbian groups. These and other such collectivities had a say—whether or not it was admitted—in the construction of analytical categories used to approach educational issues. Such categories tended to override differences of class and to render them almost invisible. As Sherry Ortner (1991, p. 169) noted,

Class is not a central category of cultural discourse in America, and the anthropological literature that ignores class in favor of almost any other set of social idioms—ethnicity, race, kinship—is in some ways merely reflecting this fact. . . . At the same time, it is clear that class is a "real" structure in American society.

During the late 1990s, a renewed interest in the conditions of labor in America made anthropologists of education return to the issue of class.[14]

A second notable category in U.S. educational ethnography is *generational difference*. The exploration of youth cultures and countercultures, under the influence of Paul Willis' classic study in England, has lent a particular interest to the series of studies that center on adolescent males and females in the contexts of schooling. Life history and biographical approaches are enriching the temporal dimension of this focus as well. This literature is having an important influence on educational ethnography worldwide.

A third characteristic is attention to the *local community*. In U.S. ethnography, the basic unit of work and analysis tended to be the local school district and community, whether a rural town or the inner city.[15] This category reflects the administrative organization of a school system that confers a certain autonomy to the local level that is difficult to find in Latin America, except perhaps in countries such as Chile, where recent municipalization of the schools has influenced research.

In contrast, other distinctions are more visible in Latin American educational ethnographies.

Poverty is one of these. Once referred to as the *popular classes*, or as the *working classes*, now simply named *the poor*, these groups are generally lumped together and further distinguished from *the extreme poor*. In Latin American countries, these two categories are the undeniable *majority*. In Mexico, a relatively "developed" country, around 70% are officially poor, that is, do not earn enough to cover elemental needs, and a third of these are extremely poor.[16] In all of Latin America, half of the children are born and raised in families earning less than two dollars a day. Whether this structure can be reconsidered in terms of class entails much debate; however, it is certainly the overwhelming cause of a differential experience of schooling. People living in such extreme poverty are not able to keep their children in school, even when free public schooling is available to them, which is often not the case.

A second category, largely overlapping with the first one, is *rural population*. Once referred to as *campesinos*, this group still represents 25% of the population in largely urban Mexico and even greater proportions in other Latin American countries. This has posed to researchers the whole question of rural schooling and of alternative educational policies and their relationship to rural cultural configurations, including both the Indian and the *ranchero* traditions mentioned above.

A third overlapping category is that of *internal migrant workers*. In Mexico, temporary migrant workers are generally landless and travel long distances to work in both national and U.S. agricultural fields, with nearly a million accompanying children. Some eventually settle in the cities, contributing to the creation of new urban cultures that preserve many resources and strategies of rural life. Needless to say, patterns of migration pose particular problems for schooling and research.

These social categories reflect dominant historical tendencies north and south of the border. However, each one also allows us to observe things that are less visible, but nonetheless present, in the other region. For example, the stress on *majorities* in Latin America suggests reconsidering U.S. distinctions. The myth of a "mainstream majority culture" in the United States may hide many internal regional and cultural differences. Conversely, the prominence of minorities defined along ethnic grounds fragments the actual majority population in a country where the only true minority is that which holds economic and political power. As noted, people grouped as minorities are collectively majorities in many large cities in the United States.

The Latin American tradition of *mestizaje*, for all its conceptual problems, also offers a vantage point for rethinking U.S. realities, where new spaces of cultural hybridization are emerging that resist categories cut along the racial, ethnic, and national origin lines. For example, children of "mixed marriages" are becoming increasingly visible, though they are often forced to opt between conflicting identities.[17] Educators are learning to value processes in which the linguistic and cultural resources of immigrants are pooled to meet the demands of living in the United States. These funds of knowledge influence "mainstream culture"—as seen, for example, in the increasing tolerance for, even popular appropriation of, nonstandard English, and the emerging patterns of solidarity in informal sectors. Perhaps much might be found in common in the plight of the children of the landless in Latin America and the children of the homeless in the United States.

Conversely, ethnographic research from the United States, together with globally reaching media coverage, has made Latin American scholars increasingly aware of formerly invisible differences that take on local significance through research. For example, in Argentina, the presence of new immigrants from other countries, such as Bolivia and Korea, has prompted research that questions essentialist views of cultural difference and places issues of power and exploitation at the center of the debate.[18] Furthermore, studies on racial discrimination in the United States have made Latin American scholars examine local forms of racism in a different way by taking into account local histories of construction. The same may be said for gender and ethnic differences as researchers construct finer descriptions of the school experience of particular children and youth.[19]

EMERGING SITUATIONS, EMERGING THEMES

Finally, these realities are changing dramatically, in both the United States and Latin America. Emerging situations will redefine both actual collectivities and social categories of difference in the near future. These situations will also challenge our vision of schooling, culture, and society. There are some foreseeable themes.

Transnationality crosses different levels of society. Actual social boundaries are changing. Migration patterns now connect the Mexican state of Michoacán much more closely to Chicago than to the Mexican capital, for example. At the other pole, the youth of the Latin American ruling classes, free to cross borders, are increasingly studying in U.S. colleges, and their education is producing lasting changes in culture, business, and politics in the region. One consequence of transnationality will be a redefinition of borders. While national boundaries are being increasingly patrolled, they are nevertheless fragmented and permeable. At the same time, new internal borders are being set up, particularly between classes, that may be ever tougher to cross in the future. These developments may both enable and constrain the free flow of culture (Hannerz, 1992).

New forms of labor exploitation are appearing in both the north and the south. The increase in economic migration is related to this process, as opportunities for stable employment vanish. Of particular concern to education is the rise of child labor, in both agricultural and manufacturing work, as it affects permanence in school systems. In Mexico, and perhaps other countries, attempts to serve child workers through parallel and multitiered school systems may deepen the social construction of difference among children along class lines, reversing the trend toward equal public schooling for all that marked the past century.

Most of us are unaware that *war* is being currently waged on our continent, since the media has deliberately camouflaged it. Signs include the growing military occupation of the rural regions (often rich in natural resources) where indigenous people live, and the emergence of paramilitary bands that do the dirty work of controlling and killing local dissidents. Recent wars are not like the civil insurrections that marked the mid-twentieth century, such as the Cuban and the Nicaraguan Revolutions, or the all-out counterinsurgency wars of El Salvador and Guatemala. They are "low intensity" wars, waged from above with resources, training, and instructions provided by the U.S. military, that are progressively being escalated to regular military operations, often masked as campaigns against narcotics. They are also linked to vast economic interests, such as trade in drugs and arms, and the control of oil and biodiversity.

One product of these wars is the increase of so-called displaced people, in fact internal refugees, driven from their homelands by military occupation and paramilitary violence. In Colombia, some estimate a million and a half *desplazados*; in Chiapas, Mexico, some 20,000 people live in conditions where schooling is nearly impossible and new forms of dependency are engendered. Warlike situations, and the use of low intensity warfare techniques, can also be found in the north, in the inner-city tension between security forces and minorities, and in the emerging violence in U.S. schools and neighborhoods.[20]

On a more hopeful note, *new social movements* are also emerging, spaces where solidarities are constructed. In the past, labor, civil rights, and feminist movements as well as liberation movements have had a decisive influence on educational thought and practice. The new social movements have not yet been well documented. They challenge our traditional categories of political organization, tend to be decentralized, even horizontal, and stress ethical principles as much as political postures. A few take the traditional form of student and workers' movements. Some, such as the *Sin Tierra* movement in Brazil and the *Zapatista* movement in Chiapas, or the Seattle protests, have acquired international renown. Other organizations are just desperately attempting to resist war and poverty. Many movements remain local and modest in appearance, yet share with others a broad consensus, such as the intent to foster autonomous civil life rather than to take over state power. They will all surely have an effect upon education in both the United States and Latin America and upon our perceptions of difference as they are reconstructed along the lines of new ethical and political cultures.

CONSTRUCTING CIVILITY IN SOCIETIES OF DIVERSITY

This final point leads to another theme of this year's conference, the issue of *civility*. Civility may be construed, in our times, as the possibility of living together in diversity. It may be understood as a basic agreement among all parties for conducting public business, including schooling, as Fred Erickson (1984) argued some time ago. Civility implies renouncing all use of force, including the primary source of violence in our countries to-day, that coming from the "legitimate public security forces." In its classic form, civility forgoes coercion in any form and advocates communication (Habermas, 1985). However, the traditional concept of civility does not do justice to the processes that must now be identified and generated in order to meet popular demands. This concept is often associated with a social order constructed in a particular time and place, in the emerging European cities of modernity; it is a word linked to cities, or to the courtly societies and their habits, as Elias (1998) argued.

From this origin, the term has led to the notion that the political and social space that might accommodate diversity peacefully should somehow be constructed along the lines set out by the European model. It is often thought that those countries in America that are considered closest to the European tradition, including Canada and the United States, but also Argentina, Chile, and Uruguay, have the strongest civil society. I don't believe this to be the case. The essence of *civility* was also created, for example, in Córdoba, under medieval Arab rule, where Christians, Jews, and Muslims interacted. It was achieved in Yugoslavia during many decades before the war. It was promoted by Gandhi during the struggle for independence of India. It is found in local forms in different civilizations and communities worldwide. It is only by drawing on these diverse traditions that we may hope to reconstruct civility in our times.[21]

How is civility played out in schooling? De Certeau (1968) claimed that schools have been a space for the construction of civility as well as a space for the construction of state power. However, schooling is changing rapidly through some of the processes mentioned above. National governments soon will no longer sustain full free schooling for all; trends toward diversification and privatization are taking hold. Emerging collectivities increasingly mistrust official school systems as well. Schools are being subjected to the destructive actions of warfare and violence. Given such changes, it is now an open question whether schooling can remain a site for the construction of civility. In any case, research on how we construct diversity, both socially and academically, and how we may overcome some of the discriminatory and destructive effects of our categories of difference, will inform future efforts to respond to this question.

One possible response is what in Latin America, following European usage, is understood as intercultural education (Godenzzi Alegre, 1996; López and Küper, 1999). *Interculturalism*, unlike multiculturalism, attempts to focus on what occurs between groups in order to understand the dynamic and creative cultural processes in context. This perspective has also taken seriously the problem of the asymmetry of power among different groups as it affects differential power, prestige, and access to cultural patrimonies. Current positions on interculturalism maintain that cultural diversity should be made available through education to all children, rather than only promoted within "bicultural" programs designed for those marked as "others" and used as a condition for their assimilation into "mainstream" societies. Perhaps the effort to construct an intercultural educational milieu for all would contribute to a sort of civility that would render the study of ethnic and racial difference as a cause of conflict and failure unnecessary while at the same time creating a civility that might celebrate diversity rather than uniformity.

I have attempted to contribute to this task by deconstructing the ways in which difference has been configured in Latin American countries, in contrast to the categories taken for granted in the United States. I would stress that these categories are subject to change, as we may observe in the schools and communities that we approach as ethnographers or practitioners. In each of these contexts, the effects on policy and politics of the ways we label groups and speak of diversity will become increasingly evident. Our attempts to foster mutual recognition of educational research north and south may serve to forge a language that is more sensitive to some of the current issues and changing realities involved in each context.

NOTES

Keynote talk presented at the opening session of the Eighth Interamerican Symposium on Ethnographic Educational Research, held at Indiana University, October 1999. I thank the many comments received during and after the presentation that have helped me amend the text.

1. On the historical construction of whiteness, see, for example, Jacobson (1998).

2. Latin America itself is a category with a history, in this case promoted originally by the French, who challenged both Anglo and Iberian hegemonies in America and proposed the term Latin to demarcate a region that might justify their own claims.

3. The colonial regime produced an elaborate "caste system" to classify the offspring of mixed marriages. However, some claim it had little effect. Both privilege and power continued to be concentrated in the hands of "pure" Spaniards and the "whiter" castes. Both the proportions and the degree of intermarriage of the African population with Native and European people varied from one region to another. In Mexico, with 10% African population during the colonial period, intermarriage was almost total. See Lomnitz (1992).

4. For analyses of the construction of minorities, see Burguière and Grew (2000).

5. On the history of Altar, see Lizárraga García (2000).

6. Meaning "from the state of Oaxaca" in a despective diminutive form.

7. As cattle ranching and farming have declined in the region, a major source of income is linked to crossing illegal workers, and goods, into the United States.

8. See Reina (1997).

9. Many are also speakers of Spanish and of other Indian languages.

10. See Bonfil (1987, 1991).

11. See Hannerz (1992) and Keesing (1994).

12. See Ortner (1991).

13. See de Certeau (1968).

14. See, for example, Schneider (1997) and Tapia (1998).

15. However, this is changing rapidly with globalization.

16. See Boltvinik and Hernández Laos (1999).

17. See, for example, Ifekwunigwe (1999). Legal obstacles to mixed marriages were only recently abolished in some southern U.S. states.

18. Work in Buenos Aires under Neufeld and Thisted (1999), in Rosario by Achilli (1996), and in Brazil by Gentili (2001) explores this direction.

19. The work of U.S. ethnographers in Latin America contributes valuable insights along these lines. See for example, Levinson (2001). Hopefully, future exchange might allow studies in the opposite direction, as some researchers are currently planning.

20. See Bourgois (1995) for a revealing discussion.

21. For further reflections along this line, see Rockwell (1999).

REFERENCES

Achilli, Elena. (1996). *Práctica docente y diversidad sociocultural.* Rosario: Homo Sapiens.

Anderson, Benedict. (1983). *Imagined communities.* London: Verso.

Boltvinik, Julio, and Hernández Laos, Enrique. (1999). *Pobreza y distribución del ingreso en México.* Mexico City: Siglo XXI.

Bonfil, Guillermo. (1987). *México profundo.* Mexico City: Grijalbo. (*Mexico profundo.* Austin: University of Texas Press, 1996.)

Bonfil, Guillermo. (1991). *Pensar nuestra cultura.* Mexico City: Alianza.

Bourgois, Philippe. (1995). *In search of respect: Selling crack in El Barrio.* Cambridge: Cambridge University Press.

Burguière, André, and Raymond Grew (Eds.). (2000). *The construction of minorities: Cases for comparison across time and around the world.* Ann Arbor: University of Michigan Press.

Czarny, Gabriela. (1997). Los maestros como constructores de interculturalidad en una escuela pública de la ciudad de México. In M. Bertely and A. Robles (Coords.), *Indígenas en la escuela*. Mexico City: Consejo Mexicano de Investigación Educativa.

de Certeau, Michel. (1968). *La prise de parole*. Paris: Desclée de Brouwer. (*The capture of speech and other political writings*. Minneapolis: University of Minnesota Press, 1998. Spanish trans. *La toma de la palabra y otros escritos*. Mexico City: Universidad Iberoamericana, 1995.)

Elias, Norbert. (1998). The development of the concept of Civilité. In N. Elias, *On civilization, power and knowledge* (S. Mennell and J. Goudsblom, Eds.). Chicago: University of Chicago Press, pp. 75–82.

Erickson, Frederick. (1984). School literacy, reasoning, and civility: An anthropologist's perspective. *Review of Research in Education* 54(4), 525–546.

Erickson, Frederick. (1987). Transformation and school success: The politics and culture of educational achievement. *Anthropology and Education Quarterly* 18(4), 335–356.

Gentili, Pablo. (2001). A exclusão e a escola: O *apartheid* educacional como política de ocultaçao. In Pablo Gentili and Chico Alencar (Eds.), *Educar na esperança em tempos de desencanto*. Petrópolis: Editora Voces, pp. 27–43.

Gibson, Margaret. (1997). Complicating the immigrant/involuntary minority typology. *Anthropology and Education Quarterly* 28(3), 431–454.

Godenzzi Alegre, Juan (Ed.) (1996). *Educación e interculturalidad en los Andes y la Amazonía*. Cusco: Centro de Estudios Regionales Andinos Bartolomé de Las Casas.

Gruzinski, Serge, and Wachtel, Nathan. (2001). Cultural interbreedings: Constituting the majority as a minority. In André Burguiere and Raymond Grew (Eds.), *The construction of minorities: Cases for comparison across time and around the world*. Ann Arbor: University of Michigan Press, pp. 194–212.

Habermas, Jürgen. (1985). *The theory of communicative action, Vol. 1. Reason and the rationalization of society*. Boston: Beacon Press.

Hannerz, Ulf. (1992). *Cultural complexity: Studies in the social organization of meaning*. New York: Columbia University Press.

Ifekwunigwe, Jayne O. (1999). *Scattered belongings*. New York: Routledge.

Jacobson, Matthew Frye. (1998). *Whiteness of a different color: European immigrants and the alchemy of race*. Cambridge, MA: Harvard University Press.

Keesing, Roger M. (1994). Theories of culture revisited. In Robert Borofsky (Ed.), *Assessing cultural anthropology*. New York: McGraw-Hill, pp. 301–312.

Levinson, Bradley. (2001). *We are all equal: Student culture and identity at a Mexican secondary school*. Durham, NC: Duke University Press. (trans. to Spanish, to be published by Santillana, Mexico.)

Lizárraga García, Benjamín. (2000). *Altar y los altareños*. Altar: Ayuntamiento de Altar, Sonora.

López, Enrique, and Küper, Wolfgang. (1999). La educación intercultural bilingüe en América Latina: Balance y perspectivas. *Revista Iberoamericana de Educación* 20, 17–87 (available online at www.campus-oie.org/revista/rie20f.htm).

Lomnitz, Claudio. (1992). *Exits from the labyrinth: Culture and ideology in the Mexican national space*. Berkeley: University of California Press. (In Spanish,

Las salidas del laberinto. Cultura e ideología en el espacio nacional mexicano. Mexico City: Joaquín Mortiz Planeta, 1995.)

Neufeld, María Rosa, and Thisted, Jens Ariel (Comps.). (1999). *De eso no se habla: Los usos de la diversidad sociocultural en la escuela.* Buenos Aires: Editorial Universitaria de Buenos Aires.

Ogbu, John U. (1987). Variability in minority school performance: A problem in search of an explanation. *Anthropology and Education Quarterly* 18(4), 318–334.

Ogbu, John U., and Simmons, Herbert D. (1998). Voluntary and involuntary minorities: A cultural-ecological theory of school performance with some implications for education. *Anthropology and Education Quarterly* 29(2), 155–188.

Ohnuki-Tierney, Emiko. (2001). Historicization of the culture concept. *History and Anthropology* 12(3), 213–254.

Ortner, Sherry. (1991). Preliminary notes on class and culture. In Richard Fox (Ed.), *Recapturing anthropology: Working in the present.* Santa Fe, NM: School of American Research Press, pp. 163–190.

Patthey-Chavez, Genevieve. (1993). High school as an arena for cultural conflict and acculturation for Latino Angelinos. *Anthropology and Education Quarterly* 24(1), 33–60.

Reina, Leticia (Coord.). (1997). *La reindianización de América: Siglo XIX.* Mexico City: Siglo XXI.

Ribeiro, Darcy. (1972). *The Americas and civilization.* New York: Dutton.

Rockwell, Elsie. (1998). Ethnography and the commitment to public schooling: A review of research at the DIE. In Gary Anderson and Martha Montero-Sieburth (Eds.), *Educational qualitative research in Latin America: The struggle for a new paradigm.* New York: Garland Press, pp. 3–34.

Rockwell, Elsie. (1999). El "occidente," los otros y la construcción de un nuevo espacio público [The West, the "others" and the construction of a new public space]. *Revista CIDOB d'Afers Internationals* 43–44, 121–125, 279–284 (bilingual French-Spanish edition). Available online at www.cidob.org/castellano/publicaciones/Afers/43-44rockwell.html.

Rosaldo, Renato. (1989). *Culture and truth: The remaking of social analysis.* Boston: Beacon Press.

Schneider, Jo Anne. (1997). Dialectics of race and nationality: Contradictions and Philadelphia working-class youth. *Anthropology and Education Quarterly* 28(4), 493–523.

Tapia, Javier. (1998). The schooling of Puerto Ricans: Philadelphia's most impoverished community. *Anthropology and Education Quarterly* 29(3), 297–323.

Vaughan, Mary Kay. (1997). *Cultural politics in revolution.* Tucson: University of Arizona Press.

Part II

Research Projects and Interpretation

Chapter 2

When Policy Moves Fast, How Long Can Ethnography Take?

Geoffrey Walford

THE CURRENT CONTEXT

Within the United Kingdom questions about the quality and relevance of educational research have recently been at the center of a prolonged public, and sometimes acrimonious, debate. This debate is far from being isolated to the United Kingdom, as it was two major reports from CERI and from Australia that originally sparked the concern (Australian Research Council, 1992; CERI, 1995; see also Rudduck, 1998). These reports led the British Economic and Social Research Council to commission two reports that reviewed "the position of research into education in the United Kingdom with a view to increasing the Council's knowledge of the particular problems facing educational research and its development over the next decade" (ESRC, 1993) and that considered the educational organization and management of research (Ranson, 1995a) (see also Gray, 1998; Ranson, 1998).

A further "strategic review of educational research" was commissioned by the Leverhulme Trust and conducted by David Hargreaves and Michael Beveridge (1995), and a sustained critique of educational research was launched in 1996 by David Hargreaves in a much publicized speech given at the annual Teacher Training Agency conference. In that lecture he argued that much educational research was irrelevant to the needs of teachers and policymakers. He called for an end to

second-rate educational research which does not make a serious contribution to fundamental theory or knowledge; which is irrelevant to practice; which is uncoordinated with any preceding or follow-up research; and which clutters up academic journals that virtually nobody reads. (Hargreaves, 1996, p. 7)

This contribution was influential and much debated (Hammersley, 1997). The intervention was indirectly responsible for two further highly critical and contentious studies of the educational research literature (Hillage et al., 1998; Tooley and Darby, 1998), which have themselves been the subject of considerable criticism. But the result of this critique and debate is that the Labor government has been led to emphasize the need for educational research to have relevance for teachers, policymakers, and others involved in educational practice. This has become linked to the call for teaching to be a "research-based profession" (Davies, 1999) and to increasing pressure from government and other research funders for researchers to justify their activities in more directly instrumental ways.

Most of the discussion about the relevance of educational research has been cast in terms of the potentially direct influence on teaching and learning. Teachers are seen as the primary "customers" for research and the expectation is largely the rather crude one that research should help teachers by showing "what works" in the classroom. Other potential "customers" for research are less in evidence, but it has been recognized that the results of some educational research might also be beneficial to "policymakers." It is within this context that a consideration of the relations between ethnography and education policy is crucially timely. I would certainly not wish to argue that all ethnographic research should strive to be of direct benefit to policymakers, but in this chapter I wish to explore the extent to which it might be possible for some ethnographic studies to have a more direct impact on policy.

THE NATURE OF POLICYMAKING

Before examining two examples where I have attempted in different ways to link ethnography and policy, it is necessary to discuss the concept of policy and policymaking. It is far from straightforward. There has now been considerable empirical and theoretical work on the nature of policy development and implementation, and it is abundantly clear that the whole process is far more complex, dynamic, and interactive than any of the traditional linear or staged models suggest (see, for example, Mazmanian and Sabatier, 1981; Ranson, 1995b; Sabatier and Mazmanian, 1983). There have been many attempts to describe and analyze this complexity, and the models produced have frequently been highly contested. However, it is evident that policy is not made "once and for all" by people called "policymakers." Any attempt to make change within the educational system is the result of negotiation and compromise, and even where a change is incorporated in law, the nature of the change that results to practice is often far from clear. This ambiguity and lack of clarity is not necessarily due to poor drafting of the law but is usually the result of constraints within which most legislation comes to be enacted.

Stephen Ball's models of "policy as text" and "policy as discourse" are highly illuminating ways of beginning to understand this complexity. Ball's (1993, 1994) account of his models of policy remains tentative, but he identifies the challenge of relating "together analytically the ad hocery of the macro and the ad hocery of the micro without losing sight of the systematic bases and effects of ad hoc social actions: to look for the iterations embedded within chaos" (Ball, 1994, p. 15). He puts forward what he sees as a postmodern understanding of policy where "two theories are probably better than one" (p. 14), and outlines what for him are "two very different conceptualizations of policy" (p. 15). For Ball, "policy as text" draws upon some of the insights of literary theory and recognizes the complex ways in which textual representations are encoded as a result of compromises and struggles. Along with Codd (1988), he rejects the technical-empirical approach to understanding policy implementation, where there is a quest for the authorial intentions presumed to lie behind the text. He recognizes that texts contain divergent meanings, contradictions, and structured omissions and that "a plurality of readers must necessarily produce a plurality of readings" (Codd, 1988, p. 239). It is not, of course, that *any* reading is possible. While authors cannot control completely the meaning of their texts, they make great efforts to try to exert such control by the means at their disposal. Only a limited range of readings is possible, but that range permits a diversity of forms of implementation.

Where the concept of "policy as text" allows for social agency and the making of meaning, it may be, as Ball (1994, p. 21) argues, that this misses what Ozga (1990) calls "the bigger picture." "Perhaps it concentrates too much on what those who inhabit policy think about and misses and fails to attend to what they do not think about" (Ball, 1994, p. 21). The idea of "policy as discourse" links to those of Foucault (1977) and many others, and emphasizes the limitations on what can be said and thought, and also who can speak, when, where, and with what authority. Policy as discourse gradually builds over time, such that some interpretations and some patterns are more likely than others. Policy as discourse sets boundaries to what actors are allowed to think and do. In practice, of course, actors are embedded within a variety of discordant and contradictory discourses, but some discourses are more dominant than others. Those discourses that are supported by the state have an obvious dominance in circumstances linked to the law and acts of parliament.

Ball's work, and that of most others working in this field (for example, Corbit, 1997), has been mainly concerned with relationships between policy texts at the government level and how these policy texts are read within schools. Ball's own model, for example, was developed from his work on the implementation of the 1998 Education Reform Act within schools and has focused on such areas as the national curriculum (Ball, 1990), local management of schools, special educational needs (Bowe and Ball with

Gold, 1992), changes in teachers' work, competition between schools, and school leadership (Ball, 1994). In these cases, once the policy text has been published, the prevailing policy discourses frequented by actors provide constraints on and opportunities for what they can think and do. The reading of these policy texts is made at the level of school governors, headteachers, teachers, pupils, and parents, and is limited or expanded by the particular range of policy discourses that they inhabit.

This is not always the case. In my own work on sponsored grant-maintained schools (Walford, 2000a), which were a new type of school where sponsors helped to fund a school in return for a guaranteed continuing role in maintaining its religious or philosophical ethos, the final decision to accept or reject an application was made by the secretary of state for education and employment. While the application process demanded that actors at the local, micro level initiate and develop proposals, raise funds, and promote their idea for a new grant-maintained school, the final micro and all-important decision to accept or reject was made at what must be thought of as the macro level. It was the current discourse of government that was the final structuring context that led to success or failure. In such a situation, policy as text and policy as discourse need not be seen as two very different conceptualizations of policy, but as complementary conceptualizations.

What is of note here is that the idea that some people are "policymakers" while others implement "policy" simply does not hold. Even where there is a specific policy text, that text will always contain divergent meanings, contradictions, and structured omissions. Different readers will necessarily produce a plurality of readings. In this sense, they are also "policymakers." However, they make policy within the limitations on what can be said and thought, and also who can speak, when, where, and with what authority. Policy as discourse acts such that some interpretations and some patterns are more likely than others. These discordant and contradictory discourses within which we are all embedded are thus, in some sense, also makers of policy through their discursive effects.

THE NATURE OF ETHNOGRAPHY IN RELATION TO POLICY

This is not the place to discuss the detailed definitions of what might be considered as ethnographic research. There are many discussions, and a simplified version of my own is given in Massey and Walford (1998). There, and elsewhere, an attempt is made to identify what might be seen as the minimum requirements for a research project to be seen as ethnographic, as opposed to, say, just qualitative or naturalistic. We identified seven key elements: (1) the focus on the study of culture, (2) the use of multiple methods and thus the construction of diverse forms of data, (3) the direct involvement and long-term engagement, (4) the recognition that the researcher is the main research instrument, (5) the high status given to the accounts of participants and their understandings, (6) the engagement in a cycle of hypothesis and theory building, and (7) the focus on a particular case rather than on any attempts to generalize. These seven points are open to question and accept a rather modernist view but are echoed by others (e.g., Gold, 1997). Point three is of particular importance in considering the relation between ethnography and policy.

The ethnographer believes that "observation of culture in situ" (Denscombe, 1995, p. 184) is the best way of getting to know it intimately. Hence Woods' (1994, p. 310) description of the "most prominent features of an ethnographic approach" as "long-term engagement in the situation as things actually happen and observing things first-hand." Ethnographers work on the premise that there is important knowledge that can be gained in no other way than just "hanging around" and "picking things up."

The principle of engagement by the researcher contains two elements: human connection with participants and an investment of time. There is an assumption that as the researcher becomes a more familiar presence, participants are less likely to behave uncharacteristically. Gold (1997, p. 394) explains: "The fieldworker uses face-to-face relationships with informants as the fundamental way of demonstrating to them that he or she is there to learn about their lives without passing judgment on them." The idea is that participants "perform" less and that as trust builds they reveal more details of their lives. So the success of an ethnography depends on the researcher developing and maintaining a positive personal involvement with participants (Denscombe 1995, p. 178), staying as close as possible to what and who is being studied, and returning perhaps many times to the field.

Part of how an ethnographer learns about a culture is through a process of enculturation, which takes time. Traditionally, it takes a very long time. The importance of extended engagement is underlined in very many accounts of ethnography (for example, Hammersley and Atkinson, 1995, p. 222; Mac an Ghaill, 1991, p. 109; Pollard, 1987, p. 106). Participants and settings are said to need time to show what is going on. As the researcher enters the culture more deeply, new questions and avenues open up, requiring further investigation. "Blitzkrieg ethnography" (Rist, 1980), where the researcher spends only two or three days in the field (and where there are associations of high damage to those observed), is therefore a contradiction in terms: a prolonged period of investigation is said to be essential for an ethnographer to get to know the ways of a culture.

Yet, policymaking and policy evaluation move fast. One of the major reasons put forward for the lack of utilization of *all* educational research is that the research time scale is often much longer than policymakers are prepared to wait before acting. Not only is there the political imperative to take action and be seen to have achieved change before the next election, there is also the moral imperative to help the children and young people currently in schools. Being politicians, policymakers will already have beliefs about desirable change and will have outlined these in political manifestos.

If this problem exists for most educational research, it is greatly magnified with ethnographic work (Finch, 1986). To take some well-known examples from England: Burgess' study of a comprehensive school, initially related to the raising of the school leaving age in 1972 and conducted just after that time, was only published in 1983; Ball's study of banding and mixed-ability teaching was published in 1981 and relates to 1973–1975; Palmer's research into class, gender, and ethnicity in a comprehensive school, published in 1998, is based on research conducted in the early to mid-1980s. It is quite evident that the time necessary to conduct, analyze, and write such studies makes them unusable by policymakers at any level as evaluations that might directly lead to changes in policy. By the time such studies are published, so much else is likely to have changed that no direct recommendations for action can be made.

There is another element to the mismatch between ethnography and policy that relates to time. As the process of doing ethnography is both time consuming and time extensive, few established researchers are able to conduct ethnographic studies. The majority of full-length ethnographic monographs in education are derived from the researcher's *first* extensive ethnographic experience—usually their doctoral work. Often, it is only at the beginning of an academic career that ethnographers will be able to devote three years to the task. After that, the demands of teaching and administration (and perhaps a desire for a more comfortable life) mean that only intermittent short periods of fieldwork are conducted. Thus, extended ethnographic work is often conducted by young and relatively inexperienced fieldworkers whose status and lack of experience contrast sharply with the high status and experience of most major policymakers. This difference in status between researchers and those who are involved in developing "policy as text" is a major inhibitor to research affecting policy. While we may well wish to argue that research should not be evaluated according to the status of the researcher, it is clear that the political world is more likely to give weight to the work of those who already have established academic reputations. It is thus desirable for ways to be found by which such academics can continue to conduct ethnographies.

A FOCUS ON THE POLICY TEXT

As I've said, in Stephen Ball's model, "policy as text" is one of a pair of models that can be used in a rather postmodern way to illuminate complexity. One way that ethnography can relate to policy is through researching "policy as text." Such research examines the variety of ways in which a particular legislative or "top down" policy is interpreted and put into action at the local level. In essence, ethnographic work that investigates the effects, for example, of tracking or banding, of new courses for 15-year-olds, or of new types of schooling might be seen as focusing on the "policy as text" aspect of policymaking. How might ethnography relate more closely to this aspect?

If the desire of the ethnographic researcher is to engage with this aspect of the policy process, traditional ethnographic methods need to be modified. Political and practical realism demands that ethnographers with some status are involved in the research and that ways are found to "compress" the time needed for the study, analysis, and writing. The traditional time scale of ethnographic work needs to be compressed such that the results of such studies of policy as text can still be relevant to ongoing policy issues. I offer as an example my research that focused on a new type of school—the City Technology College (CTC).

The initial public announcement of the CTCs was made during a speech by Kenneth Baker (then a new secretary of state for education) on October 7, 1986 at the Conservative Party Annual Conference. He outlined how a pilot network of 20 CTCs was to be created which would be jointly funded by central government and industrial sponsors. The initiative was explicitly presented as one of a number of new measures that were intended to "break the grip" of left-wing local education authorities and one designed to offer new hope and opportunity to selected young people and parents. As the name suggests, City Technology Colleges were to provide a curriculum rich in science and technology, but they were also designed for a specific group of 11- to 18-year-olds from the "inner city." One major feature was that they were to be private schools, run by independent charitable trusts, with the sponsors having a major influence on the way in which the colleges were managed. These sponsors were also intended to provide substantial financial and material support. While central government would provide recurrent funding on a scale similar to that of local authority schools, it was expected that additional funding would be provided by the private sponsors.

The CTCs were thus firmly linked to the idea of widening and improving educational provision in urban areas, particularly the disadvantaged inner cities, where the government believed the local authority system was often failing children. The attack on the Labor councils, which controlled practically all of the inner-city local education authorities, was not made explicit in the booklet but was plain from many political speeches at the time.

The reaction to the announcement of CTCs was not as the government would have wished. Apart from the expected negative reactions from the teacher unions, the local education authorities, and the Labor opposition, there were very few industrialists who showed their "wish to help extend the range of choice for families in urban areas." On the contrary, many were openly hostile to the idea. It took until February 1987 for the first site and sponsor to be announced. The northern part of Solihull bordering onto Birmingham was to have a college sponsored by Hanson plc, and Lucas Industries. A little later, just before the general election, two more sponsorships were made public. In practice, the scheme rapidly stalled. As is well known, the considerable difficulties in attracting sufficient sponsorship and in finding appropriate sites for the CTCs continued. The program stalled at 15 CTCs, with about only 20% of capital funding having been provided by sponsors and the bulk of the capital expenditure and practically all of the current expenditure being provided directly by central government (Walford and Miller, 1991; Whitty et al., 1993).

I have described elsewhere (Walford, 1991b) why I decided to try to conduct a critical ethnographic study of the first of these CTCs, and I've discussed aspects of the process of doing that research. What is relevant here is that I decided to conduct a "compressed ethnography" where I visited the school about two days a week for a term—a total of about 225 hours over 29 days between October to Christmas 1989. In practice, this was all the time I could spare and all the time that the school was prepared to allow me. But as the ethnography was embedded within a wider qualitative study of the politics behind the CTC and its effects on neighboring schools, this was sufficient to be able to say something worthwhile. The ethnography furnished four of the eight chapters of the resulting book (Walford and Miller, 1991).

The study of this one college was conducted as part of a wider study of the whole City Technology College program, but the slow process of take-up of the initiative meant that we knew that any publications from the wider project would be delayed several years (Whitty et al., 1993). The second two colleges opened two years after the first. The date of publication of the book (1991) is highly significant in the context of this paper, for a general election was expected, and finally came in April 1992. I wanted something published before that election, for I had the somewhat naïve hope that it might slightly influence the results. One of the main audiences for the research was thus "the general public"—the policymakers at the micro level. In the end, it was they who had to reaffirm or reject the educational policies of the Conservatives, which I saw as deeply damaging and divisive. I obtained a contract for the book before I had access to the college, and the manuscript was due with the publishers in April 1990. If the book was to have any influence on that election, I saw it as necessary to investigate the "policy as text" quickly and to get the results of the study published rapidly. I missed that deadline by a little, but not much.

It was not that I knew what I would find in the college itself. My ethnographic work brought unexpected surprises, but I interpreted the whole broader policy in terms of a larger thrust toward the privatization of education (Walford, 1990), which I found deeply worrying. In fact, the ethnographic work gave many insights about the wider policy that I had not expected and provided many examples of how "policy as text" is interpreted at the micro level in ways that were probably unexpected by many at the center.

It is, of course, impossible to know if the book had any effect whatever on the 1992 general election. As it was, the Conservative Party was re-elected for another term. The book received some good reviews and a little popular press comment, but it is unlikely that it swayed many people's votes. It did not even appear to have any effect on local politics. Perhaps one of the problems that many researchers have is that they have too grandiose a view about the importance of their own work. While recognizing that generally no one piece of research will alone have great influence, we still hope that our own research may be the exception.

A FOCUS ON THE POLICY DISCOURSE

If there are limitations in the way that ethnography can relate to and critique particular policy initiatives, perhaps there are greater possibilities in focusing on understanding and informing "policy as discourse." What I am suggesting here is that ethnographers should study the particular wider discourses within which policies are established. They may be able to influence policy through generating and introducing new discourse, which may then be taken up by those involved at all levels of policymaking. Rather than the focus being on particular individual policies, the focus is cases within a wider context of discourse. My second example of a study that hopes to relate ethnography to policy is a comparative project that involves ethnography, interviewing, and document analysis in England and The Netherlands. It is funded by the Spencer Foundation for three years (1998–2001) and is examining and comparing the two countries' current national and local policy and practice on faith-based schools. The particular focus is on Muslim and evangelical Christian schools, both of which are fully funded by the state in The Netherlands. In contrast, only two Muslim schools are state-funded in England, while no evangelical Christian schools have yet been funded.

The comparison between Britain and The Netherlands is particularly appropriate as recent British policy on the funding of religious minority schools, in the 1993 Education Act, drew in part on the Dutch experience through a process of so-called "policy borrowing." The research examines the possibilities and limitations of this particular case of policy borrowing, and considers wider issues associated with the practice of policy borrowing. Information is being gained about current government policy and practice through published documentation and a series of interviews with politicians, officials, and religious leaders in each country. In addition to broad issues of policy, these interviews focus on the potential and real equity effects of state-funded faith-based schools.

The ethnographic aspect of the research consists of a series of case studies of schools and their local environments in each country. Four case studies are being conducted in each country—two being of Muslim schools and two of evangelical Christian schools. The case studies selected for more intensive study are chosen because of their particular historical role in the development of policy rather than their statistical significance. There is no intention of looking at "typical" schools, but at specifically chosen schools that are important in understanding the implementation of overall policy in each country. Their selection has thus required substantial preliminary research on overall policy. Each school site will be visited for a total of three weeks over a period of about a year. Thus, I am using a form of "compressed ethnography" (Walford, 1991b) to build an account of the nature of each school and to try to understand the possible effects of state funding on the culture of each school. In order to indicate why I chose to select the schools that I have, it is necessary to describe some of the background to the project.

The research relates directly to the 1993 Education Act which, among other changes, gave powers to the then newly established Funding Agencies for Schools to assist in the establishment of new grant-maintained schools. The act allowed independent sponsors to propose the establishment of new schools and if the secretary of state approved individual cases, the way became open for England and Wales to have state-funded schools that have the aim of fostering, for example, Muslim, Buddhist, or fundamentalist Christian beliefs or that wish to promote particular educational philosophies. In particular, existing faith-based private schools could apply to become reestablished as sponsored grant-maintained schools (see Walford, 1999, 2000b).

In a similar way to CTCs, the overall policy has not been as successful as the original promoters of the 1993 legislation had hoped. Very few schools or promoters have managed to meet the demands made on them during the application process. Many have fallen by the wayside before their applications were passed to the secretary of state for consideration, and only 14 schools in England (and one in Wales) have successfully become grant-maintained under these new regulations.

The position in The Netherlands is very different. For supporters of a greater diversity of state-funded schools, including faith-based schools, the Dutch system presents several features that appear to be highly desirable. The most significant of these features are that since 1917, state and private schools have been financed by the state on an equal basis and that about two-thirds of all primary and secondary pupils are taught within private schools. It is open for any group of parents or others to apply to the Ministry of Education and Science to establish new schools, and if the relevant criteria are met, these new schools become state-funded. This means that, in addition to the state schools organized by the municipalities, The Netherlands has Roman Catholic and Protestant Christian schools, Islamic, Hindu, and Jewish schools. There are also several secular schools that promote particular educational philosophies such as those of Montessori, Dalton, Jenaplan, and Freinet.

One part of this research is an attempt to try to describe and assess the ways in which particular policies have been implemented. I have already written about the ways in which the sponsored grant-maintained schools legislation has played out, and somewhat similar papers will be written on the Dutch case. But the research is not linked to a simplistic attempt at "policy borrowing." Looking at the educational systems of other countries and observing what "works" there has an obvious appeal to politicians and policymakers, who are looking for rapid solutions to perceived difficulties or who wish to legitimize changes of direction within the educational system. If a particular policy is seen to be successful elsewhere, it is argued, it can be made to "work" in the home country, too. But, in practice, wrenching particular policies from their historic, economic, political, and social roots can result in unanticipated consequences as those in the host country react to the new implant. As Phillips (1992) argues, it is the sociocultural setting that keeps a country's particular educational policies in place, and the rather different sociocultural setting of the borrower country that provides resistance to the implantation of ideas from other systems. While it is highly instructive to examine the educational ideas and structures of other countries, there are severe constraints on using this information in new contexts.

What the ethnographic part of this comparative project seeks to do is to understand the schools within their sociocultural settings. The focus is much more on understanding the similarities and differences between the situations in each country, such that the ethnographic work is attempting to investigate and describe the nature of each of the chosen schools and to relate this to wider cultural differences. In practice, this is very close to attempting to understand the wider policy discourse within each country and to describing how the case study schools have developed within the constraints that such a policy discourse represents.

What is of interest here is that in understanding and describing the policy discourse of other countries, such a study will automatically extend (to some small degree) the policy discourse in the home country. Here, then, ethnography can have an influence on policymakers at all levels by seeking to extend and modify the policy discourse. By examining the scope and limitations on what can be said and thought, and also on who can speak, when, where, and with what authority, the study can expose and challenge current discourse and begin to develop new discourses. Policy as discourse gradually builds over time, such that some interpretations and some patterns of policy become more likely than others. By introducing contradictory discourses the ethnographer may be able to restructure the boundaries around what actors are allowed to think and do. While actors are still embedded within a variety of discordant and contradictory discourses, with some discourses more dominant than others, the new discourse may gradually grow in strength as it is used by the researcher and others.

LONG-TERM ENGAGEMENT

Every academic I know has problems with lack of time. For my present project, I do not have three clear years to undertake the research. I still have administrative, teaching, writing, and editing commitments in addition to this research. I also wish to study eight schools. Clearly this is also a case where "compressed ethnography" is again being undertaken. In all, I shall spend about three weeks in each of the schools—24 weeks in all. Many would argue that this is no longer ethnography, but I would wish to counter this with the idea that "the direct involvement and long-term engagement" need not necessarily mean that the researcher is actually in the site for a single extended period. What the present research is beginning to show me is that repeated periods of "compressed ethnography" might be as effective as a longer period of continuous fieldwork.

It has usually been assumed that when ethnographers talk of long-term engagement, this necessitates continuous engagement. While this may be the ideal, the practicalities and pressures of modern academic life may mean that long-term but discontinuous engagement may be necessary. No doubt many will see this as too great a compromise, but my own experience is that there may even be advantages to such a process. In the current study I am visiting each school for only a week at a time, but on second and third visits it seems to me that I am greeted as an "old friend." The gap is quickly restored and the fieldwork proceeds. Indeed, it is almost as if I had been there for longer than a week on the previous occasions and not as if this was simply the second or third week of an ethnographic study. It is still too early in the research to make any clear statements about this, but it seems that the fact that I have a "long-term engagement" is important in its own right—even though I have not been in continuous contact with each school between visits. The time you have "known" someone may be as important as the continuity of knowing.

With our increased individual geographical mobility, many of us now have friends who we see only irregularly and infrequently, yet with whom we can easily reestablish a deep and trusting relationship. When we meet, we are quickly able to enter into that relationship again, update ourselves on what has happened during the gap, and move the relationship forward. I would suggest that a similar process can happen with intermittent compressed ethnographic visits. Indeed, the absences may well actually improve the quality of the data generated, as those involved in the school see a need to update the researcher on what they believe has changed during the absence. Data generation thus has a genuine purpose that makes sense to those involved, and the researcher almost automatically receives multiple perspectives from the various actors involved. Continuous involvement may actually have the disadvantage that the actors see no need to give an account of their perspectives as the researcher has "been there all the time."

CONCLUSION

There is currently great concern that educational research should relate more closely to practice. Issues related to time provide problems for all forms of educational research but are a particular inhibitor for ethnographic work. I would not wish to argue that all ethnographic research should be policy oriented, but it is worth considering how some studies might be focused such that they more directly relate to policy.

I have argued that insights can be gained into dilemmas of time by considering the nature of ethnographic study in relation to two theoretical ways of examining policy—policy as text and policy as discourse. This suggests that there are several different purposes to which ethnographic work might be put. If ethnography is to examine "policy as text," there is a clear need for it to be done faster through "compressed ethnography" if there is to be a greater chance of the study still being of direct relevance to policy once completed. But there is perhaps more value in seeking to understand "policy as discourse." This involves a focus on the wider cultural and discursive influences on policymaking and may result in influencing the process of policymaking through developing and extending educational discourse.

Both ways of relating to policy may require compressed ethnography, but it is suggested that traditional ideas of continuous long-term engagement with fieldwork sites may be usefully modified into several shorter periods of engagement spread over an extended period. There may even be some advantages to be gained through such a strategy for capturing the changing discourses of participants.

NOTE

The research reported in this chapter was in part made possible by a grant from the Spencer Foundation. The data presented, the statements made, and the views expressed are solely the responsibility of the author.

REFERENCES

Australian Research Council. (1992). *Educational research in Australia*. Canberra: Australian Government Publishing Service.

Ball, S.J. (1981). *Beachside comprehensive: A case-study of secondary schooling.* Cambridge: Cambridge University Press.

Ball, S.J. (1990). *Politics and policy making in education.* London: Routledge.

Ball, S.J. (1993). What is policy? Texts, trajectories and toolboxes. *Discourse* 13(2), 10–17.

Ball, S.J. (1994). *Education reform.* Buckingham: Open University Press.

Bowe, R., and Ball, S.J., with Gold, A. (1992). *Reforming education and changing schools.* London: Routledge.

Burgess, R.G. (1983). *Experiencing comprehensive education.* London: Tavistock.

CERI. (1995). *Educational research and development: Trends, issues and challenges.* Paris: OECD.

Codd, J.A. (1988). The construction and deconstruction of educational policy documents. *Journal of Education Policy* 3(2), 235–247.

Corbit, B. (1997). Implementing policy for homeless kids in schools: Reassessing the micro and macro levels in the policy debate in Australia. *Journal of Education Policy* 12(3), 165–176.

Davies, P. (1999). What is evidence-based education? *British Journal of Educational Studies* 47(2), 108–121.

Deal, T.E. (1985). The symbolism of effective schools. *Elementary School Journal* 85(5), 601–620. Reprinted in Westoby, A. (Ed.) (1985), *Culture and power in educational organisations.* Buckingham: Open University Press.

Denscombe, M. (1995). Teachers as an audience for research: The acceptability of ethnographic approaches to classroom research. *Teachers and Teaching: Theory and Practice* 1(1), 173–191.

ESRC. (1993). *Frameworks and priorities for research in education: Towards a strategy for the ESRC.* Swindon: ESRC.

Finch, J. (1986). *Research and policy: The uses of qualitative methods in social and educational research.* London: Falmer.

Foucault, M. (1977). *The archaeology of knowledge.* London: Tavistock.

Gold, R. (1997). The ethnographic method in sociology. *Qualitative Inquiry* 3(4), 387–402.

Gray, J. (1998). An episode in the development of educational research. In J. Rudduck and D. McIntyre (Eds.), *Challenges for educational research.* London: Paul Chapman Publishing.

Hammersley, M. (1997). Educational research and teaching: A response to David Hargreaves. *British Educational Research Journal* 23(2), 141–161.

Hammersley, M., and Atkinson, P. (1995). *Ethnography: Principles in practice* (2nd ed.). London: Routledge.

Hargreaves, D., and Beveridge, M. (1995). *A strategic review of educational research.* London: Leverhulme Trust.

Hargreaves, D.H. (1996). *Teaching as a research-based profession: Possibilities and prospects.* Cambridge: Teacher Training Agency Lecture.

Hargreaves, D.H. (1997). In defence of research for evidence-based teaching: A rejoinder to Martyn Hammersley. *British Educational Research Journal* 23(4), 405–419.

Hargreaves, D.H. (1999). The knowledge-creating school. *British Journal of Educational Studies* 47(2), 122–144.

Hillage, J., Pearson, R., Anderson, A., and Tamkin, P. (1998). *Excellence in re-*

search on schools. Research Report RR74. London: Department of Education and Employment.

Mac an Ghaill, M. (1991). Young, gifted and black: Methodological reflections of a teacher/researcher. In G. Walford (Ed.), *Doing educational research*. London: Routledge.

Massey, A., and Walford, G. (1998). Children learning: Ethnographers learning. In G. Walford and A. Massey (Eds.), *Children learning in context: Studies in educational ethnography, Volume 1*. Stamford, CT: JAI Press.

Mazmanian, D.A., and Sabatier, P.A. (Eds.). (1981). *Effective policy implementation*. Lexington, MA: Lexington Books.

Ozga, J. (1990). Policy research and policy theory: A comment on Fitz and Halpin. *Journal of Education Policy* 5(4), 359–362.

Palmer, A. (1998). *Schooling comprehensive kids*. Aldershot: Ashgate.

Phillips, D. (1992). Borrowing educational policy. *Oxford Studies in Comparative Education* 2(2), 49–55.

Pollard, A. (1987). Studying children's perspectives—A collaborative approach. In G. Walford (Ed.), *Doing sociology of education*. London: Falmer.

Ranson, S. (1995a). *The future of educational research: Learning at the centre*. Swindon: ESRC.

Ranson, S. (1995b). Theorising education policy. *Journal of Education Policy* 10(4), 427–448.

Ranson, S. (1998). The future of educational research: Learning at the centre. In J. Rudduck and D. McIntyre (Eds.), *Challenges for educational research*. London: Paul Chapman Publishing.

Rist, R.C. (1980). Blitzkrieg ethnography: On the transformation of a method into a movement. *Educational Researcher* 9(2), 8–10.

Rudduck, J. (1998). Educational research: The prospect of change. In J. Rudduck and D. McIntyre (Eds.), *Challenges for educational research*. London: Paul Chapman Publishing.

Sabatier, P., and Mazmanian, D. (1983). Policy implementation. In S.S. Nagel (Ed.), *Encyclopedia of public policy*. New York: Marcel Dekker.

Tooley, J., and Darby, D. (1998). *Educational research: An Ofsted critique*. London: Ofsted.

Walford, G. (1990). *Privatization and privilege in education*. London: Routledge.

Walford, G. (1991a). City Technology Colleges: A private magnetism? In G. Walford (Ed.), *Private schooling: Tradition, change and diversity*. London: Paul Chapman Publishing.

Walford, G. (1991b). Researching the City Technology College, Kingshurst. In G. Walford (Ed.), *Doing educational research*. London: Routledge.

Walford, G. (1997). Sponsored grant-maintained schools: Extending the franchise? *Oxford Review of Education* 23(1), 31–44.

Walford, G. (1998). Reading and writing the small print: The fate of sponsored grant-maintained schools. *Educational Studies* 24(2), 241–257.

Walford, G. (2000a). A policy adventure: Sponsored grant-maintained schools. *Educational Studies* 26(2), 113–118.

Walford, G. (2000b). *Policy, politics and education-sponsored grant-maintained schools and religious diversity*. Aldershot: Ashgate.

Walford, G., and Miller, H. (1991). *City Technology College.* Buckingham: Open University Press.

Whitty, Geoff, Edwards, Tony, and Gewirtz, Sharon. (1993). *Specialisation and choice in urban education: The City Technology College experiment.* London: Routledge.

Woods, P. (1994). Collaborating in historical ethnography: Researching critical events in education. *International Journal of Qualitative Studies in Education* 7(4), 309–321.

Chapter 3

Contradictory Logics in the Social Construction of Teaching in Argentina: An Ethnography of the Notebook of Professional Performance

Graciela Batallán

I

An ethnographic analysis of the daily evaluation of teaching in Argentina using the *Cuaderno de Actuación Profesional* (Notebook of Professional Performance) allows for increased familiarity with the identity of teachers' work as a process of social construction. Although the concepts of social construction and symbolic interactionism established by Alfred Schütz and Herbert Blumer (Blumer, n.d.; Schütz, 1974) describe the uninterrupted enactment of reality via everyday interactions between social actors, their application in this chapter intentionally adds a temporal (or historical) dimension to this theoretical framework, leading to the understanding that the stream of social consciousness depends on the cognizance and abilities of the actors involved (Giddens, 1987).

The social construction of teaching is considered to be the result of state intervention (by means of the implementation of legislation and statutes), working in conjunction with the interests of the actors involved in the daily workings of the school system. The processes of coercion and negotiation involved in the evaluation of teachers' work, which may be identified by studying the contents of the *Cuaderno*, reveal a kind of "microphysics of power" (Foucault, 1979) within which the orientation and contingencies of governmental policies, and the practices and applications traditionally attributed to the characteristics of school life, interact side by side.

This power struggle, which involves teachers participating as protagonists at the local level, emerges as a result of the specific nature of their work as educators. This means that the power that the teacher wields in the classroom originates from his/her exclusive authority with regard to the relatively autonomous interpretation and application of the curricula, courses, programs, and disciplinary standards. However, there is no corresponding teachers' power or participation in governmental decision making with regard to the educational content and orientation of school knowledge. Rather, the teaching profession has traditionally been absent from this particular dimension. My hypothesis is that this absence of teachers from the policymaking sector explains the laborious construction of the identity of teachers as a social sector throughout the entire history of the educational institution in Argentina. Such an identity can be seen in the antagonistic dichotomy of the terms "work" and "profession."

Research carried out on the practice of teaching with groups of educators has identified a sense of conflict surrounding the definition attributed to the notion of "work" and the varied semantic meanings of the term "profession." This denomination, commonly used among teachers, makes reference to their autonomy and independence from the State, despite the fact that the actual content of teaching practice remains dependent on the latter and that they continue to demand labor conditions and benefits as employees of the very government from which they claim independence (Batallán and García, 1992).[1]

The Notebook of Professional Performance is part of the Professional Evaluation and Promotion System. This system (evaluation-rating-classification) combines the use of several different methods and analyses for defining a teacher's performance. The result is the incorporation or exclusion of teachers from the promotion circuit of the so-called teaching profession's "career ladder." Each teacher has a personal dossier compiled from the results of these methods and analyses, which identifies them as a state employee. In addition to each teacher's personal history (affiliations, level of seniority, titles or accreditations, level of education completed, etc.), the dossier also includes details of their annual salary, which is based on evaluation of their teaching in the classroom and of other extracurricular school activities usually assigned to them. The daily evaluation carried out by the teacher's "senior supervisor" (*superior jerárquico*) is that which is traditionally reflected in the comments detailed in the Notebook.

I focus my ethnographic attention on this particular tool because the negotiation regarding the meaning attributed to the teacher's task originates at the local level. The increasingly discordant criteria and interpretations held by representatives of the hierarchical strata (superintendents monitoring principals and principals overseeing teachers) and whoever occupies the subordinate position give rise to a special contractual arrangement particular to the school environment, which is regarded as a semi-domestic realm. As we shall later see, the colloquial rhetoric of the Performance Notebook identifies it as a "cultural object" that highlights the particularity of the school environment.

Although for governmental authorities negotiation surrounding the duties and rights of the profession carries undertones of labor union activism—for example, in demands by the sector for active participation in methods of promotion or advancement up the career ladder—this arbitration initially emerges from subtle and ingenious agreements and pacts made within the school environment.[2] Within this realm, "objective" evaluations are permitted—allowing the institution to override authoritarian arbitrariness and recognize individual professional merit—yet they exist alongside strong disagreement by members of the various hierarchical strata over their definitive results.

The elaboration of different strategies by teachers and principals alike to circumvent regulations imposed by legislation puts into question the power and authority that derive, respectively, from the unique characteristics of the daily task of teachers in the classroom and the hierarchical structure of the educational system. The outcome is generally the cancellation or suspension of any kind of genuine evaluation of the extent of teachers' knowledge and, therefore, of the main requirement for professionalization of the sector. We shall return later to this point.

An objective evaluation of the teachers' performance (of the kind to which professionalization policies aspire) that relates to the specific intellectual dimension of teaching cannot be carried out due to the incompatibility of the different logics behind its organization. The contradiction of such attempts at evaluation is as follows: on the one hand, the dynamic and contextualized status of teaching that allows a teacher to have relative autonomy and, on the other, the subordination that exists within the bureaucratic structure of the educational system, which assigns the teacher the extracurricular tasks befitting an employee of the State. Given the specific nature of the school as a childhood realm, these contradictory logics give rise to a permanent dynamic of negotiation, which is congruent with the imprints of family and home life that influence the environment.

This chapter considers two converging aspects: (1) that of educational policies and labor legislation (teaching statutes) and (2) that of the evaluation practices employed in schools, as detailed in the Notebook of Professional Performance (the Notebook, or *Cuaderno*). The time frame under discussion begins in 1954 and concludes in 1989.

II

Given that they regulate the rights and duties of educators, the statutes that govern teaching practice form part of the legislation that defines the so-called teacher's "profile." The statutes also establish the criteria and methods of administration that have defined advancement in the profession or promotion to leadership positions. Political and pedagogical criteria applied to teaching at different historical moments reveal that performance evaluation has played an important role in several different statutes. The latter also indicate the extent of the participation of labor unions in the official bodies that mediate in the teaching profession, such as the Board of Classification and Discipline. The following statutes are cited as examples of legislation introduced to effect change in the politico-pedagogical criteria applied to teaching as well as in the extent of participation of the teaching profession: General Juan Perón's 1954 Argentine Teachers' Statute, the 1958 Teaching Staff Statute introduced by the Ministry of Education and State Justice Department, and the Municipal Teachers' Statutes of 1978/1983 and 1985.[3]

Although the Notebook is not always mentioned in the teaching statutes—with the exception of the Teaching Statute of 1958—it has traditionally been used as a tool for the evaluation of teachers within the school system, and its use may be traced as far back as 1930. Its appearance takes on the form of the classic hardcover notebook, similar to those used by schoolchildren in Argentina. Some teachers have more than one, while others compile their professional vitae in a thick, numbered 200-page notebook.

Up until 1958, the process of evaluating teaching practice in schools, as recorded in the Notebook, was conceptual, involving, according to the format of the comments (later indistinctly referred to as "observations," "records," "entries," "reports," or "performance"), a qualitative method of grading, phrased as "Satisfactory," "Good," or "Very Good." The latter classification was often accompanied by an exhortation of encouragement, such as *"Way to go, keep it up!"* or simply *"Congratulations!"*

The first page of the Notebook bears a calligraphic notation of a standardization table of 16 points, listing the categories to be evaluated and their corresponding scores. The categories relating specifically to performance evaluation are: (11) Outstanding Participation in School Events or Projects, (12) Initiative, (13) Special Notes of Encouragement, (14) Absences, (15) Activities at School, (16) Other Qualities, and (17) Other Considerations.

The teacher begins his/her career at a school, and all professional achievements are recorded in the Notebook, which will then accompany him/her to other jobs at other schools. During the school year, the Notebook is safeguarded by the administration of the educational establishment where the teacher works. It belongs to the teacher, but he/she must acquire permission to remove it, use it, or borrow it, given that it must be made available at all times to the school authorities. Different concerns or observations made by the principal of the school and, occasionally, those made by the inspector or superintendent of the school district are recorded within its pages. Notations for each school year begin with an "opening" or introductory paragraph, followed by descriptive comments of encouragement or "work monitoring." The year concludes with a note of "closure," or summary:

On today's date, I hereby inaugurate this Notebook of Professional Performance, belonging to Ms. Laura González, a fourth category teacher at School [Number] ... in the Province of Buenos Aires. This Notebook comprises 189 blank pages.

I am pleased to record that Ms. Laura González, a recently qualified educator, has proven to be an outstanding teacher. It is evident that she has already acquired the complete trust of the students in her class, given the interest shown by the children in listening to her explanations and the respectful devotion they display when relating to her. Her influence is strongly evident among her students, who are orderly, hard working, and well disciplined. Very well done!

The school has concluded another academic year. Evaluating Ms. González's performance at the end of this school year, I am pleased to record that her conduct has been exemplified by her respect for her superiors and her obvious affection toward her students. A teacher's accomplishments reflect the success of the school and of the country as a whole, and for this reason, I should like to express my full satisfaction with Ms. González's performance and to proffer my warmest congratulations. The full range of her achievements, her almost perfect attendance, her dedication to her students' education—without a doubt one of the greatest hopes for the future of mankind—as well as the artistic and esthetic qualities and minute detail which she has developed in her approach to her daily teaching practice make her worthy of the highest commendation for the outstanding results achieved in her work.

The comments recorded in the Notebook acquire the status of legitimate documentation when authenticated with the relevant signature and the date on which they were written. The standard procedure currently in use involves the active participation of the teacher concerned who, by signing his/her name next to the word "Notified," thereby indicates agreement with the nature of the comments made.[4]

The Notebook may be considered a typical literary piece (Bajtin, 1982). It contains a summary of the basic principles assigned to the school system during the creation of the Argentine state: a mission of civilization and salvation, combined with the basic school principles of morality and civic-mindedness. Nevertheless, coexisting with this strong sense of tradition, which remains evident in the style of its prose, the Notebook is also testament to changes in education policy on two different levels: on the one hand, changes in the current educational climate, since a teacher's work is now assessed according to the immediate learning results achieved by students (a concept which explains the parallelism between the criteria for evaluation of students and those applied in evaluating teaching practice) and, on the other, changes in the role of the state employee status assigned to the teacher, which transcends the boundaries of the profession. This role infuses the teaching task with characteristics of political subordination, as exemplified by the following comment from 1952:

On the third day of this month, with students from the 3rd and 5th grades in attendance, Ms. [. . .] gave a special lecture on the second presidential term of General Perón. My hearty congratulations on her brilliant speech, which was heard with the utmost interest and widely discussed by her listeners.

The Notebook also reveals heterogeneity in the interpretation and application of established evaluative criteria, thereby creating a rift between different protagonists in positions of authority within the local school environment. In this sense, the model or "profile" that defines this evaluation process manifests both continuity with and separation from its original framework of meaning. In the same way, the linguistic formulae used in its composition, tied in to a certain number of key phrases—according to the particular period of time—comprise a private code within the school environment, further sustaining the tradition surrounding the profession of teaching.

Rosario, April 14, 1943

Ms. Lucrecia Langue

Dear colleague:

It is indeed a pleasure to be able to sing someone's praises, particularly when such praise is richly deserved. The first observation I must make since your transfer to this shift, although not merely restricted to the reasons outlined herewith, is to express an admiration in your work worthy of the congratulations of the school's administration. During your short time with us, you have shown unequaled enthusiasm and commendable industriousness. You have proven to be caring with the children, an excellent team member with your colleagues, and enthusiastic and attentive to all suggestions and recommendations put forward by this Administration.

May your good work continue along the same path that you have chosen to tread with such conviction and inspiration.

Best wishes,
Rosa E. de Escobar[5]

As mentioned earlier, in addition to its testimonial role, the Notebook is specifically mentioned in the regulations of the Teaching Staff Statute of 1958, authored by the Ministry of Education and Justice, as "necessary information for evaluation" of the teacher. It is considered part of the Dossier of Personal Performance and thus is afforded the status of an official document in which "the capabilities and skills of the teacher" are recorded. The Notebook provides the material upon which the "objective" observations of the dossier are to be based, translating to "a scale of categories and their corresponding numeric values."[6]

Following an initial trial period in 1959, the new guidelines for evaluation in schools were not implemented until 1961, establishing that "numeric evaluation would replace conceptual evaluation." The teacher's annual salary continues to be noted calligraphically in the Notebook, stip-ulating four main categories for consideration in evaluation: (1) general and professional education, (2) teaching and leadership skills, (3) industri-ousness and team spirit, and (4) attendance. Each category—along with its deductions—has a maximum of 10 points. The classification of "Outstand-ing" is awarded to anyone who accumulates a total of 40 points.

Despite the fact that the Notebook is not mentioned as an evaluation tool in any legislation or decree apart from the 1958 statute, its existence as a monthly record of teachers' performance has always been essential. The comments regarding "work monitoring" or "professional perform-ance" (after 1958) form the basis for the development of the category that contributes, together with "Other Background," to the construction of the "order of merit" (priority of position). This category will then allow the teacher to apply for transfers or promotions up the career ladder.

The Notebook's existence as a documentary element in the compilation of the dossier's contents is particularly significant in situations where com-plaints are filed. This explains its elliptical recording methods that, gener-ally speaking, tend to avoid direct expressions of opinion. Usually, with the exception of serious incidents, the administration prefers not to use the Notebook as a weapon against the teacher, in order to avoid the comments written within its pages compromising or having any negative effects on the general daily life of the school or on "the future of a colleague."

Generally speaking, poor professional performance is concealed behind the reiteration of certain statements that evolve from the monitoring of a teacher's work which, without dispensing with the "positive" style of writ-ing, merely emphasize secondary aspects of the teacher's performance. In the enigmatic code of the Notebook, the tactic of subtle suggestion or in-dication, both essential and practical for use within the framework of a permanent evaluation, translates to an underlying warning that such con-duct might limit future possibilities for transfer to another school. The fol-lowing comments in the Notebook of the same teacher are from 1965 and 1984, respectively:

I hereby declare my attendance at this meeting, called by . . . , with the purpose of investigating a situation brought to my attention by the parents of upper first grade students regarding the performance of Ms. Ester Lisio. I have spoken to the prin-cipal, who has been made aware of the situation and who will take the appropriate action. Several mothers in attendance voiced their concerns regarding the teaching procedures implemented by Ms. Lisio, which have not created any serious situations nor had any negative repercussions on her students. . . . Generally speaking, the students' level of achievement is satisfactory. Nevertheless, I have met with the teacher concerned to implement an extensive revision of her course, in order to further establish the extent of her knowledge. I have discussed relevant and appli-cable educational techniques with Ms. Lisio, as well as appropriate treatment of her students. She has indicated her understanding and acceptance of the observations I have made with regard to her performance.

Action taken by this administration. Comments made and signed by the mother of a student: I can only deduce that perhaps due to her brief time at this school and, consequently, an underdeveloped teacher-student-parent relationship, this teacher has not been successful in building the natural and emotional bond that would make her work so much more agreeable. . . . It is recommended that she attempt to control her reactions, avoiding any behavior outlined in point "K" of article 180. . . . A simple word, gesture or friendly smile will do so much more than a cold and expressionless remark.

Nevertheless, despite the unusual written warning, the comment written at the end of the Notebook reads:

Don't give up the fight, don't allow your enthusiasm to wane, and you will be successful.

In extreme instances, where "serious" (immoral behavior) or "difficult" (repeated nonfulfillment of professional tasks) problems are evident, the Notebook is set aside and the teacher's evaluation is recorded directly into the "Reports," which summarize performance, and are placed in the dossier, which then remains strictly within the school's administrative files.

III

Reflecting changes in education policy over the course of 60 years, the content and style of the Notebook's comments can be divided into four main phases, which each indicate differences in the direction taken by the system of teaching evaluation in schools. Although this research includes analysis of the evaluation system from 1946 to 1992, my investigation concludes in 1985, given that this was the year during which the current crisis surrounding the professional evaluation system[7] began. I have categorized the four phases as follows:

• Conceptual evaluation (1931–1957)
• The technico-professionalist transition (1958–1975)
• Technocratic consolidation (1977–1983)
• The bureaucratic evaluation system crisis (1984 to present day)[8]

Throughout the approximately 60 years of teaching evaluation methods researched for this chapter, changes in the use of and meaning attributed to the Notebook have been identified. After the first phase, and despite maintaining the tradition of comments handwritten by senior supervisors (principals evaluating teachers, superintendents evaluating principals), the Notebook progressively ceased to be the only tool congruent with conceptual evaluation. Its contents—from the second stage onward—were incorporated into a "summary table" or Performance Sheet, with a numeric correlate. During the third phase, coexisting with the Notebook was an evaluation process precoded into a score table and aimed at implementing strict control over teachers' work. This had the effect of increasing fiscal rationalization while fragmenting any appreciation of talent, skills, and attitudes.

The categories detailed in this table are laid out in vertical and horizontal columns, in double-entry chart format. In the vertical column, the "summary tables" award a maximum of 10 points in each of 10 categories for good professional performance, divided as follows: (1) Responsibility, (2) Knowledge, (3) Results, (4) Initiative, (5) Astuteness, (6) Quality, (7) Personality, (8) Industriousness, (9) Cooperation, and (10) Personal Demeanor. In the horizontal column, each of these characteristics is graded according to a scale of categories and their corresponding numerical values. Each *category* is assigned a score from 0 to 10 according to its conceptual classification of Poor, Satisfactory, Good, Very Good, Outstanding, or Exceptional. This system is the one still in use today.

Nevertheless, above and beyond the changes that have taken place in the orientation of teachers' work in schools, in the standardization of evaluation criteria and in the fragmentation of the individual with regard to his/ her skills and attitudes, the comments written in the Notebook make reference to three main areas of performance. These areas of observation include: (1) classroom performance, (2) collaboration with the school, and (3) fulfillment of the role of state employee (attendance and punctuality). In these particular areas of prescribed performance (upon which less emphasis is placed nowadays) there are almost always references to the teachers' ability to keep an orderly classroom and develop the morality of the children in their care. Such skills were especially emphasized and valued, as revealed in this comment from 1955:

The teacher showed up on the set date . . . and set about assisting with the enrollment of 2nd grade students. An intelligent, dynamic, hard-working and responsible educator, she has dedicated herself wholeheartedly to her students from her very first day on the job. Her classroom has been orderly on a daily basis, and her teaching imparted with the noble mission of concentrating first on the moral development of the children, and then on their physical and intellectual learning. I am pleased to commend this teacher on her performance.

The insistence of "professionalist" attempts (primarily initiated at the beginning of the phase referred to as "technocratic consolidation") to designate the Notebook as an objective evaluation tool clashes with the hyperbolic literary style of its colloquial text, which is almost epistolary, deriving from the far reaches of ancient tradition. Such a style is revealed in the following comments from 1964 and 1973, respectively:

I have inspected the students' notebooks in my periodic review of this and other classroom grade levels. The extent of the work carried out—i.e., the series of graded exercises and their selection—all completed at the precise time at which the teacher's curriculum had planned for each assignment to be completed during the school year, has been highly efficient. I am pleased to point out that the daily scheduling of exercise completion and correction of mistakes for both mathematics and Spanish reveal both the dedication and progress of the students.

Report on teacher skills:
On this date, I visited Mrs. González's 7th grade geometry class, in which the students were learning how to calculate the surface area of polygons. . . . The students were working at the chalkboard, solving problems and responding enthusiastically, demonstrating that their knowledge had been effectively acquired. There is a harmonious study environment, a mutual understanding in the teacher-student relationship. I left the class highly impressed, and congratulate Mrs. González on her good work.
Rating: 40. Outstanding.

Despite the minute detail to which the observation guidelines aspire, certain characteristics or types of conduct, such as "Personality," "Astuteness," or "Personal Demeanor,"[9] which cannot be translated strictly into a numerical score, can cause problems.

She wanted to lower my score . . . so I tried negotiating with her; after all, we're living in a democracy now. . . . I had already made a supreme effort to implement changes, so she was facing a very tricky situation with me, as I didn't want to change anything else and she did. So she decided that at the end of the year, she was going to lower my score. . . . The situation was starting to get personal. . . . When she approached me about this, I asked her, "On what grounds are you going to lower my score?" and that was when all hell broke loose. . . . From a personal point of view, she couldn't stand what I was doing, but I told her that she had no valid reason whatsoever for lowering my score. . . . I asked her, "What is it about me that bothers you so much? Is it the way I dress? Something I've said?" She replied in the negative to all my questions. . . . So I said to her, "You and I can sit down with a cup of tea and talk about a lot of things, but when it comes to educational issues, we'll never see eye to eye." . . . When the time came for her to assess me, she told me she was going to lower my score because some of the parents had been having problems with me. I tried to discuss the matter with her further, but she couldn't give me specific examples. I told her to think very carefully about what she was going to do, because I would challenge her decision. She was taken aback, and told me that if I challenged her, I would not be allowed to take my vacations. She wanted to scare me. . . . Here [at this school], emotional threats and intimidation are frequently used to manipulate. Teachers are often afraid of the principal, so there's a lot of acquiescence. . . . For example, until this country became a democratic state, no one even knew about the Statutes; they were kept locked away by the Administration and no one read them. No one knew what his or her rights were. When the time came for her to compile my evaluation, we started looking into the criteria for the "Initiative" category, and saw that it was completely ridiculous to lower my score. We inspected all the categories in which she wanted to lower my score and saw that she had absolutely no recourse. The end result was that we negotiated, and she only lowered my score by a single point. (excerpt from an interview with a teacher, Buenos Aires, 1992)[10]

The style used in writing the comments retains the underlying objective of using encouragement and praise as a persuasive tool for the improvement of behavior and, simultaneously, displays the type of familiarity promoted in the daily school environment, as shown in this comment written in 1976:

I am delighted to record that I am able to discern excellent qualities in you as a teacher, which are more than appropriate for the fulfillment of leadership tasks; you have a well-defined personality; you are capable and intelligent, and possess ample common sense; you are enterprising, always excellently prepared, and are familiar with all school regulations currently in effect. For these reasons, I have the utmost confidence of your success in your new role of responsibility, which will doubtless be extremely satisfying, although occasionally filled with problematic experiences, but which will contribute to the success of our school, and prove to be highly beneficial to your students. With much warmth and affection, I wish you outstanding achievement at the school where you have been placed in charge, and would like to express my satisfaction at having had the opportunity to work with you. My heartiest congratulations for a job well done.

IV

The continuity of the Notebook's style as a formula that reveals strong links to the school environment clearly demonstrates the deceptive use of the concept of "profession" (in the sense of "expert") for teachers' work and the lack of moderation in the demands made in such work. Thus, the hegemonic status of the behaviorist model of teacher evaluation is surrounded by a permanent air of instability.

The idea of "profession" as attributed to a specific activity refers to exclusive familiarity with a field of knowledge whose particular characteristics are established by parameters enforced by those within the field through their ongoing practice. Generally speaking, the professional nature of occupations is linked to their relative autonomy and to public recognition of the specialized knowledge that those involved in the field possess. In the case of teachers, their "professionalism" describes their capabilities with regard to their subject knowledge and their rating in the area of pedagogy. Nevertheless, these characteristics and the determination of competent performance are rendered more complex by teachers' position of subordination within a hierarchical structure enforced by the State as well as by the specific tasks required of them with regard to the discipline or socialization of children. In practice, evaluation of the professional performance of teachers has been as much a result of the various directions taken by education policy—those which have alternately prioritized or ignored some of the characteristics of teachers' performance—as the specific negotiation processes by which the educational sector has sought to define itself both within and before the State.

In the milestone achieved by the professionalization of teachers in the law of 1958, which was passed largely due to pressure from labor unions following the overthrow of the first Perón government, demands for definition of the structure of the teaching occupation primarily called for dispensing with the obligation to comply with official ideology, on open competitions for positions of responsibility, on autonomy within the classroom environment, and on the provision of adequate training and refresher courses. Teachers wanted all this without having to relinquish the labor rights granted by the Perón government to all state employees.[11] The status of being civil servants has defined the "career" of teaching as a bona fide profession.

The professionalization of the job according to its location in the hierarchical pyramid affords teachers the rights of responsibility for authority and administration, but this also ties them down to the status of state employees. The specific pedagogical skills required for "promotion," apparently endorsed by the objective control of competition, are blurred and made insignificant by the extent of the requirements that emerge from performance evaluation. This means that competition, as a tool for evaluating a candidate's command of a specific field of knowledge in so-called liberal professions, becomes disfigured by the superimposition of requirements for school evaluation. In this sense, the weight that elements like *"Collaboration with the School"* and *"Fulfillment of the Role of State Employee"* have in a teacher's evaluation end up turning the boundaries of the definition of teaching—as a profession essentially concerned with the link between pedagogy and knowledge—into something vague and indistinct. This has the effect of expanding (although in an implicit manner) the tasks or areas relevant to performance of the job. This is illustrated in the following Notebook comments, written in 1950:

If a teacher's accomplishments reflect the success of the school and of the country as a whole, I should like to express my complete satisfaction and to proffer my warmest congratulations. The full range of her achievements, her almost perfect attendance, her dedication to her students' education—without a doubt one of the greatest hopes for the future of mankind—as well as the artistic and esthetic qualities and minute detail which she has developed in her approach to her daily teaching practice, make her worthy of the highest commendation for the outstanding results achieved in her work.

The category of "*Collaboration with the school*," which, depending on the particular period in history, is infused with politically partisan connotations, can either work in favor of or against a teacher, independently of their classification as an educator in the strictest sense of the word. The category "*Other Qualities*" also appears to carry significant weight, acquiring definition—like a blank check—according to the particular period in time, or to the whims of the senior supervisor. In this category, "spirit of initiative" or "leadership abilities," for example, are considered positive attributes, even when they neglect to strictly correlate with educational aptitude and ability.

Extremely active and very dedicated to her work. The well-ordered quality of her written tasks and the care she takes in her educational and instructive activities deserve the congratulations of the deputy administration. She has shown excellent collaboration with the common goals of the school.

Basis: Influence, tact and disciplinary abilities.
Ms. González possesses a strong personality, and is able to maintain order with her mere presence alone. She has managed to gain the respect of students and parents alike, and they in turn have a great deal of admiration for the reliable nature of the knowledge she imparts. Her extensive moral predominance inspires a strong sense of commitment, bringing honor to the reputation of the school.

Under the headings "*Other Information*" or "*Other Collaborations*," comments such as the following may be found:

She has been responsible for the Post Office Savings scheme (afternoon shift), a position she has fulfilled with the utmost success. She worked with third graders for the first time, and her work this academic year has been extremely fruitful.

She accomplished the goals established for the Second Five-Year Plan with true and astute Argentine spirit. Her extremely efficient classes proved to be in keeping with the principles of the invaluable educational project being developed by the country's government, and she imparted these classes to her students with a missionary-like zeal.
    Summary of principal's assessment: Very good, congratulations.

V

Thus, we hereby come to the crux of the issue under discussion, given that the process of evaluation comprises two logics that are not always completely compatible: (1) the logic of evaluation of the specific (educational) tasks of teachers in explicitly contextualized situations (the class-room and the area of complementary extracurricular school activities) and (2) the logic of state bureaucratic-administrative organizations and their systems of employee promotion.

Analysis of a "quasi" legal document such as the Notebook clearly shows that legitimization of the teacher's work, achieved through evaluations and the enforcement of regulations whose end effect is the standardization of the profession within a bureaucratic structure, results in the categorization of teachers in an ambiguous realm that affords them neither the simple status of subordinate executor nor of a professional in the strictest defini-tion of the word. Given the specific characteristics of the school environ-ment, which is predominantly populated by children and rigidly controlled by state policy, where, then, does the professional status of this occupation fit in?

It would seem that the teacher's power of action resides in the role he/she fulfills mediating between the State and students' families. Mutual re-lations render the school a place of inflection between society and the State. Such attributions and expectations vary both according to the political cli-mate of the time as well as to the capacity for control and participation of the community (parents and guardians) and the teaching sector alike.

The virtual heterogeneity of the school system with regard to local con-ditions and circumstances maintains, nevertheless, a common denominator in the form of a prevailing understanding of childhood, which lends a sense of permanence to traditional relationships within the school environment. Working with children (and "for" children in accordance with the ideology of the profession's vocation) lends school life a unique quality, character-ized by strong influences deriving from family relationships and home life. In the daily encounters of school life, mutual assistance in contending with authorities exists side by side with rivalry among peers. The need for har-mony and the continual instability characterize an extremely fragile type of relationship, which nevertheless must be developed within a framework of trust and complicity. The act of caring for young children and the ne-cessity of connecting the adult world to the logic of such care have a ten-dency to infantilize teachers and establish a kind of analogy between the work environment of teachers and the world of the children they teach. Similarly, the authority/subordinate relationship within the school environ-ment primarily takes the form of oral communication, and is based upon the level of sincerity of whoever gives his/her "word."

However, both sides prefer to implement safety measures alongside the practice of this custom, or tradition. As we have already seen, in matters of negotiation, verbal communication is preferred over written fact, given that it is attributed greater moral significance. The written word conveys a formal, threatening tone, and given the diverse range of tasks attributed to the job, does not necessarily convey absolute professionalism. Everyday practice within schools indicates that the use of written communication may make a mockery of—indeed, does make a mockery of—the important documentary quality institutionally attributed to it:

What really happens is that everything ends up being distorted. So everyone gets 100 because no one wants to put the career of a colleague in jeopardy. . . . It depends on the criteria used by each principal; I could give a teacher 85 for something, and at the school next door, another principal might give a much worse teacher 100. And the one that gets promoted is the one who got 100. Do you see what I mean? It's dangerous. The four hundred schools out there don't use the same criteria; even though a point system is used, each principal uses a different method for awarding points. (excerpt from an interview with a principal)[12]

Because the fields of observation describing "professional performance" that are detailed in the Notebook widely encompass all educational tasks fulfilled, the consequent evaluation clearly indicates that the type of work assessed is based upon the ideology of a "family-oriented business." Evaluation is also based on the principles attributed to fulfillment of responsibilities as an employee of the State (ideological-political status and the duties of a subordinate employee), which place greater emphasis on loyalty over autonomy.

We may therefore conclude that the implementation of an objective evaluation of the performance of teachers aimed at within the framework of neo-liberal educational reform is especially difficult, given that the specific "intellectual" nature of the job is in contradiction with the obligation of these employees to comply with and subordinate themselves to state regulations and political contingencies. Apparently, both the bureaucratic-promotion ladder logic and the occupation-specific logic of the school environment, strongly influenced by family relationships and home life, require basic characteristics of "activism" and "initiative," fundamental for the sustained continuation of institutional goals, rather than pedagogical expertise.

The anachronism that this form of evaluation reveals today allows us greater understanding of the difficulties faced in defining the identity of teachers' work. Thus, due to the parameters laid down by the forms of academic evaluation documented in the Notebook, the teaching profession is conditioned by the contingencies of the government in office and the social and political meanings the State attributes to the field of education, rather than focusing, as it should, on the psychological development of children.

Overcoming this dilemma requires extensive discussion about the problem of the power struggle within the school environment, clearly distinguishing the power imposed by the verticality of the bureaucratic organization of the educational system from the area of autonomy and legitimate power that the teacher possesses with regard to the specific nature of his/her work. At the same time, the status of early childhood, entitled to certain legal rights, allows us to consider the school environment as a democratic and participatory institution.

NOTES

A preliminary version of this chapter was presented at the Fourth National Congress of Anthropology, Olavarría, Province of Buenos Aires. Its content is based on the results obtained from research entitled "The Social Construction of the Teacher's Role in Argentina: An Anthropological Approach," carried out by José Fernando García, Daniel Suárez, Patricia Maddonni, and Liliana Dente (UBACyT, 1990–1994, University of Buenos Aires, Final Report [mimeograph]).

1. This theory has been expanded upon in other works produced during a prolonged line of research on the problems of teaching as a perspective for analysis for the understanding of the social processes that take place in schools. Development of this theory has been assisted on several occasions by the co-participation of groups of teachers involved in Workshops for the Research of Teaching Practice. See Batallán, 1998; Batallán and Díaz, 1990; Batallán and García, 1987, 1992; Batallán in collaboration with Morgade, 1987.

2. It is important to mention the participation of the teaching profession on the Board of Classification and Discipline, an official body responsible for monitoring and supervising the methods of advancement and transfer of teachers.

3. Despite the fact that Argentina is a federal state and its provinces have their own teaching statutes, the weight of decisions made in the federal capital (mainly analyzed in the research under discussion) allows for a generalization of the aforementioned demarcation.

4. The teacher's signature involves a certain degree of participation, given that they have the full right to sign "in disagreement" of the comments noted. However, this is, generally speaking, an unusual procedure in the school system.

5. Transcript of a comment written in 1943 in the Notebook of Professional Performance belonging to a former teacher at the Serena School in Rosario, Argentina. (Participant in the New School movement in the city of Rosario [for the purpose of analysis, names have been changed to protect the protagonists' identities], research file material.)

6. The behaviorist model of evaluation was first implemented in Argentina in the 1960s. It was originally based on the experimental psychology of Watson and Skinner.

7. These criteria were developed as a way of responding to an interest in providing a parallel analysis of the first teaching statute introduced by the Perón government (1945–1956), with the concepts expressed in the Notebook. The climax of the crisis came in 1985, during the second year of the Radical presidential term of Raúl Alfonsín, during which, following a period of promotion of democratization in education, the process began to fail.

8. In the second phase, three different stages can be identified: (1) developmental orientation (1958–1968), (2) rationalist restructuring of planning (1969–1972), and (3) the incipient participation of teachers (1973–1976). This brief period of

time may be considered an interregnum before the initiation of the subsequent phase, which in accordance with the policies of the last military dictatorship left a strong technocratic imprint on the nature of the evaluation system.

9. For example, the category of "Personality" is predefined as: "Intellectual capability, good physical and mental health, sound judgment, the ability to fulfill one's role." Greater difficulties are encountered in trying to establish the conceptual criteria that come under the category of "Personal Demeanor." In this particular category, the classification of "Outstanding" is awarded to the teacher who: "stands out for his/her personal talents, who is highly discreet and correct, has impeccable personal and professional presentation, is noticeably respectful to his/her colleagues and tries to instill in his/her students ethical conduct and an important sense of values." In the same category, the classification of "Exceptional" is deserved if the teacher "possesses exceptional personal demeanor, is outstandingly discreet, has an exemplary presentation, displays remarkable attitudes of respect to those around them, and continually endeavors to instill his/her own personal exemplary behavior in his/her students."

10. Interview conducted by Patricia Maddonni, Buenos Aires, 1993.

11. The populist nature of the Perón government was revealed in the implementation of a multiclass model (alliance between capital and labor), in an international postwar context that favored Argentina's trade balance and allowed the economy to flourish. The development of national industry and redistribution policies made Perón a charismatic and self-regulating leader. With regard to the teaching sector, the so-called Teaching Statute of General Perón of 1947 ensured the same labor rights to teachers as had already been afforded other state employees. Nevertheless, despite the advance that this legislation constituted, ideological imposition, favoritism, and exclusion for political reasons provoked strong opposition from teachers, along with professional demands for their occupation (open competitions for promotion to positions of authority, rejection of ideological imposition in education, openness, etc.).

12. Interview conducted by Patricia Maddonni, Buenos Aires, 1993.

REFERENCES

Bajtin, M. (1982). *Estética de la creación verbal.* Mexico City: Siglo XXI.

Ball, S. (1989). *La micropolítica de la escuela. Hacia una teoría de la organización escolar.* Barcelona: Paidós.

Batallán, G. (1998). ¿Puede ser la docencia una profesión? Contradicciones en el contexto de una escuela democrática. *Revista de la Academia* No. 3 (Santiago, Chile), 123–135.

Batallán, G. (in collaboration with Morgade, G.) (1987). El niño y el conocimiento de la realidad social en la escuela. In Nora Elichiry (Comp.), *El niño y la escuela.* Buenos Aires: Nueva Visión.

Batallán, G., and Díaz, R. (1990). *Salvajes, bárbaros y niños. La noción de patrimonio en la escuela primaria.* Cuadernos de Antropología Social Año II No. 1, Universidad de Buenos Aires.

Batallán, G., and García, J.F. (1987). Trabajo docente, democratización y conocimiento. *Revista Paraguaya de Sociología* No. 65 (Asunción, Paraguay), 31–

47.

Batallán, G., and García, J.F. (1992). Especificidad del trabajo docente y la transformación escolar. In A. Alliaud and L. Duschavsky (Comps.), *Maestros: Formación, práctica y transformación escolar*. Buenos Aires: Miño y Dávila.

Berger, P., and Luckmann, T. (1984). *La construcción social de la realidad*. Buenos Aires: Amorrortu.

Blumer, H. (n.d.). La sociedad como interacción simbólica. Servicio de documentación de Sociología. File No. 369, Universidad de Buenos Aires.

Bourdoncle, R. (1991). La professionnalisation des enseignants: Analyses sociologiques anglaises et américaines. *Revue Française de Pédagogie* No. 94 (Paris).

Burbules, N., and Densmore, K. (1991). The limits of making teaching a profession. *Educational Review* 5(1).

Carlson, D. (1986). Teachers, class, culture and politics of schooling. *Interchange* 17(4) (Toronto, Canada: OISE).

Contreras, J. (1997). *La autonomía del profesorado*. Madrid: Morata.

Foucault, M. (1979). *Microfísica del poder*. Madrid: La Piqueta.

Gadamer, H. (1977). *Verdad y método*. Salamanca, España: Sígueme.

Gauthier, C., Tardif, M., and Belzile, C. (1994). La professionnalisation: Un meta modele reunnissant la demarche scientifique et praxeologique en education? Paper presented at the Deuxieme Biennale de l'Education et de la Formation, La Sorbonne University, Paris, France, April 9–12.

Geertz, C. (1987). *La interpretación de las culturas*. Barcelona: Gedisa.

Giddens, A. (1987). *Las nuevas reglas del método sociológico*. Buenos Aires: Amorrortu.

Giroux, H. (1990). *Los profesores como intelectuales. Hacia una pedagogía crítica del aprendizaje*. Barcelona: Paidós.

Graubard, A. (1981). *Liberemos a los niños*. Barcelona: Gedisa.

Hargreaves, A. (1996). *Profesorado, cultura y postmodernidad*. Madrid: Morata.

Kob, J. (1976). Problemas del rol en la profesión docente. *Revista Educación* 14 (Instituto de Colaboración Científica, Tubingen).

Labaree, D. (1992). Power, knowledge, and rationalization of teaching: A genealogy of the movement to professionalize teaching. *Harvard Educational Review* 62(2), 123–155.

Lawn, M., and Ozga, J. (1988). ¿Trabajador de la enseñanza? Nueva valoración de los profesores. *Revista de la Educación* No. 285 (Madrid), 191–215.

Offe, C. (1986). La abolición del control del mercado y el problema de la legitimidad. In *El estado en el capitalismo contemporáneo*. Mexico City: Siglo XXI.

Rockwell, E. (1985). Etnografía y teoría en la investigación educativa. *Dialogando* No. 8 (Red de Investigaciones Cualitativas de la Realidad Escolar, Santiago, Chile).

Rockwell, E. (Coord.). (1995). *La escuela cotidiana*. Mexico City: Fondo de Cultura Económica.

Schütz, A. (1974). *El problema de la realidad social*. Buenos Aires: Amorrortu.

Snyders, G. (1981). *No es fácil amar a los hijos*. Barcelona: Gedisa.

Tenti Fanfani, E. (1989). Universidad y profesiones. In V. Gómez Campo and E. Tenti Fanfani, *Universidad y profesiones*. Buenos Aires: Miño y Dávila.

Chapter 4

Spatiotemporal Fluidity and Culturally Relevant Pedagogy in the Latino Diaspora

Stanton Wortham and Margaret Contreras

Culturally relevant pedagogy uses students' home cultures as a resource, in two ways. First, teachers draw on students' cultural beliefs and practices to teach the standard curriculum more effectively. Second, teachers incorporate students' cultural beliefs and practices into the classroom in order to develop students' knowledge of and pride in their home cultures. Many teachers accomplish both these goals in their classrooms (cf. the cases described in Freeman, 1996; Ladson-Billings, 1995; Rose, 1995; and the references in Osborne, 1996). But in some cases these two goals conflict. This chapter describes a case of culturally relevant pedagogy in which some students end up choosing between academic success and their home culture.

The case involves an interesting type of culturally relevant pedagogy developed by the second author. In her years living in Colombia and in experiences with her own family, she noticed that many Latino homes have more fluid spatiotemporal boundaries around activities than Anglo homes typically allow. In many Latino homes, including ones that we visited in the community described in this article, people tend to participate in several activities at once. They move smoothly among chores, conversations, television, homework and other activities—not serially, but by competently participating in more than one activity at once. Many Anglo homes and mainstream U.S. institutions like schools tend to discourage multiple simultaneous activities and to demand focus on one activity at a time. Noting this apparent mismatch between Latino and mainstream Anglo practices and concerned to provide culturally relevant pedagogy for her Latino students, Margaret Contreras designed her ESL (English as a Second Language) room to be more like a Latino home. She allowed multiple simultaneous activities, and she encouraged fluid boundaries among these activities. Her Latino students and other Latinos who visited the room reported that Margaret succeeded in making her classroom feel more like a Latino home.

Despite this success, however, most school staff and some Latino students did not react as Margaret had hoped. Staff appreciated Margaret's rapport with the Latino students, and they often drew on her cultural expertise. But in interviews they sharply distinguished between the culturally relevant "tutoring" that Margaret was doing and the "instruction" in academic subject matter that they were doing. They perceived Margaret's room as chaotic and undisciplined—as the kind of place in which rigorous teaching and serious learning were unlikely to happen. Some Latino students, mostly girls, did manage both to succeed in school and to appreciate the aspects of their home culture embedded in Margaret's room. But many others, mostly boys, chose to identify completely with their home culture and to reject the mainstream Anglo values represented by the school. This latter group used Margaret's room as a Latino haven in the midst of the Anglo school but not as a tool to help them succeed academically.

This chapter has two goals: (1) to describe how an innovative type of culturally relevant pedagogy for Latino students was appropriated in practice (2) and to illustrate how the two goals of academic success and cultural empowerment can conflict in complex ways in some cases. The first section reviews theories of culturally relevant pedagogy and discusses how its two central goals might conflict. The second section describes the case of Margaret Contreras' ESL room and describes the phenomenon of fluid spatio-temporal boundaries. The third section describes how staff and students at the high school reacted to Margaret's innovations. The conclusion suggests two reasons why Margaret was unable in many cases to help students both succeed academically and preserve aspects of their home culture: first, she did not have sufficient power or institutional support to convince other school staff that her culturally relevant pedagogy might make sense; second, in this context there seem to be conflicts between the students' home culture and the values embedded in mainstream schooling.

CULTURALLY RELEVANT PEDAGOGY

U.S. schools that serve linguistic and cultural minority students need culturally relevant pedagogy for at least two reasons. First, minority students—and especially U.S. Latinos—more often drop out of school than students from mainstream backgrounds (Losey, 1995). When teachers incorporate minority languages and cultures into the classroom, minority students learn more academic content and are thus more likely to attain educational credentials that will open opportunities for them (Allen and Boykin, 1992; Genesee, 1987; Osborne, 1996). Allen and Boykin (1992), for instance, describe values and practices found in many African-American cultural settings. As one component of their argument, they claim that African-American homes often contain high sensory stimulation, with overlapping visual, verbal, musical, and kinesthetic cues. Allen and Boykin show that classrooms which incorporate multiple channels into the learning of academic content—for instance, by encouraging students to listen to music and move while they are working on academic tasks—allow African-American students to learn more than they would have otherwise. This increases the chances that the African-American students will succeed in school.

Second, U.S. schools need culturally relevant pedagogy because well-intentioned efforts to help minority students often inadvertently undermine students' home cultures. Most programs aimed at linguistic and cultural minority students intend for these students to *assimilate* to the mainstream values and practices represented by the school (Cummins, 1993; Freeman, 1996; Ladson-Billings, 1995). Most practitioners and policymakers do not intend to eliminate or devalue students' home cultures. But, as Valdés (1996) clearly shows, interventions that aim to acknowledge cultural differences and help minority students "overcome" these differences often undermine students' cultural traditions. Valdés describes, for instance, programs that teach U.S. Latino mothers how to raise their children "better." These programs have good intentions: to counteract the mismatch between the mainstream Anglo expectations found at school and the different cultural expectations found in most rural, working-class Mexican homes. Valdés argues, however, that these programs presuppose Anglo models of child rearing based on individualistic values—values that conflict with the collectivist, family-oriented ones commonly found in rural Mexican culture. From an anthropological perspective, neither of these cultural perspectives is better or worse. But when authority figures from schools and agencies teach Latinos how to "improve" their child rearing, they undermine these Latinos' confidence in the value of their own culture.

For these two reasons—to facilitate minority students' academic success and to avoid undermining their home cultures—several theorists have recently developed comprehensive approaches to culturally relevant pedagogy (Cummins, 1993; Ladson-Billings, 1995; Osborne, 1996).[1] Ladson-Billings (1995) provides a concise account, arguing that culturally relevant pedagogy should have three crucial aspects: minority students must experience academic success that is recognized by mainstream standards and institutions; they must maintain and develop both competence and pride in their home cultures; and they must learn to recognize and criticize exclusionary practices that hurt members of minority groups. Cummins (1993) and Osborne (1996) advocate similar approaches to culturally relevant pedagogy. As Cummins puts it, minority students should have a positive orientation toward both their own and the dominant culture, and they must not perceive themselves as inferior because of their language and culture. Cummins and Osborne also agree with Ladson-Billings that culturally relevant pedagogy should actively counter the disempowerment that minority students face in the larger society, by explicitly teaching about the social processes that accomplish such disempowerment.

These advocates of culturally relevant pedagogy acknowledge that sometimes minority students choose between mainstream success and affirming their own cultural identities. Ladson-Billings (1995) cites Fordham and Ogbu's (1986) claim that some African-American students see academic success as "acting white" and feel that they must fail in school in order to affirm their identities as black people. While acknowledging that this happens, Ladson-Billings argues against "caste" explanations that present blacks as a monolithic group (e.g., Ogbu, 1987). Instead of seeing African-American students' disproportionate school failure as the inevitable result of structural factors—as if most black students must inevitably choose between academic success and cultural pride—she argues for heterogeneity and the possibility of transformation. Ladson-Billings supports her argument empirically, with ethnographic descriptions of classrooms in which culturally relevant pedagogy helps African-American students *both* succeed in school *and* embrace their home culture. She describes students who do not see school success as antithetical to their identities as African Americans. Others have described similar successes accomplished with culturally relevant pedagogy among U.S. Latino students (Freeman, 1996; Rose, 1995).

In arguing for structural complexity and the possibility of transformation among minority students, Ladson-Billings (1995) and other contemporary advocates of culturally relevant pedagogy move beyond a simple "difference" hypothesis in their explanations of disproportionate minority school failure. The difference hypothesis explains disproportionate school failure by citing the unrecognized divergence in cultural styles and values between mainstream schools and minority communities (e.g., Bourdieu and Passeron, 1970/1977; Michaels, 1981). On this account the gatekeepers who run schools assume that mainstream Anglo practices and values are naturally superior, and they unwittingly (and wrongly) interpret minority practices and values as evidence of academic deficits. Although this difference hypothesis may hold a grain of truth, it has been criticized on two grounds. First, in recent years many have described *various* factors that likely contribute to disproportionate minority school failure, in addition to a mismatch in cultural values, and they have argued that single-factor explanations cannot suffice (e.g., Cummins, 1993; McDermott, 1987; Suárez-Orozco and Suárez-Orozco, 1995; Valdés, 1996, 1997).

Second, minority cultures are much more heterogeneous and minority students are much more hybrid than the difference hypothesis allows (Heath and McLaughlin, 1993; Ladson-Billings, 1995). In reality, most minority students and many teachers have varying degrees of competence in more than one set of cultural practices and values. The encounter between minority students and mainstream schooling is thus more complex than a simple conflict of monolithic cultural styles. It involves, instead, more subtle adjustment and negotiation among the multiple repertoires available to both teachers and students. Minority students *are* often unjustly stigmatized and disempowered in these school interactions, but we need more subtle tools than monolithic descriptions of cultural style in order to explain how this happens (for alternative tools see McDermott and Tylbor, 1995; Wortham, 1994). We must go beyond structural variables to examine what happens as minority students encounter educational policies in practice.

But if cultural differences are complex and fluid, and do not in themselves explain disproportionate minority school failure, why do we need culturally relevant pedagogy? Allen and Boykin (1992), Cummins (1993), Ladson-Billings (1995), and others argue that students can benefit from the incorporation of their home cultures into schooling even though this will not eliminate all the disadvantages they face. Advocates of culturally relevant pedagogy agree that multiple factors impede minority students' school success, and they acknowledge that cultures are heterogeneous and that individuals are hybrid. (In fact, culturally relevant pedagogy intends to *foster* the hybrid cultural identities of linguistic and cultural minority students because it emphasizes *both* competence in the mainstream curriculum *and* celebration of the home cultures.) It is important, then, to distance culturally relevant pedagogy from the "difference" hypothesis. Contemporary advocates do not claim that culturally relevant pedagogy will by itself eliminate all the major factors that produce exclusion and disadvantage in our educational system. But they claim that it can nonetheless help in many cases.

As Freeman (1996), Levinson and Sutton (2001), and others remind us, however, we often find discrepancies between reforms as envisioned by education policymakers and the realities of practice. This chapter examines a case of culturally relevant pedagogy, in order to see how this reform plays out in one particular context. In this case culturally relevant pedagogy worked for only some of the students being served. Other students faced an apparently exclusive choice between academic success and their home culture. In describing the cultural conflict that produced this exclusive choice and the academic failure of some of these students, we are *not* returning to a simple "difference" explanation for minority student failure. Instead, we will describe the complexity of students' responses to this instance of culturally relevant pedagogy, and thus we will illustrate how minority students respond in diverse ways to education policy.

FLUIDITY IN AN ESL ROOM

Havertown[2] is in a small rural New England town far from any sizable Latino community. About 200 Latinos, mostly from Mexico or Southern

Texas, live in Havertown. (Only 1% of U.S. Latinos live in the Northeast, where they comprise 0.3% of the total population—cf. Saenz & Greenlees, 1996—but small diaspora communities like the one in Havertown are becoming increasingly common.) Virtually all of the adults have come to work at a local meat processing plant. Turnover is very high, as families regularly leave town for other jobs or to return south. At any given time, about 50 Latino children are enrolled in the local schools (comprising about 2% of the total school population). Margaret Contreras worked at the high school for three years as a bilingual paraprofessional, where she designed and staffed an ESL room for the Latino students. All the Latino students in Havertown schools attend mainstream classes, but many are pulled out of one or two classes a day in order to work in the ESL room in that particular school. Each ESL room is staffed by a bilingual paraprofessional, and certified ESL teachers come to the rooms to offer formal classes for "limited English proficient" students. For logistical reasons, however, the certified teachers rarely used Margaret's room, so she made it available to all Latino students at the high school. The first author, together with two research assistants, observed Margaret's ESL room daily for two months and interviewed teachers and students, as part of a two year ethnographic study of the Havertown Latino community.

Latino adolescents have mixed feelings about life in Havertown. On arrival they usually suffer culture shock at being transplanted into a community so devoid of Latinos. Margaret spent many hours with new students—often in tears—who refused even to leave the ESL room for fear of the unfamiliar, totally Anglo world of the school. The adolescents miss their Spanish-speaking friends and Spanish-language radio (although many families do have satellite dishes and watch the Spanish-language cable network Univisión). Due to the lack of friends, relatives, and familiar activities, they often find rural American life sterile and boring. The transience of Latino families also takes a toll. As reported by Stull, Broadway, and Erickson (1992), the turnover of workers in this sort of meatpacking job can be 6 to 8% a *month*. Turnover among Havertown Latinos approaches this at times. Even children from families resident for several years often speculate that they will be leaving soon, and this expectation disrupts their commitments to school and friends.

On the other hand, many adolescents and their parents appreciate the quality of the schools, which they consider far better than those in southern Texas or rural Mexico. Some parents remain at extremely difficult jobs so that their children can finish school in Havertown. Many adolescents and their parents also value the lack of drugs and gang violence. Students report that they feel safe in Havertown, and parents worry less about the bad influences their children might fall under. The primary reason for these Latinos' presence in Havertown, however, is work. As described comprehensively by Griffith and Kissam (1995), the employment prospects of many agricultural workers based in southern Texas have become less secure in recent years. These workers now value a *steady* job above all else, and they find that in Havertown. The jobs are exhausting, often dangerous and unpleasant, and pay the minimum wage. But workers get steady work and ample overtime year-round, and there is no shortage of new workers interested in the jobs.

Finding Margaret Contreras' ESL room at Havertown High can be a challenge. You must go through the cafeteria and almost out the back door of the school, then enter the self-contained special education room for seriously disabled students. Through this room, past the eager stares of the disabled students, you will find a small room that must have been designed as a large storage closet (measuring about 12 feet by 9 feet). As you enter, you will see Margaret's small desk and chair immediately on your right. On the far wall are a filing cabinet, a desk with a computer, a map of the world and many Spanish-language posters. Compressed against the two side walls are two or three other desks and chairs, a combination TV-VCR, a bookcase filled with Spanish-language books and books on bilingual education, plus more posters and students' work. A prominent portion of the right hand wall contains a gallery of half a dozen hand-drawn pictures, each containing the nickname of a male Latino student and an artistic depiction. One, for instance, says "El Tomate" in stylized letters and has a picture of a humanoid tomato that is supposed to resemble ninth grader Paco. Margaret refers to this artwork as "legal graffiti." The boys take pride in their pictures and consider it a mark of friendship to be given a nickname and enshrined on the wall.

If you visit Margaret's room in the morning, and if you are a mainstream Anglo, this small space will contain a dizzying amount of activity. Margaret sits at her desk, filling out forms and intermittently answering questions from the three students in the room. Jesús Villalobos and his friend Paco Moreno have been released from their ninth grade math class, which is at the moment taking a test. They are doing worksheets that they must finish before taking the test themselves. They alternate between Spanish and English, and between a conversation about a recent fight and their math homework. Jesús occasionally turns to the back wall and teases Teresa Fuentes, who is sitting behind him writing a paper on the computer. She sometimes teases back, but more often she ignores him. One of the few African-American students in the school enters the room, greets Margaret, and then remarks that no one saved a chair for him. He borrows one from the special education room, sits down beside Teresa, and proceeds to discuss the paper assignment that she is working on. At this point we have four students, one teacher, one ethnographer, two or three conversations, and three different types of schoolwork going on in a little over 100 square feet of space.

On this day, Margaret had promised Jesús the opportunity to watch an educational video on the ancient Maya. Later in the period they turn on the VCR. Margaret continues with her paperwork, and Teresa continues with her paper, but both apparently attend to their work and the video simultaneously. Even more remarkable to the Anglo ethnographer (the first author), when he and Margaret begin a conversation in the corner, the students manage to attend to that, too. Teresa chimes in at exactly the right moment to contribute to the conversation, while still making progress on her paper and apparently learning something about the Maya. Toward the end of the movie other activities do stop for a few minutes after Jesús remarks about one of the Mayan Indians that "his lips are like mine." Margaret uses this comment to start a discussion of "ethnic" appearance and its consequences, which becomes a discussion about how some Latino males have been getting stopped by local police recently.

In this brief description of Margaret's ESL room we can see all three central components of culturally relevant pedagogy, as defined by Ladson-Billings. Margaret supports and encourages the students' academic work, and Jesús, Paco, and Teresa do get some academic work done during their time in the ESL room that morning. She encourages the students to speak Spanish and to learn about and take pride in their home cultures. And she helps them confront the exclusion and discrimination that they and their compatriots too often face in the United States. But when asked, Margaret does not immediately identify herself as a "culturally relevant teacher." Instead, she often refers to herself as a "proud mother," and to the students as "*my* students." Her first goal in establishing this ESL room was to gain the students' confidence, such that they knew she cared about them regardless of how they behaved. And the students do treat her in many ways like a mother. Jesús, whose own mother is in Mexico several months out of the year, brings Margaret presents and is particularly affectionate on Mothers' Day. Other students confide in Margaret, sharing secrets that they tell no other adult.[3]

Margaret's maternal role is only one way in which her ESL room resembles a Latino home. Latino families are unusually close and highly value mutual support (Rothenberg, 1995; Suárez-Orozco and Suárez-Orozco, 1995; Valdés, 1996). Margaret has managed to establish a quasi-familial support group among most of the Latino students at the high school. By her third year in Havertown, when we did our ethnographic observations, most Latino students were interested in one another's lives and were willing to support one another academically and personally. More than half the Latino students in the high school would regularly gather in the ESL room during homeroom period, in the 15 minutes before school, to chat or help each other finish up homework. Once we saw a newcomer from Mexico, a young woman named Carmen, who had been in the United States only a couple of months and knew little English, dive right in and help another Latino with his English-language science homework when she recognized the concepts from her schooling in Mexico. Carmen also spearheaded a project to include the children of a Oaxacan family who had until then been isolated in the school and community. These children spoke Spanish as a second language, after their indigenous language, and also looked physically very different from most of the other Latinos. Carmen boosted their self-confidence by telling them how Oaxacan artists had influenced Mexican art in an important way, and thus she managed to bring them more into the Latino group at Havertown High.

So Margaret's ESL room resembled a Latino family in at least three central ways. First, Margaret herself was maternal. She had high standards, but she cared for her students unconditionally. Second, she encouraged students to be close and supportive of one another. In her room other students were not seen as competition or as distractions but as *resources* to help others both succeed academically and develop pride in their home cultures. Third, Margaret allowed more fluid spatiotemporal boundaries around activities. Students often participated in more than one activity, in the same place and at the same time. This third characteristic is perhaps the most striking because of the contrast between the extreme spatiotemporal compartmentalization of activities in a typical school and the fluidity of Margaret's ESL room.

Based on her own experiences in Colombia and with her Colombian husband and his family,[4] Margaret had noticed more fluid spatiotemporal boundaries around activities in many Latino homes. People in such homes do not focus on one activity at a time, serially, but instead participate in several activities simultaneously. Margaret decided to make her ESL room more culturally relevant by implementing this more fluid organization of activities there. In doing so, she was implementing an uncommon type of culturally relevant pedagogy. She went beyond curriculum materials that draw on Latino cultures and beyond the use of Spanish to incorporate a culturally familiar way of organizing time, space, and student participation. She was thus following a more "ecological" view of education and development in which teachers go beyond content and language and also recognize less explicit aspects of minority students' cultural practices (Azmitia et al., 1996; Irvine, 1990; Rogoff, 1991).

Ethnographic work by the first author showed that Margaret's observations about spatiotemporal fluidity were accurate for the Havertown Latino community itself. The level of noise and activity in the typical Havertown Latino home overwhelms a typical Anglo. The entire extended family, plus visitors, generally occupy the central area of the house—usually the kitchen and living room. Many activities often go on simultaneously, and in the same place: the TV is on; children are doing homework; more than one conversation is occurring, in person or on the phone; people transact business activities (selling things to visitors, filling out tax forms, etc.); some of the women are cooking; music is playing; neighbors are dropping by to borrow something or to chat; and family members are coming and going on various errands. Most amazing to the Anglo observer is that people seem able to attend to several of these activities at once. While making progress on their homework or their tax forms, people chime in at exactly the right moment with some comment for the ongoing conversation. There is generally a feeling of warm togetherness in such a scene, which is readily extended to guests. Havertown Latinos report that they like this arrangement in the home because it allows them to communicate and help each other with the various tasks and because it makes them feel connected to the group. One adolescent was horrified when the first author asked why he didn't do homework alone in his room. He would feel alone and uncomfortable there, he said, and he would also be cut off from others' help and encouragement.

Other ethnographic work on Latinos has described a similar pattern of spatiotemporal fluidity. Vélez-Ibáñez (1993, 1996) calls it the "simultaneity" of activities in time and space. He reports that spatiotemporal boundaries between activities are generally more fluid among Latinos than among Anglos. Some other researchers refer to this pattern in passing. Vásquez, Pease-Alvarez, and Shannon (1994), for instance, describe scenes from daily Mexican-American home life that involve the TV blaring, children playing noisily, and adults and older children engaged in academic or business tasks at the kitchen table. Gallimore and Goldenberg (1993) describe children moving from activity to activity among adults in Mexican-American homes. Sabogal, Marín, Otero-Sabogal, Marín, and Perez-Stable (1987), among many others, describe the closeness among Latino family members that underlies the high spatial proximity between Latino family members.

Rogoff, Mistry, Göncü, and Mosier (1993) provide an extensive and systematic description of simultaneous participation in multiple activities. They compare typical household organization and child-rearing practices among rural Indian, rural Guatemalan Mayan, middle-class Turkish, and middle-class U.S. families. The two middle-class settings involve much more segregation of activities than the two rural settings. In the rural homes, many more activities go on at once—ranging from adult work to caregiving to socializing. And rural adults and children, especially the Guatemalan Mayans, often attend simultaneously to more than one activity, with each "uninterrupted by the other, with each line of attention maintained as smoothly as if there were no other focus" (Rogoff, Mistry, Göncü, and Mosier, 1993, p. 50). Remarkably, by 20 months of age the Guatemalan toddlers are significantly more likely to attend simultaneously to multiple activities than U.S. adults.

No Havertown Latinos are Guatemalan Mayan, although there are a few Guatemalans who undoubtedly have some indigenous ancestry. But we seem to be observing in Havertown a similar pattern of multiple activities and simultaneous attention to the one Rogoff, Mistry, Göncü, and Mosier observed in Guatemala (and to some extent in rural India). This spatiotemporal fluidity most likely occurs among Mexican and Central American rural working classes in particular and not among Latinos of all social classes. Rothenberg (1995) describes substantial differences between rural and urban Mexicans, and notes the often-cramped quarters of the rural working classes in Mexico, which often force several activities into one space. (Note, however, that Vélez-Ibáñez (1993) suspects middle-class Mexican households also have more fluid spatiotemporal boundaries than Anglo ones, so this pattern is likely culturally as well as economically distributed.) It is also important to note that Latinos do, of course, have some spatial and temporal differentiation in their activities. Eisenberg (1986), for instance, describes family members going outside on the stoop to relax and socialize after chores are done. More fluid boundaries also do not mean that Latinos tolerate constant interruptions. Valdés (1996) describes how respect for parents keeps children from interrupting their activities until the parents finish. We have observed such boundaries among Havertown Latinos, too. We claim merely that the spatial and temporal boundaries between activities are *more* fluid among many rural, working-class Latinos than among middle-class U.S. Anglos.

Mainstream Anglo homes have relatively firm spatial and temporal boundaries around activities, with an expectation that people will focus on one activity at a time: children often do homework separately in their rooms until they are finished, and if they need help an adult goes to their room; people watch TV in the living room, and the TV is likely to go off when dinner or another activity commences; parents pay bills at a desk in an office or study. More research would be required to document the extent of this difference among various groups,[5] but a difference in degree of spatiotemporal fluidity clearly exists between mainstream Anglos and the less Americanized working-class Latino families in Havertown.

As a central component of her culturally relevant pedagogy, Margaret organized her ESL room in a more Latino way with respect to spatiotemporal fluidity. Most often she and the students participated in more than one activity simultaneously. Students could enter and leave the room at will, without regard for passes. There was deliberately no clock. While in the room students were expected to work on something, but they were allowed to wander off topic for a while before going back to their task. The next section reports that while Latino students appreciated Margaret's culturally relevant pedagogy, Anglos often misunderstood it. Margaret successfully convinced some Anglos, like the first author, that fluid boundaries do not mean lack of substance, but rather a different organization of it. Most Anglo school personnel, however, were not convinced of this.

RESULTS OF MARGARET'S CULTURALLY RELEVANT PEDAGOGY

Margaret clearly succeeded in creating a Latino haven at Havertown High. One of our research assistants, who was raised in a Mexican family in Texas (and was feeling homesick while a student in New England), felt so at home in Margaret's room that she spent 100 hours more than we had originally planned doing research at the school. She described the ESL room as a "home away from home." The Latino students also appreciated the warmth and communal feeling of Margaret's room. By Margaret's third year more than half of the Latino students at the high school could be found there every morning at 8:00 A.M., and they often went out of their way to attend these gatherings. On one morning Paco arrived at this gathering rather disheveled and apparently exhausted. He reported that Jesús would not make it to school that day because they had been out playing pool until 2:00 A.M. the night before. Someone asked him: "So what are you doing here?" He replied, apparently without irony: "Because I wanted to be here with Mrs. Contreras."

Most Anglo school staff, however, did not share the Latino students' appreciation of Margaret's work. Some of them complained that in her quasi-maternal closeness with the Latino students Margaret was "not professional." By this they meant that she inappropriately blurred the boundaries between school and home. Margaret visited the students at home sometimes, and she invited them to her home occasionally. A professional, according to other school staff, maintains distance from students, both in order to maintain authority as a representative of the institution and to avoid possible legal liability. On one occasion, our homesick research assistant ran into the conflict between this professional code of conduct and Margaret's more familial approach. She and an adolescent Latina had become close, and they were observed walking hand in hand on school grounds. School authorities immediately made it clear that this sort of physical contact with students was absolutely forbidden. From the assistant's perspective, Latina friends and relatives often hold hands as a way of feeling closer. But from the school's perspective, legitimate concerns about sexual harassment and legal liability require a no-touching policy. In this case our assistant simply stopped all such physical contact with students, without any serious damage to Margaret's efforts at culturally relevant pedagogy. But in other ways the school's negative reaction to Margaret's innovations revealed a more serious conflict of values that did undermine Margaret's efforts.

Because of its more fluid spatiotemporal activity boundaries, many Anglo school staff found Margaret's ESL room overwhelming and chaotic. With a few exceptions, most school staff interpreted the multiple activities and fluid boundaries in Margaret's room as evidence of sloppy academic work. As they conceived it, Margaret might be doing successful "mentoring," and perhaps occasional "tutoring," but she did *not* do "instruction." Mere tutoring, as they conceived it, could be done in the midst of other activities, but academic instruction designed to cover a specified subject matter in a specified time cannot coexist with such distractions. From this perspective, students in Margaret's room seemed to be "hanging around" or straying off task, and staff feared that "not much gets done there." (Many staff also did not like Margaret's disdain for hall passes.) When asked by the first author to speculate about why Margaret's room operated the way it did, few staff mentioned cultural factors. Most attributed it to Margaret's personality, claiming that she was too "social" as a person. The one differing opinion came from a second-generation Italian-American teacher, who said that his cultural heritage made him feel right at home in the simultaneous activities going on in Margaret's room.

So Margaret and the Anglo school staff had differing interpretations of activities in her ESL room. Margaret saw it as culturally relevant pedagogy. Most Anglos saw it as chaotic and unprofessional. This conflict had both practical and theoretical implications. Practically, Margaret managed to run the ESL room as she wanted for three years, but she then decided to leave Havertown High because of conflicts with the administration. She was a paraprofessional, and thus she had little power and very limited job security.[6] Theoretically, the conflict between Margaret and the school illustrates how culturally relevant pedagogues can face a hard choice between academic success and instilling pride in students' home cultures. Anglo school staff, although perhaps less well-informed about Latino cultural patterns than they might have been, had a reasonable argument: given the way U.S. schools are organized, with individual academic achievement rather than community-building as the primary goal, with standardized curricula and assessments, and with discrete academic subject matters and compartmentalized academic activities, Margaret's approach might not have been the best preparation for U.S. school success.

We can treat this as an empirical question: Did Margaret's culturally relevant pedagogy help Latino students both succeed in school and develop pride in their home cultures, or did it impede their academic performance? Without doubt, her approach built a Latino community and developed students' pride in being Latino. By Margaret's last year the room had become a haven for virtually all the Latino students. Even those fluent in English and at the top of their class came to the room to chat, to do their work, and to help others. One academically successful girl, who had sworn only a year earlier never to speak Spanish again, was willingly translating passages and tutoring other students in Spanish. Many students opened up enough to discuss sensitive topics like boyfriends and pregnancy with Margaret. The students also came to care for each other. Whenever someone was in trouble, many people were concerned about the problem and willing to help. So Margaret succeeded in building community and providing a culturally familiar space within the school.

This in itself had some positive effects on Latino students' academic performance: formerly disruptive students were less so; students skipped school less often; and students would attempt assignments in Margaret's room that they would not have bothered with otherwise. Nonetheless, it seems that Margaret's efforts did not substantially improve Latino students' academic performance. As the first author has described elsewhere (Wortham, 2001), Havertown Latino adolescents divide into two groups with respect to school success: some (mostly girls) value school and do well, while others (mostly boys) do not value school and end up dropping out. Many Havertown Latino adolescents face the bind described by Suárez-Orozco and Suárez-Orozco (1995) and others: they are caught between the more traditional Mexican values of their parents and the mainstream U.S. values they see in the media and among their Anglo peers. For complicated reasons, sketched in Wortham (2001), the Latina and Latino adolescents in Havertown adopt different adaptive strategies when faced with this conflict.[7] Latinas behave like Ogbu's (1987) "voluntary" or "immigrant" minorities. While in school, they adopt the school's values and work hard on academic tasks. At home they think of themselves as Mexican or Mexican American (Guatemalan or Guatemalan American) and share many of their parents' values. Latino male adolescents, however, behave more like Ogbu's "involuntary" or "caste" minorities. Both at home and in school they consider themselves Mexican, and they do not accommodate to the school's expectations. They expect to work in the trades or in manufacturing, like their fathers, and they do not see school success as necessary to this goal.[8]

This gender difference in attitudes toward school pre-dated Margaret's arrival, and it has lasted beyond her time in Havertown. In order to examine the impact of her culturally relevant pedagogy on the Latino students, then, we need to look at the two genders separately. The adolescent girls who were doing well in school before Margaret arrived continued to do well academically during her three years. Margaret was able to give some personal attention to particular students, and this probably helped some Latinas make it to college when they would not have, or encouraged them to go to better colleges than they would have. But she did not have a large academic impact on them. Margaret's culturally relevant pedagogy influenced these Latinas primarily by developing pride in their home cultures. In school, some of them had been downplaying their Latino background. But Margaret helped them see academic success and being Latina as mutually compatible. Thus these girls accomplished two central goals of culturally relevant pedagogy—to succeed academically, by mainstream standards, and to develop pride in their home cultures—but Margaret herself deserves credit only for the latter result.

With the boys, almost all of whom did not do well in school, Margaret also succeeded in developing their pride in being Latino. These boys had been proud of their Mexican heritage before Margaret's arrival, but she brought some official sanction to this pride. By valuing their home culture and by teaching them some of the accomplishments of Latino peoples, Margaret helped these boys resist the devaluation of their language and culture that too often occurs in mainstream U.S. society. Despite her efforts, however, these boys did not succeed academically in school. Most came to see the school as less hostile, and they did improve their grades somewhat. But most ended up failing one or several courses, and most have by now dropped out of high school. These boys could not reconcile their aspirations as rural, working-class Mexican men—to be the head of their own household, to work hard in the trades or at physical labor and support a family, to remain close to their own extended family—with the expectations of the school that they will "better" themselves and move as individuals beyond their families and their home culture.

So Margaret's culturally relevant pedagogy accomplished one of its goals for both groups of Latino students—to develop pride in their home cultures. The significance of this accomplishment became clear in the academic year following Margaret's departure when the ESL room reverted to a more traditional style. The room is now used almost exclusively by LEP students for formal instruction. Whereas before there might have been six or eight students in and out of the room during a given period, now we have observed no more than three. Student activities are much more spatially segregated now, with staff using a table in an adjoining room for students working on unrelated projects. There is no longer student work on the walls. There is also a new clock. LEP students and those who were formerly successful in school are doing about as well as before. These students, however, report that "everyone misses Margaret." Even though current staff are effective instructors, these students miss the support and camaraderie of the old room. Tellingly, students no longer know much about what other Latinos in the school are doing. When asked how some other Latino student is doing, people often report that they "haven't seen her." We have also observed teasing among the Latino students—particularly the less successful calling the more successful "school-girl" and the like. Losing Margaret has been more difficult for the less academically successful but non-LEP students. These students report that they no longer go to the ESL room. Current staff tries to motivate them with extrinsic reinforcements like grades, but these are in most cases not working. Current staff has good intentions, but because they are perceived as less supportive, many students will not give them a chance.

CONCLUSIONS

Clearly something was lost when Margaret and her culturally relevant pedagogy left Havertown High. But we argue that the situation is not as simple as it may seem. Margaret's culturally relevant pedagogy helped in some respects, but it did not help all the Latino students both succeed academically and develop pride in their home cultures. It may be that, with more power and institutional support, Margaret could have implemented her pedagogy more widely across the school and thereby could have helped more of the Latino students succeed academically.[9] But we argue that Margaret also ran into the deep conflict between rural Mexican and mainstream U.S. values described by Valdés (1996). Valdés reminds us that mainstream U.S. schooling practices presuppose culturally specific values and assumptions, particularly an emphasis on *individual* accomplishments and the freedom to choose one's own life course that academic credentials can bring. She describes how rural, working-class Mexicans value reciprocity and loyalty to the family over individual glory and how these more collective values lead some Mexicans and Mexican Americans to forego academic successes for the sake of maintaining their connections with others.

Valdés ends her book on what seems a painful note. She argues that we should not define "success" as only individual academic success. People like the Latino males in Havertown may be perfectly successful, by their standards, if they drop out of high school and remain loyal, contributing members of their families. Valdés argues, further, that we should not try to wipe out this alternative value system through well-intentioned efforts to help Latino students "succeed" by mainstream standards. We call this ending "painful" because Valdés realizes that mainstream Anglo values will not easily coexist with the more communal values she describes. In fact, due to larger social and economic forces, mainstream Anglo values seem to be spreading and undermining more communal values in various parts of the world. We are left, then, with a hard choice: to encourage the male Latino adolescents in Havertown to pursue academic success, as defined by the school, would seem to undermine their own cultural values; but to encourage them to reject mainstream schooling will close off many opportunities that they may not at this point fully understand.

Our description of Margaret's culturally relevant pedagogy has also shown, however, that educators face this hard choice with only some Latino students. The Latina adolescents did not encounter an either-or choice between home and host cultures, and they benefited from Margaret's culturally relevant pedagogy. The different adaptive strategies adopted by Latino and Latina adolescents led them to appropriate Margaret's educational strategy differently. Sometimes the important differences between minority and mainstream U.S. cultural values force students and their teachers to make hard choices. But sometimes minority students and their teachers can, through culturally relevant pedagogy, manage both academic success and cultural celebration. Whether academic success and home cultural values can coexist in any given setting seems to depend on details of that setting and the people in it.

NOTES

Portions of this chapter appeared in our article "Struggling toward a culturally relevant pedagogy in the Latino diaspora," *Journal of Latinos and Education* 1

(2002), 133–144. We would like to thank the National Academy of Education and the Spencer Foundation for supporting this research through a grant to the first author. We would like to acknowledge the insight and work of our research assistants, Levania Davis and Gerardo Joven, whose help has been indispensable. We would also like to thank Pablo Chavajay, Norma González, Genevieve Patthey-Chávez, Carlos Vélez-Ibáñez, and Ana Celia Zentella for suggestions and comments.

1. In the terms often used to describe bilingual education, these theorists advocate an "additive" and not a transitional or assimilationist approach to linguistic and cultural minority students (Genesee, 1994; Lambert and Tucker, 1972). Minority students should learn both their home language and culture and the mainstream language and culture. With such an additive approach to bilingual education, minority students learn the standard curriculum *better* than under transitional or assimilationist approaches (Bialystock, 1991; Dolson, 1985; Genesee, 1987, 1994).

2. All names and many identifying details have been changed.

3. One might expect that Margaret's maternal self-presentation would lead to lax discipline. But in fact she accomplishes discipline in a less institutional, more home-like way. Rothenberg (1995) and Valdés (1996) describe how working-class Mexican children are often particularly concerned not to upset or disappoint their mothers. In many cases Margaret does not have to resort to extrinsic reinforcement like grades and detentions with her students because they know she cares and they do not want to let her down.

4. Osborne (1996) reviews many ethnographic studies that show how non-minority teachers—with relevant knowledge and sufficient motivation—can teach culturally relevant pedagogy. Margaret's own ethnic identity is hybrid. She was born a New England Anglo, not far from Havertown, but she considers herself partly Latina. She lived for several years in Colombia, where she met her husband. And she has four Latino children with him. She once remarked that when she was pregnant with these children and exchanging blood with them, she herself became physically part Latina. Her pride in Latino cultures and her ability to speak Spanish were important to many of her students.

5. Harvey (1996) and Postone (1993) argue that the typical Anglo conception of linear, segmented time and space—in which time and space form empty containers into which activities are organized—has emerged only recently in capitalist societies. Society needed to compartmentalize time into measurable units when labor became a commodity and a measure of value. Among medieval Europeans the "hour" was invented in the thirteenth century, and the "minute" became common only in the seventeenth century—as capitalism was firmly taking hold (cf. LeGoff, 1980). The more fluid spatiotemporal organization that Rogoff, Mistry, Göncü, and Mosier (1993) observed in rural Guatemala and India, and that we have observed among Havertown Latinos, is characteristic of people more insulated from the capitalism of the modern West. Note, however, that Grossberg (1993) argues that the transition from modernism to postmodernism in the West might be bringing us back toward a more simultaneous, fluid spatiotemporal organization.

6. See Hamann (n.d.) for a discussion of bilingual paraprofessionals' roles in helping U.S. Latino students. He describes how, like Margaret, paraprofessionals are often able to advocate for Latino students and build strong relationships with them. He also describes how paraprofessionals are institutionally marginal and often devalued in the educational system.

7. Phelan, Davidson, and Yu (1998) provide a taxonomy of adaptive strategies adolescents adopt when faced with different expectations at home, among peers, and at school. In their terms, the Havertown Latinas "manage" the "incongruent" worlds of home and school by accommodating to mainstream norms in school and retaining Mexican norms at home. The boys "resist" the incongruent world of the school and adopt identities that fit at home but not at school.

8. Our research thus supports Calderón (1996), Tapia (1996), Valdés (1997), and others in pointing to the heterogeneity of U.S. Latino identities. This minority group, at least, resists characterization as one monolithic sociocultural type or another. Our results are particularly striking in this regard, as they show both "voluntary" and "involuntary" minority attitudes and behaviors *coexisting* within one very small community—and in some cases *within the same household*, with brothers and sisters adopting different stances.

9. The more successful examples of culturally relevant pedagogy described by Freeman (1996), Ladson-Billings (1995), and Rose (1995) all occurred in schools and communities with a much higher percentage of minority students. It may be that the low percentage of Latinos in Havertown makes culturally relevant pedagogy more difficult to sustain there because the curriculum in entire classrooms or the whole school is unlikely to be modified to fit the culturally relevant mode and because only a few staff will be familiar with the details of the relevant minority culture.

REFERENCES

Allen, B., and Boykin, A. (1992). African-American children and the educational process. *School Psychology Review* 21, 586–596.

Azmitia, M., Cooper, C., García, E., and Dunbar, N. (1996). The ecology of family guidance in low-income Mexican-American and European-American families. *Social Development* 5, 1–23.

Bialystok, E. (Ed.). (1991). *Language processing in bilingual children*. New York: Cambridge University Press.

Bourdieu, P., and Passeron, J. (1970/1977). *Reproduction in education, society and culture* (R. Nice, Trans.). Thousand Oaks, CA: Sage.

Calderón, J. (1996). Situational identity of suburban Mexican American politicians in a multiethnic community. In R. DeAnda (Ed.), *Chicanas and Chicanos in contemporary society*. Boston: Allyn & Bacon, pp. 179–189.

Cummins, J. (1993). Empowering minority students. In L. Weis and M. Fine (Eds.), *Beyond silenced voices*. Albany, NY: SUNY Press, pp. 101–117.

Dolson, D. (1985). The effects of Spanish home language use on the scholastic performance of Hispanic students. *Journal of Multilingual and Multicultural Development* 6, 135–155.

Eisenberg, A. (1986). Teasing: Verbal play in two Mexicano homes. In B. Schieffelin and E. Ochs (Eds.), *Language socialization across cultures*. New York: Cambridge University Press, pp. 182–198.

Fordham, S., and Ogbu, J. (1986). Black students' school success: Coping with the burden of "acting white." *The Urban Review* 18, 176–206.

Freeman, R. (1996). Dual-language planning at Oyster Bilingual School. *TESOL Quarterly* 30, 557–582.

Gallimore, R., and Goldenberg, C. (1993). Activity settings of early literacy. In E. Forman, N. Minick, and C. Stone (Eds.), *Contexts for learning*. New York: Oxford University Press, pp. 315–335.

Genesee, F. (1987). *Learning through two languages*. New York: Newbury House.

Genesee, F. (Ed.). (1994). *Educating second language children*. New York: Cambridge University Press.

Griffith, D., and Kissam, E. (1995). *Working poor*. Philadelphia: Temple University Press.

Grossberg, L. (1993). Cultural studies and/in new worlds. In C. McCarthy and W. Crichlow (Eds.), *Race, identity and representation in education*. New York: Routledge, pp. 89–105.

Hamann, E. (n.d.). Contesting unequal social reproduction: Bilingual paras' roles in helping LEP Kansans. Unpublished manuscript, University of Pennsylvania Graduate School of Education.

Harvey, D. (1996). *Justice, nature and the geography of difference*. Oxford: Blackwell.

Heath, S., and McLaughlin, M. (Eds.). (1993). *Identity and inner city youth*. New York: Teachers College Press.

Irvine, J. (1990). *Black students and school failure*. Westport, CT: Greenwood Press.

Ladson-Billings, G. (1995). Toward a theory of culturally relevant pedagogy. *American Educational Research Journal* 32, 465–491.

Lambert, W., and Tucker, G. (1972). *Bilingual education of children*. Rowley, MA: Newbury House.

LeGoff, J. (1980). *Time, work and culture in the middle ages* (A. Goldhammer, Trans.). Chicago: University of Chicago Press.

Levinson, B., and Sutton, M. (2001). Policy as/in practice: A sociocultural approach to the study of educational policy. In M. Sutton and B. Levinson (Eds.), *Policy as practice: Toward a comparative sociocultural analysis of educational policy*. Westport, CT: Ablex, pp. 1–21.

Losey, K. (1995). Mexican American students and classroom interaction. *Review of Educational Research* 65, 283–318.

McDermott, R. (1987). The explanation of minority school failure, again. *Anthropology and Education Quarterly* 18, 361–364.

McDermott, R., and Tylbor, H. (1995). On the necessity of collusion in conversation. In D. Tedlock and B. Mannheim (Eds.), *The dialogic emergence of culture*. Urbana: University of Illinois Press, pp. 218–236.

Michaels, S. (1981). Sharing time. *Language in Society* 10, 423–442.

Ogbu, J. (1987). Variability in minority school performance. *Anthropology and Education Quarterly* 18, 312–334.

Osborne, A. (1996). Practice into theory into practice. *Anthropology and Education Quarterly* 27, 285–314.

Phelan, P., Davidson, A., and Yu, H. (1998). *Adolescents' worlds*. New York: Teachers College Press.

Postone, M. (1993). *Time, labor and social domination*. New York: Cambridge University Press.

Rogoff, B. (1991). *Apprenticeship in thinking*. New York: Oxford University Press.

Rogoff, B., Mistry, J., Göncü, A., and Mosier, C. (1993). Guided participation in cultural activity by toddlers and caregivers. *Monographs of the Society for Research in Child Development* (Serial No. 236) 58(8).

Rose, M. (1995). *Possible lives.* Boston: Houghton Mifflin.

Rothenberg, B. (1995). *Understanding and working with parents and children from rural Mexico.* Menlo Park, CA: The CHC Center for Child and Family Development.

Sabogal, F., Marín, G., Otero-Sabogal, R., Marín, B., and Perez-Stable, P. (1987). Hispanic families and acculturation. *Hispanic Journal of Behavioral Sciences* 9, 397–412.

Saenz, R., and Greenlees, C. (1996). The demography of Chicanos. In R. DeAnda (Ed.), *Chicanas and Chicanos in contemporary society.* Boston: Allyn & Bacon, pp. 9–23.

Stull, D., Broadway, M., and Erickson, K. (1992). The price of a good steak. In L. Lamphere (Ed.), *Structuring diversity.* Chicago: University of Chicago Press, pp. 35–64.

Suárez-Orozco, C., and Suárez-Orozco, M. (1995). *Transformations.* Stanford, CA: Stanford University Press.

Tapia, J. (1996). Juntos y separados. In R. DeAnda (Ed.), *Chicanas and Chicanos in contemporary society.* Boston: Allyn & Bacon, pp. 75–86.

Valdés, G. (1996). *Con respeto.* New York: Teachers College Press.

Valdés, G. (1997). Dual-language immersion programs. *Harvard Educational Review* 67, 391–429.

Vásquez, O., Pease-Alvarez, L., and Shannon, S. (1994). *Pushing boundaries.* New York: Cambridge University Press.

Vélez-Ibáñez, C. (1993). Ritual cycles of exchange. In P. Frese (Ed.), *Celebrations of identity: Multiple voices in American ritual performance.* Westport, CT: Bergin & Garvey.

Vélez-Ibáñez, C. (1996). *Border visions.* Tucson: University of Arizona Press.

Wortham, S. (1994). *Acting out participant examples in the classroom.* Philadelphia: John Benjamins.

Wortham, S. (2001). Gender and school success in the Latino diaspora. In S. Wortham, E. Murillo, and E. Hamann (Eds.), *Education in the new Latino diaspora: Policy and the politics of identity.* Westport, CT: Ablex, pp. 117–141.

Chapter 5

The Role of Institutional Education Projects in the Reconstruction of the School Labyrinth

Rafael Ávila Peñagos and Marina Camargo Abello

"How beautiful is the world;
and how ugly are the labyrinths," said Adso.
"How beautiful the world would be
if there were a clue
to guide us through the labyrinths,"
replied the master.

Umberto Eco, *The Name of the Rose*

The purpose of this chapter is to share with the international research community the theoretical and methodological premises, as well as the results, of a research project on the social construction of *Proyectos Educativos Institucionales* (Institutional Education Projects—henceforth referred to as PEI).[1] This research took place within the context of the reforms initiated by the new education law in Colombia (Law 115/94), in which by state policy all schools must construct their own institutional education projects (PEI) in order to structure their capacity for self-government. This law initiated a period of transition in the management of the education system in Colombia from an excessively centralized scheme to a decentralized structure.

THE PURPOSE OF THE STUDY

Our project from the outset was designed to study primary school culture and more specifically the conceptions and practices of teachers in relation to the process of social construction of the PEI. Since the term "social construction" was from the start given a number of different interpretations, it was necessary to discuss its definition in order to find an agreement on its meaning among researchers. We agreed that this category would be understood as participatory construction. However, at the end of the first term in the field, and after working in five institutions, we arrived at the conclusion that based on the agreed definition, there had been no process of social construction.[2] Further, and more important, our interest as researchers, and the objective of the study, was not the reconstruction of the process, but rather the identification of the culture that had permitted or blocked this process of social construction. We had access to this culture through practice and from scenarios designed in each establishment.

THEORETICAL FRAMEWORK

Our project had a research component and an intervention component. For the research component, a proposal was made to understand school culture with the assistance of a theoretical framework of an ethnographic nature. The proposal was inspired by the hermeneutical tradition, and its intention was to understand the problems of education as problems of culture. In order to ensure that the approach was ethnographic, the researchers took care to satisfy four conditions required for this type of approach: (1) prolonged fieldwork (1.5 years); (2) the use of observation as a basic working strategy; (3) a theory of culture from which we focus and interpret practice; and (4) the production of an interpretive text based on cumulative records. In this project, we applied a semiotic understanding of culture. From this point of view a human is born in a horizon of meaning, influenced by a web of meanings that he/she personally has woven, and in which he/she is inextricably inserted (Geertz, 1992, p. 20). We therefore understand the school culture as a set of significations shared by teachers and administrators in the institution, which are revealed by their practices and their language.

In the intervention component, the intention was to test a method of teacher assessment designed to *facilitate* the construction of the PEI on the basis of rigorous reflection on teaching practice. It was decided to test the democratic education workshop method (talleres de educación democrática—TED), developed and systematized by the Interdisciplinary Education Research Program (Programa Interdisciplinario de Investigaciones en Educación—PIIE) of Santiago, Chile.

As we suggest in our title, the problem is not the existence of labyrinths, but the lack of clues to decipher the route. In order to guide us through these labyrinths, we have applied the theoretical and methodological tools of qualitative research.

The hunter who stretches out in the mud to stare at the tracks left by his prey, Sherlock Holmes collecting up fingerprints of possible criminals, Morelli identifying the traces of an original painting, Guillermo de Baskerville searching for tracks and deciphering enigmas in the labyrinth of an abbey, the monk concerned to interpret the scriptures, the historian who selects documentation to reconstruct the facts, the doctor who depends on symptoms to offer a diagnosis, and Freud trying to enter the unconscious through the real indicators of dreams and verbal lapses—all these examples show the impact of traceable clues, where the observer is given indicators of how to arrive at a complex reality that cannot be experienced directly by the individual.

The common premise for all these forms of knowledge is as simple as it is fertile: there are things that designate other things; there are some things that remit us to others; there are some things that reveal others to us. There are some levels of reality to which we cannot have access except through other levels. Therefore, the knowledge that characterizes these forms of knowledge is indirect, indexical and conjectural. There is an undeniable degree of randomness, as Ginzburg has said (1989, p. 147).

Qualitative research, and its underlining epistemological discourses, belongs to the constellation of disciplines that naturally are ruled by criteria of scientific application that are quite different from those that inspire disciplines derived from Galilean physics. Ginzburg calls these criteria indexical; we prefer to call them semi-logical.

We work with things that designate others, and therefore we follow marks, traces, and hints, and we try to understand and interpret symptoms and signs, whether physical or written. These we call texts. Where there is a text, there is exegesis, interpretation, and hermeneutics. All the empirical bases of our research were texts, sets of texts, mountains of texts constructed during fieldwork in the school organizations studied. And all the results of our research are readings. These are readings which, to be more accurate, are superimposed on the first readings that teachers make of their school context (Giddens, 1976, p. 158; Habermas, 1987, p. 147 ff.).

If we translate this theoretical principle to the conditions of our research, this means that when we arrive in the field with the intention of observing, but there is somebody who has gone before us in the work of observation and has seen the school from inside, that predecessor is the teacher. What researchers do is to generate scenarios of interlocution, to provoke the expression of teachers' experience through language. In the generation of these scenarios to provoke expression, and in recording their experiences, we produce the data that will be the basis of our interpretation. Therefore, data are not (re)collected as if they existed before the research, but they are produced as the result of an interactive process between the researcher and the researched.

An education institution is for us a text loaded with meanings, interesting and intriguing, but unclear, meanings, infested with contradictions, inconsistency, and suspicious comments at the margins. To approach this text with the intention of understanding it is like working into a labyrinth.

The research report is, therefore, a systematic ordering of our readings. We observe observations, we read readings, and we interpret interpretations. The results of interpretations are not verified, but documented. This qualifies them as reasonable and plausible. The hypotheses did not precede the research, and did not guide it, but they may be produced at the end of it as a consequence of the clarity arising from comprehension.

METHOD

Method of Research

We initially went to the Bogotá Education Department for help in identifying 10 public sector schools that met a previously outlined profile. We visited each identified school and, after a process of negotiation during which we motivated school administrators to participate, five schools were selected for the study. Although little importance was ascribed to this process of entering the site of research, we believe that it deserves greater attention. In this type of research it is necessary to motivate, persuade, and arrive at agreements before entering the site. One does not know whether one should enter at the grass-roots level with the teachers or with the upper branches of administration. In our case, we started with administration, which expressed great enthusiasm at the beginning. However, when we tried to secure the space and time required through formal agreement, problems began to arise. We found that the schools were fed up with offers. There were many other offers in addition to our own (the "culture institute," *El Espectador* newspaper, strategic planning, the teacher network, Universidad Nacional, etc.). The problem was not the multiplicity of offers but the absence of criteria on the part of the administration. The administration failed to define which research would be most relevant and which would not. They said "yes" to everyone and then found themselves running around to find time for new commitments, all of which would obviously be added to the routine activities of the school and subsequently cause an overload of work for the teachers.

By agreement with administrators, we selected two or three teachers in each institution to take part in an induction seminar for the TED. These initial 15 were formed as a reference group, serving as a methodological bridge between the schools and the research group. The intention was to provide this group with a greater knowledge of the methods to be employed in order to make them more able to collaborate with us. We worked in two types of sites: one we called "natural" and the other we called "constructed." In the natural sites, there were administrative meetings, academic council meetings, area meetings, disciplinary meetings, and teacher training sections. That is, these were sites that were more or less part of the institution in which the teachers themselves worked. We were present at the "natural" sites and recorded conversations on tape. In the "constructed" sites, there were the TED, some informal meetings with teachers, and the interviews. The "constructed" sites were also taped. All tapes were transcribed for analysis. The main points of reference of teacher discourse were categorized and cross-referenced against nine categories, in order to proceed to an overall interpretation. The results of these interpretations were contrasted with three types of actors: First, with the reference group, second with the teachers with whom we were working, and finally with the Chilean PIIE advisors. In addition to regular comparison and contrast among the researchers themselves, each of these actors provided feedback so that from comparison to comparison, the final interpretation was gradually constructed and triangulated.

Method in Intervention

What happened in the intervention with the TED? Each group of teachers that had taken part in the TED induction seminar tried to disseminate the TED in turn to the teachers in their various schools. Each group found its own way of convincing administrators to make space available to re-create the experience. This was a very interesting process. Although initially we intended to apply or to replicate the TED, we began to understand that it was more suitable to talk of appropriating the TED in another cultural context. With this, we began to propose to study the problems specific to the transfer of one methodological tool to another cultural context. In a second stage, each group came to the site of the reference group to share experiences with others and receive feedback to improve their own experience. Each group invented the way in which it would record its workshops, sometimes with the help of researchers. Based on their records, each group went on to reflect on their experience. The records were expanded with all comments from the members of the reference group. Something genuinely surprising and unforeseen was that the dissemination of the workshop results in the context of the reference group turned out to also be a meaningful space for the construction of information; here, the school imaginary was let loose more or less spontaneously and in a more interesting way than in the natural site. The discussions of the teachers in this site were less bound to the format of their routine agenda, thus allowing them to "get it off their chests." This was definitely one of the most important means of access for us to the school culture. Thus, the process of intervention ended by being methodologically subject to the overall research process, thereby contributing a new means of accumulating information. If there was a moment when the school imaginary took off, it was in the appropriation of the TED, brought by the teachers to the space of the reference group.

As a working experience with the international research community, this was a source of learning. We made use of telephone, fax, and e-mail to communicate with our international advisors, with whom we had continual contact. Four follow-up meetings were held, two in Santiago and two in Bogotá. There were difficulties, to be sure, and these should not be minimized, but the benefits were greater than the costs. It is important to work with the international research community, first in order to come out of our parochial world, and second to construct a supranational environment of exchange of knowledge in our fields of interest.

THE PROTO-IMAGE

Upon approaching the jungle of data accumulated in the first stage of the research, we discovered that we had to reckon with an image located at the threshold of interpretation before starting the reading of any written record. The image was not there before the process began, but it was there prior to starting the interpretation stage for the texts. It did not fall like a shooting star but came about slowly as a result of our immersion in the schools. It was something like a gestalt, a flash of recognition, and much more a film negative than a photograph, since it had yet to be developed.

As in Max Weber's ideal types, everything was there: the school, the actors, and even the framework, but there was no specificity, nothing in particular. As happens with the "faceless judges," we saw no faces, only shadows; we heard no voices, only deformations of a voice as if in a slow-motion film. Everything happened in the shadows, as if through a fog.

It was a difficult text, but it was a text; dense, but a text; misty, but a text. It revealed itself as an object, as an environment, and as a backdrop for interpretation; a contrast between object and environment, a contrast between object and background, which cannot be understood with disjunctive logic. It was a difficult text, and we believe it owed its difficulty to its prediscursive character. But it was a fertile text, and it could give us the clue to read the other items of discourse from the school imaginary.

This image, which for lack of a better term we decided to call a "proto-image,"came as the first text to be deciphered. Interpretation is shadow-boxing, but it is also a struggle against masks. It is an attempt to clarify, but also an attempt to unveil. It is like hunting for a hidden meaning (Freud), yet it is also like suspecting (Nietzsche). Therefore, it is impossible to avoid this proto-image. Like titles, proto-images mark the tone and give us the key for our reading.

The school was here and there in the image; some of the teachers were there, and also others; some of the administration was also there:

- Sharp ingenious agents, colliding with each other, grinding against each other ("if we continue with these intrigues . . .")
- Irritated vocal chords ("I also have vocal chords . . .")

- Hands that anxiously look for the word ("I would like to say . . .")
- Muscles that retract to close the mouth ("Better not say anything . . .")
- Unexpected increases of volume ("We are raising our voice . . .")
- Discussions that launch labels (the day staff, the evening staff, the rebels, the sneaks, etc.)
- Feelings of fear ("If I say it, I'm afraid that . . .")
- Feelings of guilt ("So where are we? Are we guilty or not?")
- Feelings of being undervalued ("They do not value us as teachers . . .")
- Feelings of isolation ("Each of us is an island . . .")
- Feelings of anarchy ("If there is no one running the show . . .")
- Feelings of shame ("Sorry, please excuse me . . .")
- Feelings of mutual respect ("Here we must respect each other . . .")
- Abundance of projects ("We want to do so many things . . .")
- Lack of opportunity to interact ("We have to look for the opportunity . . .")
- Shortage of time ("Give me five more minutes . . .")
- A good dose of improvisation ("We have to improvise . . .")
- "Meetingitis" ("Another meeting?")
- Useless meetings ("We spend 50% of the time on information . . .")
- Lack of decision ("We still haven't decided anything . . .")
- Absence of basic agreement ("There is no agreement between the three agents . . .")
- Excessive complaints ("This is becoming a department of complaints . . .")
- Waffling ("We still haven't got to the point . . .")
- Verbal flood of stifled frustrations ("Sorry, but we are trying to get it off our chests . . .")
- Open and hidden resistance ("You don't have the right to come tell us how it is . . .")
- Enthusiasm and clipped wings ("They've put the brakes on us . . .")

In sum, these are particles that are agitated, faces that light up, temperatures rising, frustrations let loose, intense and multiple confrontation. All these thermal metaphors make one think not only of the invasion of underground energy but also of the boiling up of rigid attitudes that unfreeze with the effect of "cultural heat." Branches moved by all kinds of wind, but more than anything, a great appetite for knowledge (the quest for all types of courses, workshops, conferences, scenarios, etc.). Sharp teachers, ingenious teachers, hard-working teachers, teachers who work their fingers to the bone, with a great sense of responsibility, overcoming all the obstacles presented by our harsh reality. But, paradoxically, there are teachers who waste their energy, who expend it the wrong ways, teachers who dissipate the energy like light from the surface of an enormous bulb instead of concentrating on a particular spot like a laser beam. There are teachers who become agitated on an overheated thermal layer by the collision of rigid attitudes, but at the same time, teachers who prepare to pass from cognitive invariance to changes in concepts and practices. A high temperature, but at the same time an approach to boiling point. A high degree of dispersion, but at the same time an approach to new forms of concentrating energy. An old paradigm of school organization crumbles, but the way has not yet been found to construct an alternative paradigm. The oldest is dying, but the new has yet to be born (Gramsci).

Metaphor has played an important role in the history of science (Elizalde, 1994, p. 43), and it will help us to come to know an unknown level of realities, from a known level. It will transfer us (metaphor means "transfer") from one form of meaning to another, and in this it helps us to translate the reading of a difficult text. It is impossible not to accept that the metaphors we have employed in the reading of this proto-image draw our attention to two central dynamics: dispersion and collision among the school actors. Our hypothesis, and this is now a good bet, is that the dispersion of the agents and the collision of their imaginaries are the results of the same paradigm of school organization.

The Relationship of School and Environment

The contrast between physical space and psychosocial space in the school organization was impressive. Physical space seems carefully limited by well-built walls of brick, which make one think of ivory towers, impermeable to the outside world. But the psychosocial space, formed by the imaginaries of all actors concerned, seems to be a porous space, penetrated by many influences of discourse from the most diverse types of organization. With the pupils, severe problems of poverty, hunger, violence, and even drug addiction come into the school, and teachers and managers have to deal with these daily. With the representatives of many organizations, an extremely wide range of discourse enters the school. But teachers and administrators also go outside the school in search of offers, and they are on the lookout for any seminar, conference, or training course offered in the knowledge market. When no offer arrives, they go out to look for them, and when they cannot be at the actual event, they find a way of getting hold of photocopies, course notes, or recordings. The ingenuity of the moonlighters in the informal economy is replicated in the knowledge market.

To give some idea of the diversity of the offers, here are a few examples:

• *El Espectador* newspaper sells a discourse which projects news as a teaching resource for context and analysis.

- Companies offer opportunities for work-study to provide a practical solution for the relationship between education and the employment market.
- The hospital joins in this pragmatic approach by offering work-study experience for services related to care for the elderly and the terminally ill.
- The staff computer technician puts pressure on the administration to tell him how to make out evaluation sheets. ("Whether you know how to evaluate or not, is not my problem; what I need is to agree with you on the sheet."[3])
- The local town council places pressure on the administration to give some attention to local problems but avoids including a budget item for education investment in its finances.
- The national Department of Education requires specific tasks to be done but combines its requirements with incentives for the best PEI and training courses for management and teachers.
- The minister of education attempts to reorganize the system and to define the competencies of the various levels but goes overboard with mountains of regulations: laws, regulatory decrees, general guidelines, suggestions for reflection on subjects to be considered, schemes that should not be considered as unique, and even forms which must be filled in.
- The teachers' union calls on the teachers when it wants to exert pressure on the State to improve employment conditions and manages to bring the school to a halt in a permanent state of tension.
- Parents begin to organize themselves to demand a "rendering of accounts" from teachers and administration, although the preference is still to maintain them at a distance in "schools for parents" instead of recognizing their right to play an active part in school government.
- Consultancy groups offer technical assistance, which ends up in training courses and fails to generate relevant documentation.
- Finally, educational researchers, such as ourselves, ask for admission to the scenes in which the teachers discuss their affairs in exchange for promises of rationalization that cannot come about except in the long term.

In summary, there is a multidirectional exchange and influence, which implies some compromise in meanings and the reconfiguration of imaginaries. There are negotiations between actors, and there is reorientation and redefinition, provoked by a constant and inevitable interaction with many different organizations. The boundaries of the school are being destroyed, and windows begin to be built to favor bidirectional flows.

The PEI-Environment Relationship

The environment—a concept that needs to be defined—is not simply a vague circle around the physical plant of the school (the neighborhood, or barrio). Rather, it is a complex network of organizations with diverse but complementary purposes, that do not necessarily relate to the neighborhood because of spatial contiguity. It is not only the city district, through the town council (*Junta Administradora Local*—JAL), that brings its demands to the school but also other organizations with divergent purposes. Through their offers of discourse, they bring their interests and ideologies. Complex networks of organizations try to involve the school, and each of them wants to take the water to its mill. But the school does not know how to respond and moves around in a turbulent environment, agitated by all types of currents, with no defined navigation charts and no compass to indicate a course.

It was interesting to the researcher that each of these offers generates a corresponding demand, which finds an echo inside the institution. In each case, there is motivation for a group of interested "clients" who then generate their projects. This situation is made more acute by the incentive policies for the presentation of projects by the Department of Education. Therefore, we find a proliferation of projects, a superabundance of projects, indeed, a Babel of projects, but with no PEI integrated or integrating the process. The document known as PEI seems to be one more project, in some cases delegated, and in others prepared by a very small group under pressure for management, who in turn are under pressure from the Ministry of Education. The PEI is a sort of floating project, with no emotional roots in the school's rank and file, who know nothing of its content or origin.

The problem, therefore, is not a lack of projects but a surfeit of projects, pointing in all directions. To use a medical metaphor: it is a kind of "projectitis" with two faces: one is positive—the emergence of a forward-looking agenda—and one is negative—a fragmentation of views.

The public school, therefore, seems to be an aggregate of private sectors, each of them with different projects, sometimes mutually contradictory, and yet there appears to be little concern over this. Branches moved by many winds have allowed themselves to be exposed to fresh air, but they create their own currents of opinion and power, without providing appropriate opportunities for the construction of shared intentions that could integrate the diversity of tendencies into a cooperative system of action.

Fragmentation means that the school cannot integrate itself into an institution with a mission and shared values. Fragmentation means that the school cannot construct itself as a body (auto-poeisis) and, even less, regulate itself. The question, therefore, as well as the problem and the challenge, is how to construct an intelligent school organization.[4]

GENERAL CONCLUSIONS

So far, we have had the reading of the proto-image. Now let us look at the conclusions at which we have arrived from reading the written text. We will concentrate on the conclusions that seem to us to be most important and of the greatest priority for the design of policies that can provide useful feedback for practices and institutions.

Attitudes to the PEI

The PEI policy comes into existence in a framework of institutional weakness in school, at a time of cultural turbulence in which, quoting Marx, "all that is solid melts into air." Truths considered to be firmly established are questioned. The authority formally recognized for teachers has been eroded.

Teachers have constructed a complex and peculiar relationship of a symbolic kind with the PEI policy. They forge their own images and their own expectations based on the text of the law. They swallow nothing whole; rather, they reconstruct on the bases of their own institutional context, their own knowledge, and their own professional experience. Official documents are not repeated or translated but rather recontextualized by teachers in their own manner, in many ways. To some extent, it can be said that the documents have been domesticated in the teachers' own image and semblance.

Although the PEI document has not succeeded in going beyond the framework of formality, something has happened which is now irreversible. The launching of the PEI in the schools has meant, in any case, that there is now a valuable opportunity:

- To set up participation laboratories
- To attempt to construct institutional autonomy, over and above the individual autonomies of each professional, especially where such autonomy is ill-conceived or distorted
- To give a new impulse to written culture, as the history of the institution
- To begin to rebuild the institution as a system of cooperative action

Teachers have begun to understand that beyond the preparation of a document, what is at stake is the reconstruction of the school as an organic whole.

Tensions between Principle and Practice

In line with our conception of the institution as a dialectical site crossed by opposing forces,[5] in which it is possible to visualize conceptions and practices seeking institutionalization but also conceptions and practices already institutionalized, we have identified throughout the project four critical tensions in school culture which should be highlighted:

- Tension between the functional administration of schools, as an institutionalized routine, and the culture of projects, as an initiative for new institutionalization.
- Tension between the culture of regulation by many (*hetero-regulación*), as an institutionalized routine, and the culture of self-regulation, as an initiative for new institutionalization.
- Tension between the culture of subordination as an institutionalized routine, and the culture of coordination, as an initiative for new institutionalization.
- Tension between the teaching practices of the classroom as an institutionalized routine and collective reflection on teaching practice as an initiative for new institutionalization.

With regard to the first of these tensions, we consider that the introduction of the culture of projects, although fragmented, offers a prospective element that may come to be a significant counterweight to the culture of functional administration of routines. A policy to reinforce this culture could contribute to a broader prospective capacity for those involved and for the practice of program design.[6]

With regard to the second tension, we consider that despite the fact that its understanding and adaptation is still in its early stages, the introduction of the culture of planning, through strategic planning and similar theoretical approaches, allows the institution to be seen as an object of self-intervention, which comes to be a significant counterweight to the habits of regulation from outside. A policy to reinforce this culture may contribute to broadening the practices and competencies required for self-regulation.

With regard to the third tension, we consider that the appearance of the culture of co-ordination, seeking more horizontal relationships among the teachers, may come to be a significant counterweight to the culture of subordination, which is expressed in the teachers' relationships to authorities. A policy to reinforce this culture may make a marked contribution to widening practices designed to harmonize intentions and purposefully coordinate actions. This would erode authoritarian relationships and the consequent manipulation that arises from them.

With regard to the fourth tension, we consider that the construction of social spaces favorable to the exercise of collective reflection on teaching practice, such as is made possible by the TED, could come to be a significant counterweight in taking teaching practice out of the classroom and away from its isolation and fragmentation as something secret or private. A policy to reinforce this collective form of reflection on teaching practice could promote a transition toward greater coordination and integration of work by teachers around a shared mission.[7]

In this process of construction-deconstruction of the school as an institution, we see the institutionalization initiatives as something that is no more than a hint in inchoate form—incipient, almost timid, somewhat fragile. That is to say, the initiatives may be domesticated by the weight of dominant routines. But at the same time, we believe that through the initiative to establish or institutionalize, there is the glimmering of a hope for a better school.

Precisely because the initiative is weak, it must be reinforced with a policy that deliberately aims at the deconstruction of the paradigm of school organization today and that is determined to create favorable conditions for the construction of an alternative paradigm of school organization.

In the work of deconstructing the school institution as a system of subordinate action and reconstructing it as a system of coordinated action, two types of complementary learning are seen to be essential: (1) to learn to make agreements on the intentions (purposes or objectives) that will guide an institution and (2) to learn to practice deliberate (conscious) coordination of actions required to fulfill those intentions. These are precisely the two types of complementary learning, and their corresponding competencies, necessary for effective teamwork. Both types of learning require new environments and spaces for interlocution between teachers, both in the process of discussion and in the decision-making process. The institution cannot be reconstructed without incorporating the agents involved in collective discussion and without affecting the structure of decision-making processes. This creates better conditions for effective participation, a reinvention of the institution, and a reconstruction of the public face of education.

Obstacles to Construction

When we speak of obstacles, we refer first to reconstruction of the school institution through the PEI.

The Teachers

"Teacher's malaise" is a category we have used to bring together a whole set of worrying images in the minds of teachers. It is a summary of all the obstacles that we identify both in the actor and in his/her working conditions. The principal symptoms are insecurity, professional identity crisis, an eroded self-image, devaluation of status, isolation in the classroom with consequent professional loneliness, limited discourse, a false conception of professional autonomy, absence of appropriate incentives, oscillation between depression and euphoria, listlessness, excess of complaints, and an overloading with activities that do not necessarily bring efficiency. There is difficulty in surviving in an institutional climate that has deteriorated through badly handled relationships, more influenced by emotion than professional responsibility. There is difficulty in responding to the growing needs of a society that changes with unprecedented speed, and difficulty in accepting the growing competition of the media for the students' attention. There is a situation of tension between teachers' professional mission and the social status of being salaried servants of the State. There is tension between the loyalty due to the school and the loyalty required by the teachers' union as the center of interest. There is tension between professional logic and union logic. Therefore, the temperature of the institution and the stress goes up, especially where the teacher is responsible for more than one job.

The Institution

The institution, for so long shaped by outside forces, seems well equipped and accustomed to perform tasks required from outside. Plagued by habits, by practices that have become routine, by procedures and rules of the game whose rationales were never examined, the institution has become rigid, static, resistant to change. Compliance with the tasks of the PEI document just becomes one more indicator of the obedience that the school habitually gives to the requirements of these outside central forces. This is the principal obstacle from the institution's point of view.

And this is the obstacle that has blocked the opportunities offered by the policy of self-regulation. A model of organization and school management made up by outside agencies accustomed to execution and obedience will not change overnight. The absence of participation in some cases and the low level of participation in others are not the result of ill will on the part of administration and teachers. This would be an explanation in terms of willful rejection. It is the result of habit-formed modes of operation of the school and more specifically of the way in which relations have been organized among those involved for the exercise of authority. In the past, for the outside central authority it was enough to have a "trickle down" system. The center was the source from which policy and orders flowed. Administrators were the transmission belts, and finally the teachers were the still waters into which policy flowed for onward transmission to students.

This was all very well set up. But it is precisely the model that it is now necessary to begin to deconstruct. The process of deconstruction has begun, but it is still in its very beginning stages. We insist that it is not the lack of will on the part of administration and teachers that has blocked participatory dynamics. It is the way in which people interact inside a system of asymmetric relations (the trickle-down effect). The central obstacle to participation lies in the real structure of decision-making processes in a vertical and authoritarian organizational model. As a consequence, the central obstacle to participation has little to do with teaching and more to do with operating plans. What must be changed in order to take teaching practice out of the classroom and bring it from the domains of privacy and secrecy to the public domain is to change the organizational matrix in which it occurs. Only in this way can we construct a new order of reference for the making of shared decisions, the construction of shared intentions, and the consequent preparation of shared operating plans.

A transition is necessary from the culture of subordination and uncoordination to the culture of coordination. In order to promote this transition, there are two main obstacles of greatest concern in the "teachers' malaise": the false conception of professional autonomy and the lack of competence to engage in teamwork. The first reinforces the fragmentation of the institution, and the second torpedoes laboratories of participation. The two reinforce each other.

Facilitators for Construction

Here, when we speak of facilitators, we refer first to the principal facilitators for the reconstruction of the school institution through the PEI.

The Teachers

Despite all the symptoms of "teachers' malaise," which we have noted, there are also some important symptoms of "teachers' health" that can be identified.

The teachers are conscious of their limitations and exhibit many indications of a great appetite for knowledge. They have increased attendance and participation in courses, seminars, conferences, and programs for the qualification of teachers—some formal, others informal, some at the undergraduate level, and others at the graduate level.

The teachers feel that they have "turned over a new leaf" and developed a new sensitivity with regard to education, multiplying spaces of discussion to question the meaning of their professional work. This shows their interest in change. Some teachers have given evidence of their broad capacity for leadership by bringing their colleagues together and opening up opportunities for discussion and reflection in an institution that resists changes of routine.

The Institution

Public schools have begun to build windows to communicate with the outside world and to remove the rigidity of their professional discourse. This obviously allows new air to enter the school environment. The school begins to break down barriers in order to sign agreements, seek consultation and training, prepare and present proposals for financing projects, and take part in interinstitutional networks for reflection. Small and isolated institutions have also looked for forms of integration with other institutions with greater resources and a higher level of development.

RECOMMENDATIONS

1. Those responsible for policy design must be more attentive to processes of participation in the generation of their policies and to the conditions of acceptance

on the part of those involved in the system. There must be a teaching and learning process in the production and socialization of policy as a condition of its effectiveness and efficiency.

2. We see "teachers' malaise" as a worrisome time bomb that must be defused as soon as possible through the design of intelligent policies. If we are really interested in the quality and efficiency of public sector education, we must improve the conditions of the leaders of the process: the teachers. And we must take steps to eradicate the conditions that generate the disease.

3. If, as we have indicated, lack of competence for teamwork is the principal obstacle to be removed from the teaching body, there is a need to design and multiply modules for reeducation and resocialization among teachers, with the aim of forming knowledge, attitudes, and predisposition for teamwork. This competence must receive first priority in the process of basic education and in processes of professional teacher formation.

4. If the current model of school organization and administration is the main obstacle of an institutional nature, there is a need to define policies that will jumpstart the capacity for redesigning the organizational model. The school's internal capacity for innovation must also be bolstered through processes of consulting and training.

5. Since the site of the Reference Group in the research project clearly showed the value of dialogue between the university—through researchers—and the school—through teachers—there is the need to design an explicit policy to provide articulation between these two institutions. Through mutual feedback, it is possible to break down the isolation in which they now find themselves, respectively. We refer more specifically to the articulation between School of Education faculties and schools.

6. If, as we have said, the experience of appropriation of the TED has shown that it is possible to make the school look at itself and the teachers to reflect on their practices, there is a need to research and explore other methods to help systematize both the processes of interaction and cooperation between teachers and the processes of reflection and exchange of knowledge. There is an urgent need for methods and strategies to systematize and invigorate teamwork.

NOTES

1. The complete version of the final report of this project, sponsored and financed by COLCIENCIAS, has recently been published under the title *La utopía de los PEI en el laberinto escolar* (*The Utopia of the PEI in the School Labyrinth*) (Ávila and Camargo, 1999).

2. In the Colombian education system, private education has an advantage over public education in terms of quantity and quality. The schools in which the researchers worked belong to the State sector in an urban context where users belong to low-income social strata of between US$350–500 per month.

3. Records of an Academic Council meeting, Bogotá, May 1997. Said by a systems advisor to an academic coordinator.

4. We refer to the category "intelligent organization" proposed by Peter Senge (1996, p. 24).

5. We drew from René Lourau (1970).

6. See our understanding of culture and school culture in the "Theoretical Framework" section.

7. We propose the expression "collective reflection on teaching practice" to contrast the private, isolated teaching practices in the classroom with the public and collective activity designed to construct shared purposes in teaching practice and the purposeful coordination of the actions of the school as an institution. These are two basic cultural preconditions for the preparation of a shared PEI and the (re)construction of the school *qua* institution as an integrated system for cooperative action.

REFERENCES

Adames, Ivette. (1997). La experiencia del PEI en Cali. In *Congreso Internacional "El Proyecto Educativo Institucional," Santiago de Cali, 1–2–3 de Octubre de 1997*. Electronic version prepared by CONEVENTOS and the Cali Education Department.

Assael, Jenny. (1996). Innovación, investigación y perfeccionamiento docente. In *Encuentro entre innovadores e investigadores en educación: Procesos pedagógicos alrededor del PEI*. Bogotá: Convenio Andrés Bello, Editorial Guadalupe.

Ávila, Rafael. (1996). *La construcción social de los Proyectos Educativos Institucionales. Proyecto de Investigación*. Bogotá: Centro de Investigaciones de la Universidad Pedagógica Nacional (CIUP).

Ávila, Rafael, and Camargo, Marina. (1999). *La utopía de los PEI en el laberinto escolar*. Bogotá: COLCIENCIAS, CIUP, and Ediciones Antropos.

Buenaventura, Nicolás. (1997). *El cuento del PEI y otras historias pedagógicas*. Bogotá: Cooperativa Editorial Magisterio.

Bustamante Zamudio, Guillermo. (1995). El PEI será lo que hagamos hoy por él. *Educación y Cultura* No. 38 (Bogotá), 5–10.

Bustamante Zamudio, Guillermo. (1995). Acontecimientos relacionados con la aparición del Proyecto Educativo Institucional. *La Revista Pretextos Pedagógicos de la Sociedad Colombiana de Pedagogía* No. 2 (Bogotá), 37–50.

Bustamente, Guillermo, Perafán, Andrés, and Niño, Libia Stella. (1994–1995). *Fundamentos normativos del Proyecto Educativo Institucional*. Medellín: mimeographed text by la Facultad de Educación de la Universidad de Antioquía, Medellín.

Caballero Prieto, Piedad. (1997). Hacia la construcción del Proyecto Educativo Institucional PEI. In *La reforma educativa en Colombia: Desafíos y perspectivas* (Eduardo Aldana and Piedad Caballero, Comps.). Bogotá: Instituto SER de Investigación and Programa de Promoción de la Reforma Educativa en América Latina (PREAL).

Calvo, Gloria. (1996). Los Proyectos Educativos Institucionales y la formación de docentes. *Revista Colombiana de Educación* No. 33 (Bogotá).

Cárdenas, Martha. (1995). El camino hacia la construcción de una escuela democrática. *Alegría de Enseñar* No. 22 (Bogotá), 10–13.

94 *Research Projects and Interpretation*

Castillo Lugo, Eduardo. (1996). *Currículo y proyecto educativo institucional: Autonomía e identidad.* Armenia: Kinesis Editorial.
Chaparro, Clara Inés, Orozco, Juan Carlos, and Martínez, Carmen Alicia. (1996). Pensar la escuela: ¿Políticas educativas vs. Proyecto Educativo Institucional? *Nodos y Nudos* 1(2) (Bogotá), 4–12.
Coy, María E. (1995). PEI: Proyecto de transformación educativa. *Educación y Cultura* No. 38 (Bogotá), 13–18.
Durán, José A. (1994). *El Proyecto Educativo Institucional: Una alternativa para el desarrollo pedagógico-cultural.* Bogotá: Cooperativa Editorial Magisterio.
El Proyecto Educativo Institucional: Una construcción de sentido. Manual para el desarrollo de los PEI. (1997). Bogotá: Editorial Santillana.
Elizade, Antonio. (1994). *Paradigmas y metáforas: Paso hacia una epistemología integradora y participativa.* Bogotá: Academia Colombiana de Ciencias Exactas, Físicas y Naturales.
Evaluación, proyecto educativo y descentralización en la educación. (1995). Bogotá: Universidad Pedagógica Nacional.
Geertz Clifford. (1992). *La interpretación de las culturas.* Barcelona: Ediciones Gedisa.
Giddens, Anthony. (1976). *New rules of sociological method.* London: Basic Books.
Ginzburg, Carlo. (1989). *Mitos, emblemas, indicios.* Barcelona: Ediciones Gedisa.
Habermas, Jürgen. (1987). *Teoría de la acción comunicativa.* Madrid: T.I. Taurus.
Ibarra Vargas, Bibiana del Carmen. (1997). *La participación de la comunidad educativa en el Proyecto Educativo Institucional (PEI). El caso de los Colegios Gonzalo Jimenez de Quesada y San Juan Bosco (Municipio de Suesca).* Bogotá: Universidad Nacional de Colombia, Faculty of Human Sciences, Department of Social Work (Degree Paper for Social Work).
Lourau, René. (1970). *L'analyse institutionelle.* Paris: Ed. de Minuit.
Lucio, Ricardo. (1995). ¿Qué tanto ayuda o entorpece el material disponible sobre el PEI? *Revista Educación y Cultura* No. 38 (Bogotá), 19–24.
Martínez, Fanny. (1995). Posible itinerario para trabajar por proyectos. *Alegría de Enseñar* No. 22 (Bogotá), 14–21.
Martínez, Marco Fidel. (1997). La experiencia del PEI en Pasto. In *Congreso Internacional "El Proyecto Educativo Institucional," Cali, 1–2–3 de Octubre de 1997.* Electronic version prepared by CONEVENTOS and the Cali Education Department.
Mejía, Marco Raúl. (1996). *La elaboración del PEI. Un conflicto entre la vieja y la nueva cultura escolar.* Bogotá: CINEP (unpublished draft).
Ordóñez Pachón, Carlos E. (1995). Los Proyectos Educativos Institucionales como discurso educativo. *Revista de la Sociedad Colombiana de Pedagogía* No. 1 (Bogotá).
Peña Borrero, Luis B. (1995). El Proyecto Educativo Institucional es una construcción social. *Alegría de Enseñar* No. 22 (Bogotá), 8–9.
Perafán, Andrés. (1995). Proyecto Educativo Institucional y currículo. *Revista de la Sociedad Colombiana de Pedagogía* No. 1 (Bogotá, February), 45–53.
Pérez, Jesús Hernando y personeros juveniles de Bogotá. (1997). La experiencia del PEI en Bogotá. In *Congreso Internacional "El Proyecto Educativo Institucional," Cali, 1–2–3 de Octubre de 1997.* Electronic version prepared by CONEVENTOS and the Cali Education Department.

Rincón, Amalia et al. (1998). *La deconstrucción: Una estrategia educativa para el Magdalena Medio.* Paper presented by CINEP at the Fair-Forum Educación Siglo XXI, Bogotá, April 1–5.

Rodríguez, José. (1990). *El Proyecto Educativo. Elementos para su diseño.* Madrid: Alhambra Longman.

Senge, Peter. (1996). *La quinta disciplina, el arte y la práctica de la organización abierta al aprendizaje.* Barcelona: Ediciones Granica.

Toro, José Bernardo. (1995). *Democracia, productividad y Proyecto Educativo Institucional (PEI): La construcción de nación como criterio orientador de la calidad de la educación* Bogotá: Fundación Social.

Torres Cárdenas, Cesar. (1995). Educación para la democracia en el escenario del Proyecto Educativo Institucional. *Revista de la Sociedad Colombiana de Pedagogía* No. 1 (Bogotá, February).

Vargas De Abella, Martha. (1996). El P.E.I. como espacio de innovación y la investigación. In *Encuentro entre innovadores e investigadores en educación. Procesos pedagógicos alrededor del PEI.* Bogotá: Convenio Andrés Bello, Editorial Guadalupe.

Villaveces Cardoso, José Luis. (1996). El Currículo y la "Nueva Escuela." In *Innovaciones en la organización de la "Nueva Escuela": Proceedings of the Second Teacher Managers Congress and the Third Congress of Bogotá Education Center Managers, Bogotá,* October 21–24.

Chapter 6

Alternative Educational Projects: Technical Developments and Political Debate in the Everyday Workings of "Nongraded" Schools in Argentina

Ana Padawer

INTRODUCTION

In this chapter I shall be referring to some of the findings from ethnographic research carried out in a series of alternative educational contexts, collectively known as "nongraded schools." These educational contexts constitute projects that have been taking place in public elementary schools (*Escuelas Públicas de Educación Básica*—EGB) located within the province of Buenos Aires, Argentina, in some instances for the last 10 years.[1]

All of the educational innovations grouped under this denomination have revised their methods of promotion and the way in which the traditional school structure is organized. Grade levels lasting a full year, which have been in place since the last century, have been replaced with groups that permit flexibility of movement from one grade to another, allowing for students to be promoted at any time during the school year.

It is my belief that these educational projects are the outcome of policies practiced at the local level by superintendents, principals, and teachers in the schools, with the aim of surmounting students' academic failure. These new policies, what we might think of as political practices, both complement and clash with the dominant educational policies in effect in the school district. The alternative political practices are based on heterogeneous educational projects which nevertheless have forged a new collective identity for themselves as "nongraded schools." In so doing, they have significantly differentiated themselves from the rest of the schools located in marginalized areas within the district.

My initial research in this area was carried out between 1993 and 1995 in an elementary school which, in order to conceal its identity, I shall refer to as Riverside School. It is an old public school recently relocated by the river, on naturally low-lying land that used to be a municipal landfill. The land frequently suffers extensive flooding from the Río de la Plata, and consequently, its limited value has attracted settlements of families from the interior of the country, or from nearby overcrowded shantytowns. The school cafeteria remains open even during the summer vacations, to serve the basic needs of those who frequently lose their few possessions during a flood.

When I began my fieldwork, the Riverside School had just initiated its first year of operation as a nongraded institution and was selected for this research project as an example of an educational innovation within the context of urban poverty. During the first of my two years at the school, I carried out an ethnographic study comprising systematic observation in three different grade levels, from which I was able to piece together the workings of the nongraded school system. I also conducted interviews with the teachers, school administration officials, and students as well as the family members of some of the children enrolled at a particular grade level.

Between 1996 and 1998, I carried out a second research project at an educational institution known as *La Escuela Pionera* (Pioneer School) among the nongraded schools in the area; once again, I have used a pseudonym in order to conceal the identity of the school. This school is located in a neighboring district to Riverside School, about 10 blocks away from the polluted river that separates the federal capital from the province of Buenos Aires. It is a neighborhood of rickety, one-story homes inhabited by manual laborers and builders, although many of the structures have since been abandoned. Due to the frequent flooding, only the roads leading to the train station, hospital, and local schools are paved.

The building that houses Pioneer School is as run-down as its surroundings. Erected by a long-gone neighborhood development scheme, the building remains under continual repair and extension. The first purpose the building served, in accordance with the immediate needs of the local population, was that of a school cafeteria. It was at this school institution that I carried out an ethnographic study comprising a series of video recordings of all the teachers, with whom I later conducted interviews in which we discussed the development of classes in a nongraded school setting.

Schools that regard themselves as nongraded do not follow an exclusively technical curriculum. The teachers and principals have developed an innovative educational project based on a sense of common identity, maintaining a somewhat oppositional stance toward conventional educational policies and pedagogical methods. This contention has manifested itself in a critical attitude, sometimes on the part of individuals and sometimes as a collective group, toward provincial state policies regarding the process of educational reform, which began in the 1980s and has been gathering momentum ever since.

Although educators have been known at times to publicly state their opposition to state educational policies, nongraded schools are still public institutions and thus require the approval of government authorities in order to continue operating. The teachers and principals from these types of schools have formed alliances and experienced conflict with both local and government education officials, and as we will shortly be discussing, these frequently turbulent interactions either make or break these nongraded schools.

However, criticism of education policy is not restricted to public opposition to government policy; it is also latently evident in pre-theoretical attitudes (Taylor, 1998) toward the relationships between education and society held by the educators at these innovative schools.[2] As I shall discuss in this chapter, after extensive research I have come to the conclusion that in some schools there is a predominant attitude of disillusionment with the current elementary education system, which has failed to guarantee the effective integration of children into society in a fair and equal manner. On the other hand, a significant number of teachers from other nongraded schools insist that the blame lies within the content of their own educational practices, insofar as they consider such practices to be supported by implicit theories and definitions of "normal" and "adapted" students that are formulated according to the social and cultural standards of the middle class.

The influence of past educational projects is evident in the creation of alternative educational proposals. I would therefore like to present a second theory in this article: in the process of institutional change that a school undergoes in order to be able to classify itself as nongraded, a common identity develops from accumulated aspects of the past (Clifford, 1995a). Using specific educational experiences from the past as a foundation, the innovations promoted in one proposal or another join forces with the former to create a new single identity; such innovations are sometimes integrated side by side in the same educational establishment. These original educational projects possess an inherently political and educational direction of their own, which allows us to comprehend why some schools are incorporating these philosophies into their own current educational methods. I would thus like to focus my discussion on the recovery of these former educational projects.

A BRIEF DESCRIPTION OF NONGRADED SCHOOLS

Nongraded schools effectively came into existence between 1987 and 1988. From that moment on, certain educational innovations began to be developed in the elementary schools of Buenos Aires that aimed to resolve the dilemma of "student academic failure."[3]

In addition to this general objective, these schools shared various other common attributes: they were all located in areas of urban poverty, reform was to focus specifically on the promotion of students from one grade level to another, and the classes were organized to include administrative classification of the students in each of the public elementary school grade levels, limiting class sizes to a maximum of 30 students, in accordance with traditional guidelines.

The largest expansion of nongraded schools took place in 1992, increasing their numbers to 40 institutions. Now, more than 10 years after the establishment of the first innovative educational project, there are officially designated 30 schools grouped under this denomination. They are located in 11 of the 16 districts into which the public elementary teaching system is divided in the province of Buenos Aires.[4]

The nongraded school system in the province of Buenos Aires promotes the creation of flexible groups in relation to the timing and methods of promotion of students from one grade level to the next. It also allows for the possibility of creating subdivisions within the levels in each group of students, dependent upon their performance in certain subjects. The decision on how to group students is left to the discretion of the teacher, who discusses the most favorable method of organizing his or her students with the school principal, as well as the possibility of working with another teacher to share responsibility for the same group of students.

The local provincial government organized a series of meetings with these innovative schools to establish common work guidelines for nongraded schools. One of the most important stipulations was that these schools should organize the duration of their elementary education in three main cycles and that decisions made on grouping and promotion should be based on "achievement profiles" (particularly for reading and mathematics) predetermined by the institution concerned. Some schools have since adopted a nongraded system for the entire public elementary school cycle, while others have opted for a more gradual change.

La Escuela Pionera (Pioneer School) was approved to operate as an innovative institution in 1987, and we know that other schools have later been identified as nongraded schools. Uncertainty over exactly which schools these were, and their numbers, has been a matter of contention among many teachers, particularly upon being appointed to a school in their own neighborhood without knowing in advance that the school had adopted the nongraded system.

In my opinion, this uncertainty is not exclusively a consequence of education officials' recording methods,[5] but also derives from the fact that in assuming the identity of a nongraded school, these institutions thus differentiate themselves from regular schools, and this assumed identity is relational in nature, not a fundamental characteristic. The nongraded aspect of the school's educational system slips in and out of existence in accordance with whether or not the local political climate supports this type of controversial identity.

The nongraded school system is a recent innovation that began in 1987, but its roots can be traced back to the birth of the public school system in Argentina at the end of the last century. The controversy surrounding "peer assistance" and "simultaneous" methods of instruction was undoubtedly over the organization and promotion of learning groups (see below). Historically, relatively little research has been carried out in Argentina regarding this controversy, and I should emphasize that most of the teachers in the public elementary schools where I collected my data professed to have no familiarity with the subject. In existing nongraded schools, some reference is made to far more recent educational innovations, in particular to the U.S. experience of nongraded schools, whose period of major expansion took place between the late 1950s and early 1970s. A far smaller number of teachers today also discuss the merits of the *Escuela Activa* (Active School), which include the *Escuela Rural Unitaria* (One-Room Rural School), an educational innovation introduced by a teacher from Buenos Aires, Luis Iglesias, in 1938.[6]

The standard interpretation offered by those involved in the educational system, and the documentation produced by schools and central organizations, is that nongraded schools are "an alternative educational proposal whose aim is to counteract academic failure, prevent dropouts and improve the quality of education"; seen as a worthwhile innovation, it is, nevertheless, frequently criticized.[7]

I agree with these interpretations insofar as I acknowledge that nongraded schools pose an "alternative" to the standard methods of education in use at graded schools. These standard, uniform methods are widely regarded as responsible for students' academic failure. This criticism of the traditional school organization takes on greater significance for students experiencing difficulties in keeping up with the requirements established by the official curriculum. Proposals for the implementation of individualized instruction and flexible grouping are aimed at providing benefits for these very students.

However, in my work, I use the term "alternative" in a different sense from these commonly held perspectives: I employ the term to refer specifically to a particular group of political-educational attitudes under discussion (Puiggrós, José, and Balduzzi, 1988). By the same token, I maintain that the term "alternative" refers to projects developed with the aim of modifying the content of education in order to adapt it to the societal context in which the experience is taking place. Thus, there is also a political aspect involved.

I believe that alternative educational projects are essentially manifestations of an oppositional political-educational identity. This is evident in the very name—"nongraded," which has an essentially negative prefix—by which this type of schools has chosen to become known. However, their differentiation from regular, graded schools is also identified in other characteristics, namely a political, ideological, and/or unionist resistance combined with a school of thought oriented toward technical-professional aspects of education.

In reports concerning the origin of the innovative methods employed by the teachers, a focal issue has been the ongoing problem of how to integrate underprivileged students into society. This concern is a fundamental part of the schools' identity, the relational difference that sets them apart from graded schools. Different pre-theoretical approaches by teachers with regard to the relationship between education and society, which maintain a central role among teachers and schools, may be identified within this common definition.

GENERAL ASPECTS OF THE HISTORY OF NONGRADED SCHOOLS

The current broad context for nongraded schools in the province of Buenos Aires is one of national and regional education policy reform, with school authorities adapting their strategies to mirror those of the state organizational model, a process known as "structural adjustment." In a nutshell, this involves a series of financial, macroeconomic and microeconomic contributions aimed at allowing countries to efficiently integrate into the global market (Tironi and Lagos, 1991).

This policy has had strong and immediate repercussions in schools, such as an avalanche of teaching staff dismissals within educational establishments. Authorities investigated the number of students per teacher as stipulated by the regulations and closed down several classes; schools underwent new categorization; and entire school staffs were displaced when the number of students did not conform to the regulations in effect.

These measures, intended to reduce the amount of public funds spent, were put into effect with the same general goal of educational policies, which aimed to prioritize elementary education. Resources were concentrated in this area in order to "qualitatively" improve elementary education standards while simultaneously improving the "efficiency" of the public education system (Carro et al., 1996; Coraggio, 1993; Grassi et al., 1994).

This political inclination is further supported by modification of the law that governs the country's educational system. The Federal Law of Education of 1992 and the Province of Buenos Aires' Law of Education, passed in 1995, call for a complete reorganization of the educational system at all grade levels, modification of content, and reassignment of the roles of central and district educational authorities and educational financing.

It is within this context that nongraded schools have been emerging— the educational project regarded as "pioneer" back in 1987 and successive innovations adopted by schools since then. As I shall later discuss in detail, the provincial government has been the main spokesperson for nongraded educational projects, and thus schools are developing their institutional reform initiatives by drawing on certain aspects of the principles directing education policy in the province of Buenos Aires, while questioning others. Likewise, the precise moment in time at which each school begins to implement its innovative system will influence its relationship with educational authorities.

The written proposals submitted by the schools to local education authorities to support their educational innovation include lists of former educational proposals, with their corresponding bibliographical references. Teachers and principals consistently refer to the same documents when asked in interviews about how they came to develop their educational innovation. Consequently, following Clifford's theory (1995b), I must concur that nongraded schools today are a feature in a historical educational time line that stretches toward the future. Common references actively create the identity of nongraded schools.

Along the lines of the same school of thought developed by Rockwell (1992) on the instructional use of written language, I have found that the use of texts to develop institutional projects that define what differentiates one school from another differs from their everyday use in class. As far as I could tell from the results of my empirical research in these and other schools, proposals written by schools are frequently based on the content of texts used in the development of official documents, teacher training courses, and the curricula of university-level instruction in education. This is most likely due to the fact that an increasing number of teachers are currently attending university or have degrees in education or educational psychology. Bibliographies frequently list texts about the history and sociology of education, as well as the constructivism applied to the learning process involved in reading and writing, pedagogy, and curriculum.[8]

In my opinion, teachers use these extensive bibliographies in an essentially persuasive manner in order to lend an air of reliability to the thoroughness of their work. References to some authors, particularly those that deal with constructivism, are included to show the aim of modifying teaching strategies in the classroom. However, these documents also contain other historical bibliographic references, related to school organization and student promotion, a theme which was supposedly initiated in 1987 but which may have originated from between three to five decades ago.

My fieldwork made me aware that even though each nongraded school developed its own educational innovation, there was an informal circulation of bibliographies and proposals authored by superintendents, principals, and teachers following visits to schools that were further along in the transformation process. This informal circulation of educational proposal bibliographies has assisted the revision of educational projects proposed by nongraded schools. Existing nongraded schools in the province of Buenos Aires do not adhere rigidly to the methods of their historical predecessors, though there is a clear logic evident in these proposals, given that elements of the past are still present and allow us to understand the complex structure of today's schools.

The process of reform of educational policies defines these initiatives as innovations pursuing the improvement of the quality of education by means of technical modification. As I shall attempt to explain, nongraded schools might have been a sterling example of positive educational reform in the province of Buenos Aires, insofar as they paved the way for educational organization in cycles, which was later adopted in the school district under the provisions of the new provincial Law of Education. However, the political and educational opposition to such measures held by teachers has resulted in the philosophies of nongraded schools posing a new dynamic of contention toward the governmental policy of the district.

PRECURSORS TO NONGRADED SCHOOLS: THE *ESCUELA RURAL UNITARIA*

Luis Iglesias was a teacher who took it upon himself to ensure the adaptation of the schooling of *campesino* (peasant) children to their particular way of life, essentially to allow them to continue working their families' land while concurrently benefiting from an education. He taught at an *Escuela Rural Unitaria* (with only one teacher) in Esteban Echeverría, in the province of Buenos Aires, between 1938 and 1957. He was determined to make school an attractive option where his students' personal experiences formed a basis for instruction. His educational project promoted peer help strategies among students and self-motivation through the use of "didactic guidelines," which allowed students to work independently without continual teacher intervention.

The ideological political issue was at the forefront of Iglesias' techniques and those of other experimental teachers with whom he associated, like the Uruguayan teacher Jesualdo Sosa and the Argentine teacher Olga Cossettini.[9] These educators developed nonconformist educational proposals during the reign of radicalism (1916–1930), which included the dissident movement embodied in the *Escuela Activa*, as well as anarchist, socialist, and communist movements within schools, grass-roots educational organizations, and labor unions (Puiggrós, 1992).

Like his colleagues, Iglesias developed his educational project by restructuring his own teaching practices and rethinking his own educational background from the teacher training college he attended. The content of instruction at teacher training colleges promoted positivist ideas in the training of teachers in Argentina, but by the middle of the 1930s, such colleges had also become the main opponent to religious education.[10] It was a time during which liberal Catholics, nationalists, landowners, conservative politicians, businessmen, and revenue agents supported the "educational reaction" promoted by "progressive teachers" like Iglesias. These are the terms used by Iglesias himself, taken from a semi-biographical account of his life (Padawer, 1997, p. 1).

Iglesias' personal crusade retrospectively recreates the period that historians attribute to the *Escuela Activa*, which occurred about a decade later. Iglesias drew upon features of the *Escuela Activa* and the spiritualism of the 1920s at the beginning of his professional career in 1935, and along the lines of the same school of thought, some years later, in 1945, published an essay entitled *La Escuela Emotiva* (The Affective School). Iglesias described himself later in his career as "more scientifically oriented and critical from a social point of view, secularist." His personal stance is linked to the second stage of the *Escuela Nueva* (New School) in Argentina (Carli, 1992).

Other conflicts throughout his life undoubtedly influenced his personal perspectives: the struggle between the Republicans and Spanish Nationalists in his early youth, and later the opposition of intellectual left-wingers to the government of General J.D. Perón. Iglesias explicitly expounded his controversial political and educational attitudes in the journal *Educación Popular*, of which he was the editor. His ideas landed him in jail at the beginning of the 1960s (Padawer, 1997, p. 2).

It is my belief that Iglesias retrospectively lent a global significance to the different conflicts throughout his life that influenced him to fight against "the reaction," an ideological position that was in opposition to the beliefs of "democratic teachers," "Sarmientists,"[11] "secularists," and "leftists." Iglesias developed his educational innovation within this political and ideological climate, based on the idealistic sense of equality promoted by public education, which was embodied in the expression of educational liberalism, spiritualism, *Escuela Activa*, and Marxism. Iglesias chose to define his personal crusades of both the past and future in these terms.

Periods of democratic government in Argentina have allowed for the widespread circulation of Luis Iglesias' publications, and since 1987, he has received extensive recognition from both government and nongovernmental organizations as well as invitations to attend education-focused events. This is the precise period in history in which nongraded schools have been developing their educational innovations, and Iglesias' experience is primarily of interest to those schools—most definitely a minority—that have explicit discussions around pedagogical policy.

PRECURSORS TO NONGRADED SCHOOLS: AMERICAN NONGRADED SCHOOLS

American nongraded schools were part of an innovative strategy to achieve flexibility in the grouping and methods of promotion of children attending elementary schools, with the purpose of addressing individual rates of learning. Grouping criteria were established which focused on students' achievement rather than their age; levels were frequently based on an assessment of reading skills, although a combination of other developing areas of cognition were also taken into account. "Continuous progress" (Smith, 1976) was the prevailing principle.

Although some American texts edited in Argentina explain the practical aspects of how to go about eliminating grade levels, some authors trace an unbroken line from nongraded schools founded in the 1930s, all the way back to pre-1850 multi-grade schools, which was when the first graded school was considered to have been established in the United States. The old controversy surrounding "peer assistance" and "simultaneous" methods is thus regarded as a historical antecedent to this initiative, according to some of its founding innovators in this country (Goodlad and Anderson, 1976; Miller, 1976).

Recent discussion on the subject has identified problems with this type of continuity (Veeman, 1995), indicating the frequent confusion between "multi-grade" and "multi-age" classes. The former corresponds to "an administrative regulation employed to address the issue of variable enrollment and classes with unequal number of students," features which could apply to rural schools or multi-grade schools from the end of the last century. The latter specifically "assimilates children of different ages in accordance with educational determinations," which is precisely where urban nongraded schools fit in.

It is my view that background elements are taken into consideration by the teachers as they formulate the identity of the alternative educational project; therefore, acknowledgment of educational systems which were the precursors to these innovations should not be regarded as a complicating factor, but more of a historical "appropriation" which lends substance to the innovation. However, it is still important to make conceptual distinctions between educational proposals, as pointed out in Veeman's discussion of the American situation.

Discussion on the continuity between schools from the end of the last century and the nongraded schools of this century (those founded in the 1960s, as well as those established in the 1990s) seems less relevant in Argentina, where I have failed to find a direct correlation, either in my fieldwork or in documents researched, between the educational proposals mentioned above. This is probably due to the fact that these historical issues are not widely discussed in teacher training colleges here. Likewise, the teachers I interviewed were not familiar with debates relating to the organization of the national education system.

In Argentina, the Federal Law of Education passed in 1883 established a public education system that was to be mandatory, free, secular, available to all, and composed of grade levels. Though the last aspect did not particularly provoke any significant amount of public outcry, it is known that the graded or "simultaneous" system was established in Europe and America following a prolonged process of reform that stretched throughout the entire nineteenth century. It is also known that the graded system faced its main opposition from the system of "peer assistance teaching," also known as "Lancaster's system" or the "monitorial method."[12]

James Thompson, chief superintendent of schools in the province of Buenos Aires from 1819 to 1821 (Weinberg, 1984), was responsible for introducing the "peer assistance method" to the Río de la Plata area. Thompson was a British Protestant who managed to gain the approval and support of both the government and Catholic majority for his innovative methodology. His educational know-how allowed for "the organization of a modern schooling process, with rational, scientifically validated guidelines which upheld the notions of efficiency that the increasingly industrialized European society demanded of its educational reform" (Narodowski, 1997).

American publications on nongraded schools were published in Argentina between 1976 and 1977, and today are available in certain bookstores and public libraries. These books provide information on how to organize a nongraded school, by means of accounts of educational innovations implemented in different American institutions and school districts. The accounts were authored either by those directly involved in these experiences or university researchers who were somehow connected to the implementation of these projects.

In these books, the nongraded classroom environment is presented as an educational project focusing on "individualization of instruction." In traditional simultaneous classes, no allowance is made for the fact that students have different learning rates and styles, different interests, and different responses to educational methods. The nongraded school system was incorporated by elementary schools and involved a reorganization of their methods of promotion according to levels of achievement, allowing students to be promoted from one class to another once they had reached a required standard. This methodology therefore focused on the learning rate of each individual student, resulting in the possibility of continual movement between levels.

This educational innovation achieved its period of greatest expansion between the end of the 1950s and beginning of the 1970s. However, by 1990, it became evident that some reorganization of school systems was starting to take place under this new strategy. Statistical revisions regarding the efficiency of nongraded schools take this fact into account (Gutiérrez and Slavin, 1992): American studies attribute the reawakening of interest in the educational innovation to the quantitative increase in the number of students repeating grades in elementary schools. The authors of this research reveal that the first programs to be implemented established nongraded classes in one subject, generally reading; later, these projects started including more subjects. They conclude that the extension of the innovation took place at a time when schools "were still promoting traditional curricula and methods of instruction," although with the passage of time, the programs included "more radical changes in curricula and methods of instruction."[13]

The results of my empirical fieldwork have revealed that American books on nongraded schools were in wide circulation among alternative schools in the province of Buenos Aires, even to the point of adopting the same denomination. American texts are cited in proposals for nongraded schools in Argentina and in shorter documents updating the details of the innovations in effect. The teachers and principals I interviewed acknowledged having read them, at least in part, or in summary form authored by their colleagues.

NONGRADED SCHOOLS TODAY: OPPOSITIONAL IDENTITIES AND RECOVERY OF PAST PROPOSALS

By the time teachers and principals from Pioneer School read the American books on nongraded schools and the text *La Escuela Rural Unitaria*, it was at least two decades after the peak period of the American experience, and 30 years after the publication of the first edition (1957) of what was likely Iglesias' most widely read book. However, as we shall see, there is a certain logic to the recovery of elements from the past.

In my opinion, historical and political context lend an atmosphere of opposition to educational innovations: the nongraded "pioneer" innovation launched in 1987 was under development during a time when the political climate favored a "return to democracy."[14] The new government introduced a far-reaching policy focusing on the dissolution of authoritarian practices in all institutions, including schools. In this context, Pioneer School, being an innovative and inclusive project, received support from certain important officials in the provincial education administration. However, structural adjustment policies were already being implemented at the macroeconomic level, and discussion on general educational policies was being initiated.[15]

By the end of the 1980s, Pioneer School counted among its staff a group of teachers interested in community service. They initiated a strike with political undertones, protesting the near-derelict conditions of the school building to local authorities. As one teacher interviewed remarked: "We were motivated by an indisputable fact: the poorest students receive the worst education."

From reports by teachers interviewed regarding the background to the educational innovation, I learned that a new principal was responsible for encouraging them to channel their frustrated energies into developing a new educational project. The staff organized special meetings to read and discuss material on the integration of normal elementary schools with special education schools, bibliographies listing publications discussing school dropout rates, and the books of Luis Iglesias.

As the principal of Pioneer School recounted in an interview, first a "publicity group" composed of principals from three schools in the same district was created to promote the virtues of the innovation. These women initiated efforts toward approval of the educational proposals they were developing. They had to deal with a significant change in the political leanings of the provincial administration, which nevertheless did not affect the development of their educational project. On the contrary, a series of administrative exceptions were made on their behalf, as a show of political support for the innovation.[16]

"At the time, the school's identification as a nongraded institution was just a feature of the reform," remembers the principal who was running the school at the time. However, this feature became a focal issue when the decision was made to eliminate grade levels and create groups of students. American texts on the subject progressively acquired greater significance as their importance was reinforced by several district superintendents who recommended these books on organized visits to area schools, which at the time were more familiar with the technical types of manuals previously promoted by these officials.

Luis Iglesias' educational proposal, which teachers associate with a proposed solution to educational problems in rural schools, has achieved a certain presence in nongraded schools located in the city outskirts. Its philosophies are actively in use in the Pioneer School, and when considering alternative proposals in terms of an identity and recovery of past proposals, this recovery does in fact—in my opinion—make sense. To begin with, both projects constitute parallel experiences of institutional autonomy and criticism of local educational authorities. Iglesias recounts that he was banished to a rural school by "reactionary" politicians and bureaucratic superintendents. There his isolation allowed him to experiment with alternative methodology. Teachers in Pioneer School have likewise protested the "educational discrimination" of poorer students by authorities, and thus have been granted permission to institute change in their school.

On the other hand, both projects possess the ideological motivation of instigating social advancement through schooling: Iglesias believed that teachers were agents of civilization because their work allowed *campesino* children access to a culture that their families could not provide. In Pioneer School, social advancement takes the form of a promise for an improvement in the quality of the lives of its students that is permitted by the extension of formal schooling. This notion is itself reinforced by the personal experiences of the teachers who come from the same area and who have been able to benefit from further education and a stable job. Along these lines, a teacher who was interviewed remembers: "I was born in this neighborhood and have always lived in the same house. I began studying downtown to become a teacher, but I had to drop out because I could no longer afford the fare for the trips or the books. Despite having a job, I didn't earn enough. The following year, the Teacher Training College opened here, in my area, and I enrolled and was in the first graduating class. This is a working class area; very few people are able to continue studying. Most people here who have a degree are teachers, and we owe it all to the Teacher Training College in the neighborhood. It's a place of study that is accessible to us."

From the point of view of those involved, continuity relates to developing a school administrative system, and promoting students based on both group heterogeneity and "peer assistance" between more capable students and less advantaged ones. For Iglesias, this involved maintaining grade levels, and for Pioneer School, establishing student groups. The idea is that the students' progress should be based on group solidarity and assistance provided by those students who are further ahead to those experiencing difficulties. As one teacher remarked while watching a video recorded in her class: "Last year I had the second level group, with four years of schooling. I taught the entire group the same class, but would assign different homework. In math, for example, I had two performance levels, but I did not separate the students in class. I wanted them to work as a group and encouraged them to choose whom to work with, and to help each other."

Although teachers in Pioneer School subdivide their classes into levels within the same group of students, they also implement a process of individual promotion, emulating the usefulness of the American system for group organization. Each teacher establishes promotion strategies every year, and the teachers are given autonomy to make decisions on criteria for promotion and groupings within their level in accordance with students' needs.

In spite of the heterogeneous nature of these educational strategies, Pioneer School teachers often question the school as an institution that, in practice, produces a definition of the "normal and adapted student." It is precisely these middle-class social and cultural standards that are leading poorer students toward academic failure.[17] This attitude is evident in teachers' and principals' own descriptions of their work and in their quest to discover their students' interests and experiences and tie them in with the content of the curricula. While watching a video recording of her students during a vaccination drive at school, one teacher reflected upon her own experiences in breaking the mold with regard to standards of normality:

It was clear to me from the very beginning that instruction in the nongraded school system was fundamentally based on the interests of the children, on providing meaningful context. The teacher had to be perceptive, to pay attention to students' interests and personal experiences and tie them into the content of the curriculum. Perhaps I understood the reasoning behind *this* feature more than the strategy of flexible methods of promotion, but then, it was also a huge change for me. The first impression made by the school is one of total chaos, but there is method in its madness.

Teachers attempt to achieve different standards of academic success with the systematic incorporation of extracurricular learning activities. The fact that many teachers come from the zone where they are teaching favors the integration of different types of content, without the typical underrating of this type of learning and the stigmatization of poor students as incapable of learning at the same rate as their middle-class peers. "Living in the neighborhood" allows parents, students, and teachers alike to share in building a common learning experience based on the nongraded system. As one teacher remarked:

I live here, so I know how hard it was for parents to understand the nongraded system. It took two or three years for them to finally accept that we work differently. . . . Here, both parents work, and children of 9 or 10 are frequently entrusted with looking after their younger siblings. That's a huge responsibility for any kid, and they're just not going to be able to perform as well in school. But by implementing the group system, we work to achieve a certain level of success: poor achievers benefit from the assistance provided by their peers.

When provincial policies in the early 1990s favored extensive budget cuts, the alternative educational projects strongly resisted the move to cut teaching staff, using as their opposing argument the authorities' very own insistence upon the importance of the "quality" of education. One teacher bitterly remembers that "there were a huge number of dismissals." However, resistance from labor unions and political factions had little effect, and the administrative exceptions that had been made for Pioneer School were cancelled for several years that followed. This was to bring about significant consequences in the development of the innovation, such as internal disagreement among members of the teaching staff over the hiring of teachers by mere qualification alone, without their necessarily displaying a genuine interest in maintaining an educational experience alternative to the traditional schooling process.

It was also around the same time that Riverside School, an institution located in a neighboring district to that of Pioneer School, began to implement a nongraded system, initiating its innovation four years later, in 1992. Some of the teachers and members of the school orientation team had developed several projects aimed at changing the structure of grade levels and methods of promotion. These changes were then discussed with the district superintendent, who recommended the American publications of nongraded schools, and put Riverside School in touch with Pioneer School.

The American innovation has been incorporated by Riverside School with a great sense of honor, just as it has likewise been implemented in the majority of nongraded schools in the province of Buenos Aires. This "recovered past" reinforces maintaining the principle of individualized instruction as a defining characteristic of the alternative educational project, making it a priority to meet the needs of students at all times in their own individual rates of learning. The vice principal thus summarized the innovation to colleagues who were visiting her school: "The idea is that the students' range of knowledge should always be increasing; there should be a continual and progressive rate of learning for each child. This project allows students to move back, but only to the level they need. They do not repeat the entire year."

This overarching principle is common to all nongraded schools, given that it was passed down from the American nongraded school experience. It can be applied to the principle of "peer assistance," as has been done at Pioneer School, or used to reinforce the goal of individual progress, as implemented by Riverside School. The existence of such heterogeneity, in my view, is a key feature for analyzing the educational orientation of each institution. In spite of sharing a common denominator, nongraded schools each have different guiding principles for their innovation.

The adaptation of Riverside School to the alternative identity represented by the nongraded school system was initiated by its participation in meetings at different schools, at the superintendent's office, and in the provincial capital, and by the authoring of proposals to convince authorities of the need for innovation and maintenance of its complete teaching staff. By late 1991, and in the years that followed, Riverside School had begun negotiations with local authorities to first obtain approval, and later support, for their innovation.

However, with regard to the push for autonomy and the criticism of local authorities, the innovative project did not emerge as radically in Riverside School as it did in Pioneer School. In the case of Riverside School, the focus of discussion with authorities and the creation of an alternative experience was at first based upon teachers' dissatisfaction with their salaries and a determination to reverse the traditional practice of "socially oriented promotions," defined as the promotion of underprivileged students from one grade level to the next without having achieved a sufficient basic standard of knowledge.

At first, teachers' dissatisfaction with their pay was made evident in sporadic demands for salary review. However, the initial threat and consequent concrete implementation of teaching staff cuts progressively incited teachers to adopt a more explicit and oppositional position toward the different declarations made by political officials and the reforms initiated by provincial authorities in general.

The pre-theoretical relationship between education and society maintained by teachers in Riverside School can be identified in their own accounts of their work. Such accounts show that the alternative educational experience was developed with the intention that school certification lose its formal quality. In this way, the different future occupations of students and the consequent heterogeneity of the developing society would depend on the students' intellectual capabilities and not on their environmental circumstances. The fundamental aim of this nongraded school is to equip teachers, via the implementation of technical methods of instruction, with the necessary means to prevent students with disadvantaged backgrounds from inevitably suffering the same fate as their parents.[18]

The determination to overcome inequality via alternative schooling is expressed in Riverside School through accounts of educational endeavor where social and cultural differences are pinpointed as predetermining factors for academic failure. A term frequently used to describe students who achieve the required standards is that they have "awakened." The lethargy that supposedly afflicts them due to a lack of basic resources is presented as a situation that may only be overcome under exceptional circumstances. As one teacher remarked, "Kids from schools located in city outskirts encounter tremendous learning difficulties. Some of them eventually 'awaken' and finish elementary school, and some may even go on to high school . . . although very few actually manage this. What we do is try to prepare them for the rigors of life as best we can."

It is my conclusion that even though Riverside School has embarked upon the implementation of an important institutional change, acknowledgement of the conditions of poverty suffered by the majority of its students, which was the principal motivation behind the founding of the school, will paradoxically result in the prior condemnation of the students to academic failure.[19]

This prediction is linked to an undervaluing of the children's formative experiences outside the classroom, which do not appear to be taken into consideration in the educational process. While explaining her proposal to other school authorities, one teacher remarked,

We make changes in the subjects comprising curricular content according to our students' needs. The children sometimes make suggestions of their own; for example, when teaching measurements, we build a box that they can use to collect things. You must be aware that many kids here scavenge items from the trash to sell. They teach us to use familiar aspects of their own environment in our methods of instruction.

The children bring their own content to the classroom, which the teachers then use to discover areas of interest. However, the latter are generally only of immediate use in jobs that require few or no qualifications, many of which are the very same jobs these students already have.

Furthermore, the wide gap between the life of the teachers and their students is emphasized on a daily basis at Riverside School by means of a distinctly evident social and cultural distancing of the teachers from the students, with areas of restricted access and formalized interaction between adults. A school psychologist working with the children ambiguously remarked,

The problem for many children lies with the frequent separations and major family upheavals they suffer. The distress of not knowing your own ancestry runs deep. . . . Many children are displaced to the homes of distant relatives or family acquaintances. But we need to be aware that they come from a different mindset; we judge their environment as seen through our middle-class eyes. What we regard as unacceptable isn't necessarily so for them.

CONCLUSION

In this chapter I have tried to show that in order to understand how nongraded schools today come into existence, their internal heterogeneity, and their temporary periods of expansion and subsequent disappearance, we first of all need to take into consideration the process of formation of identities which are oppositional to regional educational policies; second, we need to be aware of elements collected from past experiences that are evident in the proposals written by teachers today.

As long as their identities remain interchangeable, developing as a result of relational circumstances, nongraded schools will come and go: we can only confirm that there have been no more than 50 schools established in the 12 years that have passed since the first nongraded school was approved as an experimental plan by provincial education authorities. The concept of relational identity is how schools define their practices. A school may denominate itself as nongraded according to compliance with certain formal requirements, but these must be sustained by a day-to-day practice that may or may not be incorporated, depending on the local political and educational climate of the time.

The emergence of the nongraded school system may be viewed as the manifestation of a political practice that opposes regional educational policies expressed at the local level in several different ways. Even if these innovative projects, in terms of their objectives, are aimed at overcoming students' academic failure, teachers and principals alike are forced into situations of both alliance and confrontation with educational authorities and prevailing educational policies in the district.

Confrontations manifest themselves in the form of union claims and open political debates on the purpose of education today, sometimes presented by a group of educators, and occasionally put forward by an individual plaintiff. Being public schools, opposition cannot be expressed in radical measures, thus the frequent alliance with local authorities that will support the innovative process.

Underlying opposition may be identified through pre-theoretical ideas on the relationship between education and society, which are implicit in teachers' descriptions of their own practices, where they question the effectiveness of the commitment to socialize and integrate underprivileged students into society.

At Pioneer School, these pre-theoretical ideas challenge the definition of the "normal" and "adapted" student as established according to middle-class social and cultural standards. This atmosphere of criticism gives rise to the development of the educational practice of extracurricular learning activities, in search of different standards by which to measure academic success. To this end, subject profiles and methods of school organization have been redeveloped from year to year, up to the present day.

At Riverside School, the predominant attitude of teachers and school officials lends to their educational practices a sense of methodical socialization and effective integration of their students into society. The challenge posed by the nongraded system is being able to detect, by the implementation of technical methods, those students who "awaken" from the lethargy into which poverty and lack of cultural stimulation have caused them to sink. These limited expectations predicted the failure of the alternative proposal, which has since been abandoned by this school after only a few years.

With regard to the issue of a recovered past, I have concluded that the innovative experience developed by Luis Iglesias, cited with relatively little frequency in documents published by nongraded schools, has been recreated by Pioneer School, which subscribes to its critical position in political terms and its sense of autonomy in practice. The American experience, developed in strictly technical terms in documents circulating among the schools, has been proven to be more suited for incorporation into recommendations provided by school superintendents. This has probably allowed for their wide dissemination among the schools in their district.

In order to understand the heterogeneity of organizing principles that nongraded schools assume today—from peer assistance to individualized instruction—it is essential to take into consideration the use by teachers of educational elements from the past, questioning their lineal application. In their daily work in the classroom, and even when developing an educational project, teachers rely on strategies that will allow for practical solutions to problems, while discussion on the historical and political significance of these innovations takes second place, and few are familiar with the background of nongraded schools. During my research, I had the opportunity to talk with teachers and principals about the historical background of educational projects currently under development. In my opinion, they expressed interest in knowing more about the background to these projects, but considered the information to be beyond the range of their immediate needs.

The popularly held concept of nongraded schools as an unsuccessful technical innovation is based on empirical evidence of the limited application of the experience. The difficulties attributed to the innovation lie within a perceived lack of precision in its organization and methods of promotion. This so-called evidence and consequential assessment fail to appreciate the alternative nature of the proposal. In my opinion, defining a school as nongraded involves a decision by the institution to assume an antagonistic political identity within the structure of the State.

Today, despite its organization in cycles, Pioneer School is not a model institution of educational reform. Its teachers continue to discuss decisions made by educational authorities without ever reaching a consensus, and they also debate problems with the school's building infrastructure, the formal supervision of the innovation, and the relevance of curricular and content levels.

The experience of Riverside School demonstrates that, unfortunately, not all schools, nor even all alternative schools, have a teaching staff prepared to uphold this posture of distinctiveness and opposition: that is, to question the social order implicit in conventional educational practice by implementing a project that proposes a different future for children from city outskirts and rural areas who are currently suffering academic failure in the traditional methods of schooling.

NOTES

The research referred to in this chapter was carried out during my student assistantship in the Department of Science and Technology at the University of Buenos Aires. Special thanks go to my academic advisor, Professor Graciela Batallán, for her suggestions and guidance. Preliminary versions of this chapter were presented at the *Tercer Congreso Chileno de Antropología* (Third Chilean Congress of Anthropology) at the Universidad Católica de Temuco (Temuco Catholic University) in October 1998. I would also like to thank Professors Elsie Rockwell and María Rosa Neufeld for their contributions.

1. Educational reform in Argentina, established by the Federal Law of Education of 1992, mandated compulsory school attendance at the elementary level (EGB—*Escuelas Públicas de Educación Básica*) for 6- to 9-year-olds. This was to be preceded by an initial level of schooling intended for children aged 3 to 5 years, and followed by the "polymodal" level, which had an average duration of three years, the entrance requirements for which comprised conclusion of the EGB.

2. Following Charles Taylor's theory (1998, p. 167), it is my understanding that there is a "pre-theoretical comprehension of reality which appears in descriptions authored by those involved in societal institutions and practices."

3. See *Comunicación No. 4: Las Escuelas No Graduadas. Una Mirada Actualizada Sobre la Experiencia* (1998).

4. See *Programa de Escuelas No Graduadas* (1992). This includes a list of institutions and the corresponding level of the proposal's effectiveness.

5. The administrative procedures necessary for the approval of institutional change have their own time lines, which do not always coincide with school practices. This explains why a formally denominated nongraded school might have already abandoned this system in daily practice, and vice versa.

6. For information on nongraded schools in the United States, see Miller (1976), Goodlad and Anderson (1976), and Smith (1976). For details of Luis Iglesias' innovation, see Iglesias (1979, 1980a [1963], 1980b [1942], 1987, 1988, 1995) and Bianco (1992).

7. See *Escuelas No Graduadas. Documento No. 8* (1995, p. 5).

8. See the bibliographies of the following documents: *Programa de Escuelas No Graduadas*, (1992) and *Escuelas No Graduadas*. (1995).

9. Iglesias identifies his bibliographic background in the volume *Didáctica de la Libre Expresión* (1979, pp. 385–455). Within this text, he frequently cites Rousseau, Pestalozzi, Dewey, and Cousinet, whom he also mentions in some of his other books. In the appendix, he includes comments on the experiences of some of his colleagues: Olga Cossettini in Argentina; Jesualdo in Uruguay; Freinet in France, Belgium, and Spain; Lodi in Italy; and José Acosta Lucero in Mexico.

10. Principles of Christian morality were introduced to public education in the province of Buenos Aires when Manuel Fresco (1936–1940) and Minister of Education Roberto Noble came into office (Puiggrós, 1990).

11. D.F. Sarmiento held several occupations during his life, including rural teacher, journalist, senator, governor, and president of Argentina from 1868 to 1874.

12. The "Lancaster system" differed in several respects from the "simultaneous" method (Querrien, 1980; see also Pinneau, 1997): it gave faster results and focused on the teaching of rudimentary reading, math, and writing skills. The "simultaneous" system of education, on the other hand, included other spheres of knowledge such as geography, ethics, and hygiene. Discipline of the students and supervision of their work were not controlled by group activity, as they were in charity schools, but by specially appointed "monitors."

13. Gutiérrez and Slavin carried out a statistical study on the best evidence they themselves managed to collect, as well as the use of secondary data (mostly doctoral dissertations, which can be found in Washington, DC's Library of Congress), to compare the learning achievements of graded and nongraded schools (Gutiérrez and Slavin, 1992).

14. This "return to democracy" originally came into being in 1983, when presidential elections were held after eight years of military rule.

15. This period witnessed the development of literacy programs, grade and school boards, and community service days. These were all proposals put into effect by successive educational administrations (even though the provincial government went through a change in political leaning) whose aim was to promote community service in schools.

16. At the time, these alternative schools obtained authorization to relocate teachers who were not interested in participating in this educational innovation, developed a unique method for supervision of the innovation, and also worked with labor unions in selecting suitable teaching staff.

17. Although developed as a pre-theoretical approach and applied to day-to-day situations, it is my opinion that this attitude refers specifically to the theory of reproduction in its original version, remembered by teachers from their professional training. It is within this tendency that the definition of spheres of knowledge within schools comprises both a specific and arbitrary selection of cultural content in which the traditions of the dominant classes are favored (Bourdieu and Passeron, 1981). We need to bear in mind that theoretical elements inspired by these authors are in fact used in teacher training methods and are not merely confined to playing a role in discussions on the way in which the school system influences society and vice versa, but actually support specific conceptual developments.

18. The predominant attitude of these teachers and school officials gives to their educational practices a sense of methodical socialization and effective integration of their students into society. It is an attitude that could be seen as an outgrowth of classic functionalism, widely expanded in the "common sense" of public school operation. Thus, students may benefit from an education that sustains and reinforces the homogeneity necessary for the existence of society and, at the same time, ensures the continuity of an equally necessary diversity (Durkheim, 1991).

19. The trend commonly known as "American culturalism" was distinctively responsible for contributing to the field of educational research the critique of concepts of race and genetic background in determining individual characteristics, emphasizing instead the importance of cultural surroundings for the incorporation of children and youth into adult society. This perspective was used extensively in educational psychology research in the 1920s and 1930s in an attempt to explain, in cultural terms, the limited achievement of the poorer social groups and classes in schools (Souza Patto, 1990, p. 45).

REFERENCES

Bianco, A. (1992). Luis Iglesias, un maestrillo gigante. *Educoo* (9), 13–40 (Buenos Aires).

Bourdieu, P., and Passeron, J.C. (1981). *La reproducción: Elementos para una teoría del sistema de enseñanza* (2nd ed.). Barcelona: Laia.

Carli, S. (1992). El campo de la niñez. Entre el discurso de la minoridad y el discurso de la Educación Nueva. In A. Puiggrós (Ed.), *Escuela, democracia y orden*. Buenos Aires: Galerna.

Carro, S., Padawer, A., and Thisted, S. (1996). Las escuelas del conurbano y el ajuste. *Cuadernos de Antropología Social* No. 9, 53–64.

Caruso, M. (1993). *Fuentes y espacios del pensamiento pedagógico del primer peronismo. Los discursos pedagógicos del nacionalismo y de la izquierda (1943–1949)*. Informe Final de investigación, Facultad de Filosofia y Letras, Universidad de Buenos Aires.

Clifford, J. (1995a). Identidad en Mashpee. In J. Clifford, *Dilemas de la cultura*. Barcelona: Gedisa, pp. 327–406.

Clifford, J. (1995b). Los productos puros enloquecen. In J. Clifford, *Dilemas de la cultura*. Barcelona: Gedisa, pp. 15–34.

Comunicación No. 4: Las escuelas no graduadas. Una mirada actualizada sobre la experiencia. (1998). Dirección de Educación Primaria de la Dirección General de Cultura y Educación, April.

Coraggio, J.C. (1993). *Desarrollo humano, economía popular y educación. Revisión sobre informe CEAAL.* Mimeograph.

Durkheim, E. (1991). La educación, su naturaleza y función. In E. Durkheim, *Educación y sociología.* Mexico: Colofón, pp. 60–69.

Escuelas no graduadas. Documento No. 8. (1995). Dirección de Educación Primaria, Provincia de Buenos Aires.

Goodlad, J., and Anderson, R. (1976). *La escuela sin grado. Organización y funciones.* Buenos Aires: El Ateneo.

Grassi, E., Hintze, S., and Neufeld, M.R. (1994). *Políticas sociales, crisis, y ajuste estructural.* Buenos Aires: Espacio.

Gutiérrez, R., and Slavin, R. (1992). Achievement effects of the nongraded elementary school: A best evidence synthesis. *Review of Educational Research* 62(4), 333–376.

Iglesias, L. (1979). *Didáctica de la libre expresión.* Buenos Aires: Ediciones Pedagógicas.

Iglesias, L. (1980a [1963]). *Diario de ruta* (3rd ed.). Buenos Aires: Ediciones Pedagógicas.

Iglesias, L. (1980b [1942]). *Viento de estrellas* (4th ed.). Buenos Aires: Ediciones Pedagógicas.

Iglesias, L. (1987). *Aprendizaje vivencial de la lectura y escritura.* Buenos Aires: Ediciones Pedagógicas.

Iglesias, L. (1988). *Los guiones didácticos.* Buenos Aires: Ediciones Pedagógicas.

Iglesias, L. (1995). *La escuela rural unitaria* (7th ed.). Buenos Aires: Magisterio.

Miller, I. (1976). *La escuela no graduada. Una nueva solución educativa.* Buenos Aires: Ateneo.

Narodowski, M. (1997). *El mejor de los métodos posibles. La introducción del método lancasteriano en Iberoamérica en el temprano siglo XIX.* Paper presented at the Tenth Argentine Symposium on the History of Education.

Padawer, A. (1997). *La desigualdad social y la escuela primaria: una perspectiva antropológica sobre propuestas pedagógicas alternativas.* Initial research report presented to the Department of Science and Technology, University of Buenos Aires.

Pinneau, P. (1997). *La escolarización de la provincia de Buenos Aires (1875–1939).* Universidad de Buenos Aires: Ed. Flacso-Ciclo Básico Común.

Programa de escuelas no graduadas. (1992). Restricted circulation document published by Dirección de Educación Primaria, Provincia de Buenos Aires, December.

Puiggrós, A. (1990). *Sistema educativo. Estado y sociedad civil en la reestructuración del capitalismo dependiente. El caso argentino.* In A. Puiggrós (Ed.), Educational Proposal, Year 2, No. 2. Buenos Aires.

Puiggrós, A. (1992). La educación argentina desde la reforma Savedra Lamas hasta el fin de la década infame. Hipótesis para la discusión. In A. Puiggrós (Ed.), *Escuela, democracia y orden (1916–1943).* Buenos Aires: Galerna.

Puiggrós, A., José, A., and Baldozzi, J. (1988). *Hacía una pedagogía de la imaginación en América Latina.* Buenos Aires: Ediciones Contrapunto.

Querrien, A. (1980). *Trabajos elementales sobre la escuela primaria.* Madrid: La Piqueta.

Rockwell, E. (1992). Los usos magisteriales de la lengua escrita. *Nueva Antropología* 12(42) (Mexico), pp. 43–55.

Smith, L. (1976). *La realidad de la escuela sin grados*. Buenos Aires: El Ateneo.

Souza Patto, M.H. (1990). *Raizes históricas das concepções sobre o fracasso escolar*. In M.H. Souza Patto, *A produção do fracasso escolar*. São Paulo: T.A Queiroz, p. 45.

Taylor, C. (1998). *La teoría social como práctica*. Academia No. 4. Santiago de Chile: Universidad Academia de Humanismo Cristiano.

Tironi, E., and Lagos, R. (1991). *Actores sociales y ajuste estructural*. CEPAL No. 44. Santiago de Chile: Comisión Economica para América Latina y el Caribe.

Veeman, S. (1995). Cognitive and non-cognitive effects of multigrade and multiage classes: A best evidence synthesis. *Review of Educational Research* 65(4), 319–382.

Weinberg, G. (1984). *Modelos educativos en la historia de América latina*. Buenos Aires: Kapelusz/UNESCO/CEPAL/PNUD.

Part III

Position Statements and Discussions

Chapter 7

The Role of Ethnographic Research in Education Policy: A Trail to Blaze

Etelvina Sandoval Flores

THE ROLE OF ETHNOGRAPHIC RESEARCH IN EDUCATION POLICY

The title theme of this book, ethnography and education policy, due to its very nature, attracts the attention of a particular type of person: educational ethnographers, researchers who stipulate the importance of "fieldwork," of being an active presence within schools, of examining aspects of local culture, and of interacting directly with teachers, students, and parents.

Although there is a shortage of studies that shed light on researchers' incentives to define their methodological approaches, I would venture to confirm that the majority of educational ethnographers are motivated, in addition to a scientific interest in developing an understanding of the field, by a political interest in the transformation and improvement of public education. For this very reason, schools to us are not simply places where we collect data, but environments we are anxious to familiarize ourselves with in order to gather information that may help to promote change. Teachers, students, or parents are not merely "informants," but subjects who, together with the practices they implement, enact the content of education from day to day and lend significant meaning to its structure. Analyzing these practices and their implications will allow us to develop a new direction for education.

Throughout our training as ethnographic researchers, we learn that the most important aspect of our work is "to explain without casting judgment on our observations." However, we must recognize that the analytical explanations proffered are not neutral in character; we are not blank slates.

Our personal, professional, and even political views are evident in our selection of our objects of study, in our approach to these subjects, in the
way that we carry out our fieldwork, and in the methods we employ for
varying forms of analysis. They are also evident in the commitments we
undertake within our areas of research, behind which is the intent that our
work serve a useful purpose to those who have opened the doors of their
schools, their classrooms, their conceptions, and their professional lives to
our scrutiny.

The decision to become ethnographers, therefore, is inextricably linked
to our own personal and political interests, and these are in turn developed
and reinforced in our ethnographic studies. Rosaldo (1991) indicates that
the merger between analytical and ethical projects results in "the social
analyst becoming a social critic" (p. 168).

The practice of developing familiarity with the daily happenings in
schools, analyzing the meaning that subjects participating in the educational process give to their actions, and investigating the impression that
social history has left on existing school practices gives rise to analysis of
the local culture within school environments. This is the very nature of
educational ethnography. Through our approach to a closer involvement
with the school environment, we attempt to capture in our analyses the
heterogeneity of actions in, and the multiple interpretations of, the settings
that comprise today's educational exchanges. The multiple educational realities we come across often question the uniformity that characterizes "official" plans and proposals. Building a link between the two is a necessary
step, as there is little doubt that education policy regulations, conceived at
the very margin of the actual conditions that exist in schools and in the
lives of their subjects, without taking into consideration their individual
needs, will in all likelihood fail to prosper. This is precisely one of the points
at which ethnography and education policy should overlap.

RESEARCH ON THE BASIC TRAINING OF TEACHERS

I shall refer to my current research in collaboration with a group of
researchers[1] to substantiate the above statements. Despite the fact that personal circumstances, history, and the traditions of educational institutions
responsible for teacher training impart particular features to the process of
training future instructors, rarely are these institutions taken into consideration in the creation of educational policies to regulate the basic training
of teachers.[2]

In a nutshell, we are directing our research efforts toward the Mexican
institutions that train elementary school teachers; these are teacher-training
colleges (*normales*) that were officially founded over a century ago under
the principle of unifying existing systems and methods of instruction in
elementary schools.[3] However, not all teacher-training colleges are the

same, either by virtue of their historical background or the goals under which they were founded. Thus, today we encounter at least three types of teacher-training colleges. Urban schools, located in large population centers, are intended for the training of teachers destined for work in the cities. Schools in rural areas, founded during the post-revolutionary era with the aim of training the children of *campesinos* ("peasants"), train teachers to work in rural and marginalized areas. And recently created schools for the indigenous train teachers to serve the indigenous population.[4] Despite this diversity, all teacher-training colleges offer the same curricula and courses, and they are all run by the federal government. The state is required by law "to establish throughout the entire Republic, curricula and courses for elementary and secondary schools, teacher training colleges, and institutions for the continued education of elementary school teachers."[5]

Given the homogeneity in the training of elementary school teachers implicit in common programs sponsored by the Ministry of Public Education (SEP), our research attempts to identify elements of diversity derived from cultural contexts and the various types of teachers that different teacher-training colleges propose to train. To this end, our study is being carried out in four different teacher-training colleges: urban, rural, indigenous, and experimental. We employ a qualitative methodology that incorporates various elements of ethnography, histories of professional lives, and document analysis.

It is worth noting that the personal histories and interests of the participating researchers contributed to the selection of the theme of study. We are teachers, trained in teacher-training colleges, and we have all for some time now participated in teacher-training programs. However, our choice was also motivated by policy interests, given that the curricula in teacher-training colleges have been subject to multiple changes, each conveying a particular concept of the type of teacher the institution aims to train. Nevertheless, teacher training is still often considered to fall short of its expected goals, and the notion of the need to "professionalize teachers" persists. (The latter is an idea that has developed as a result of comparing teaching with the parameters of the other liberal professions, e.g., medicine and law.) Given this fact, we feel it is necessary to analyze the particular characteristics of the training that future teachers receive in different teacher-training colleges and detect the common features of this training. We do this with the aim of contributing to the disciplinary definition of the work of elementary educators and providing elements that will allow them to develop the true content of their profession. Our research aims, on the one hand, to assess the elementary level teaching profession within its own environment. On the other hand, we hope to develop knowledge that will help avoid the multiple curricular changes, frequently erratic in character, that are made to the content of teacher-training courses in Mexico.

In this chapter, I will present some initial analyses of one of the teacher-training colleges (the rural school), focusing on the influence of the socio-cultural context of the school, its teachers, and students on the type of teacher being trained there. We will observe how a specifically "rural" quality emerges within otherwise homogenous programs for the training of teachers, how the traditions of the rural school system affect developing relationships in this educational establishment between the students and between the students and their teachers and administrators, and how "the political" emerges as an extracurricular topic that carries significant weight in the training of future teachers.

Given the provisional nature of this analysis (we are about to conclude our fieldwork), I do not aspire to form solid conclusions; my intention is to show how the particular characteristics of the school context influence the basic training of teachers.

WHAT QUALIFIES A TEACHER-TRAINING COLLEGE AS "RURAL"?

Rural teacher-training colleges were founded as part of a particular moment in education policy of the post-revolutionary Mexican state. Their creation during the 1920s aimed to fulfill the following goals:

- To train teachers exclusively for the purpose of serving elementary schools in rural areas of the country in order to encourage the cultural, economic, and social development of *campesinos*.
- To allow small communities within the same area to enjoy the same benefits of general progress experienced by the rest of the country, by means of educational extension programs sponsored by the same institutions.[6]

Thus, the founding principle of these educational establishments was the training of teachers specifically intended to provide services in rural areas and to establish themselves as a driving force for the social and cultural development of the communities in which they were located. The rural teacher training colleges therefore developed their own curricula. This allowed them to meet the particular needs of communities, giving special emphasis to vocational trade and to agricultural learning. In addition, during Cárdenas' six-year term as president,[7] these institutions were given the title of *Escuelas Regionales Campesinas* (Regional Campesino Schools), where two years of the three-year courses were devoted to agricultural training and one to professional development (teacher-training college).

The buildings that housed these schools still maintain the original facilities built with the fulfillment of this goal in mind: land for crop growing, farms for animal husbandry, and workshops for instruction in vocational trade. The teachers' living quarters were annexed to these facilities, as these schools were considered to be places where students and teachers should have interaction at all times.

These institutions have been slowly succumbing to the pressure of modernization, and the spaces have either been reconfigured or enlarged in order to adapt to successive changes in the curricula: cubicles for the teachers (which addressed the need to encourage student teachers to carry out research when teacher-training courses were promoted to the same education level as a bachelor's degree), a videoconferencing room (called the EDUSAT room) for the promotion of still-evolving distance education methods, and offices for the heads of departments (research, teaching, and publication). Modernizing measures have also affected the curricula, and today rural teacher-training colleges work with the same curricula and courses as all other teacher-training colleges in the country. Although some teachers attempt to partially direct the training of some students toward rural issues by organizing field experiences in multi-grade schools,[8] including community service activities within the student teaching practicum, and above all, always making a point of referring in class to the rural environment in which they will be working, there still exists a great deal of ambivalence on the subject. There is nothing within the content of the courses that is specifically geared to the issue of teaching in rural areas, and this aspect in the training of potential teachers is therefore left open to the individual priorities and concepts of their professors.

For example, in the teacher-training college where we are currently conducting research, the indigenous issue isn't even addressed. This fact is criticized by some teachers, who point out that the Mexican state in which the school is located is largely populated by indigenous peoples. These teachers believe that therefore "its graduates are ill-prepared to work in a rural environment, much less serve the indigenous population":

There's no understanding, nor any kind of differentiation. I'm very concerned about the fact that indigenous languages are widely spoken in several areas here, and yet the kids don't speak their own language because they are forbidden to do so. . . . So the training the teachers receive instills a desire to teach in the cities. They don't like the idea of being classified as rural, nor the fact that they will be promoting educational activities in rural areas . . . and as for indigenous environments, forget it. (teacher trainer Ma. Deb.)

The student body has also changed. Originally intended for the children of *campesinos*, the rural teacher-training college in which we are collecting data used to emphasize Indian heritage as being an important factor:

On examining documents compiled during the first years of the teacher-training college's existence, I found that being able to boast Indian ancestry carried a significant amount of clout . . . When a town mayor wanted a boy in his village to be admitted to the teacher-training college, his letter of recommendation would state that the applicant was "a pure-blooded Indian" (using the latter as an influential argument in the applicant's favor). In addition, it has been found that more than half the students at the time spoke an indigenous language. (teacher trainer Mo. JL)

On the other hand, nowadays what really counts is the entrance examination. While the official line is that the school primarily admits children of *campesinos* or those who come from low-income families, there is no way of assessing whether or not students truly have such backgrounds:

We are no longer investigating the financial resources of the students, as we cannot visit all the applicants in their homes, so being the child of a *campesino* has ceased to matter. These days, there is a marked increase in the number of students who are the children of teachers, or whose fathers have widely varying professions, in contrast to the first years of the teacher-training college's existence, when most of the student body were the children of *campesinos*. (teacher trainer Mo. JL)

This situation is indicative of the continued existence of the original principles embraced by rural teacher-training colleges, combined with the introduction of new practices that are the fruit of current changes. In fact, in this rural teacher-training college (and, I suppose, in all of them), the original identifying features of the college's mission statements are preserved as a substratum on top of which modernizing measures are gradually being applied.

However, there are certain characteristics that distinguish the rural colleges from other teacher-training colleges: the boarding system, which provides a method of financial aid for continued study, thereby influencing to a large extent the type of student enrolled; the appropriate consideration of issues of rurality and poverty, which is conducive to the politicization of the student body; and certain community-oriented educational practices.

The Boarding System

One of the characteristic features of these educational establishments was the boarding system. In addition to providing financial support to poor students (the children of *campesinos* and/or indigenous people), this allowed a sufficient time frame for future teachers to train in the different trades and manual labors that they would need in order to carry out their work in rural communities. At the same time, the boarding system promoted the development of cultural activities and gave support to the region in which the school was located.

The very nature of being a boarding school automatically defines certain characteristics of the enrolled student body; they generally come from low-income backgrounds, possess a more committed sense of service, and/or have a strong desire for independence from their families. Boarding schools must also establish certain rules in order to ensure harmonious coexistence, some of which date back to the original so-called "disciplinary code" enforced during the early stages of these schools. These rules formally stipulate, in lists of regulations and penalties, the type of conduct expected of the student body. They include rules on many different aspect of school life, such as the necessary requirements for allowing students to leave the school premises, the standards of behavior that must be observed both on and off school grounds, the relationship between the students and between students and teachers, and the corresponding punitive measures imposed when violation of any rule occurs. Of course, the code is only a guideline, and it is both present and absent at the same time. I say present, because it is frequently a topic of discussion, and absent because almost nobody is familiar with its content, let alone employing it. In practice, what really works is a series of rules constructed on the basis of the original disciplinary code, which either go beyond its principles or overlook them at any given time.

These "internal rules" carry significant weight and influence in the training of future teachers; teachers must fulfill the tasks assigned to them, even if they are unpleasant, such as having to clean out the pigpens, share in the duty of cleaning the school, respect the seniority of their student representatives, and comply with decisions voted upon during their meetings. The common life based upon these rules encourages the students to consider it natural to actively participate, even to demand participation, in the decision-making process of the entire school. They have organized their ranks for this very purpose; they have elected group, team, and student committee representatives and so forth, which in reality constitute a remarkably efficient student communication network with significant political influence in everyday school life.

The Student Committee has an important role in all issues that concern the school, participates in important decision making (and also in decisions that aren't as important but that have to do with daily occurrences at the institution), and is consulted by the administration or teacher associations for its support in all projects. They especially monitor the work of the student teachers, the use of financial resources, and the care of the facilities that they consider their own, which they know are constantly under threat by educational authorities, who have branded the rural teacher-training colleges as "areas of conflict."[9]

For teachers who work in rural teacher-training colleges, living as a boarder affects their personal life since living in the same school in which they work means having to leave their family, share a house with a colleague, and most notably, be exposed to the scrutiny of the community:

"Having the teachers live with the students 24 hours a day is a very ide-alistic notion; we have no privacy" (teacher trainer Ma. Deb.).

The relationship between students and teachers in this sort of semi-permanent living arrangement lends a familiarity to their interaction, which leads to the creation of opposing factions when some sort of conflict emerges. It also has a marked influence on the inclusion of activities that are not formally part of the school curricula (some teachers feel these ac-tivities are necessary "to occupy spare time" of which, according to them, the students have an abundance). It encourages a demanding attitude to-ward the teachers on the part of the students, as they come to believe that their professors should be prepared to meet with them whenever they want (I have frequently encountered teachers working with their students at all hours of the night).

Discussion of Issues of Rurality and Politicization

> I enrolled in this teacher training college mainly because of the signif-icant financial aid we receive, because I felt that was the only way I could continue my studies.

> If we weren't studying at the teacher-training college, perhaps we would be working . . . but we wouldn't have been able to continue studying. Maybe it was the only choice we had because of our lack of financial resources. (students and future teachers)

Although not all the students attending rural teacher-training colleges are the children of *campesinos*, we know that they come from low-income families and that for them, enrolling in the school was the only chance they had of being able to continue studying and learn a profession. This is per-haps the reason why the instruction they receive from their teachers on the importance of their work in helping more needy communities is understood by the students and considered totally natural. "Going where there is the greatest need for education" and "Doing something to help the poorest segments of the population" are concepts that circulate widely among the students and that they promote as the fundamental characteristic of their future task as educators. The idea of advocating for social change reflects the original mission statement of the rural teacher-training colleges, which were regarded as vehicles for social and political change. Mexico's educa-tional authorities believe that these colleges espouse a Marxist-Leninist school of thought that they consider obsolete and incompatible with the process of modernization that is currently being promoted in teacher-training methods. However, the very nature of the students' living condi-tions is conducive to the development of an intensely political lifestyle, which the students embrace without—apparently—even questioning.

This attitude is prevalent, not only in their above-mentioned active participation in running the school but also in the atmosphere of permanent struggle that constantly surrounds them. The students are obliged to continually fight to avoid a reduction in enrollment and in the number of study grants awarded by the school, given that according to the Ministry's own brand of logic, it is essential to limit the number of student enrollments in the rural teacher-training college in order to avoid placement problems upon graduation. Yet in the minds of the student body in rural teacher-training colleges, this attitude is regarded as a direct blow against the very existence of the schools. For this reason, the enrollment figures in any given year should exactly mirror those of the graduating class, which has resulted in the rural schools being able to maintain their enrollment figures and the number of study grants they receive for several consecutive years, in contrast to most other teacher-training colleges. The same kind of struggle is played out over the issue of job placements. Almost every year, months before classes end, the students begin to petition the state authorities to guarantee jobs for all graduates, a situation that does not occur in other teacher-training colleges. However, the students eventually benefit from the hard-won victories of the rural schools.

Another aspect of the intense political activism in these schools is revealed in the nationwide alliance they have founded. Organized under the banner *Federación de Estudiantes Campesinos Socialistas de México* (Federation of Socialist Campesino Students of Mexico), problems encountered by any of their members become problems of the common cause, and the organization provides due support in any kind of conflict. The level of internal organization established by the students means that they can travel to any other rural college, as individuals or groups, to lend their support.

Thus, all students participate in and learn from practical experience what it means to be a rural student: to protest and demand their fundamental rights. Political activism has in fact already become a de facto part of the curriculum, which in the opinion of some teachers has a negative impact on their quality of education, given that complete or partial suspension of classes has become a constant. However, in the minds of the students, this type of struggle is also an important part of their training, as they embrace the philosophy that "as teachers, we need to be able to defend our rights and teach communities how to fight injustice."

Community Service

As has already been mentioned, the rural teacher-training colleges were created with the goal of connecting with the community and/or region in which they were located, and this principle is evident in certain practices that make up a large part of the schools' activities. Community service undertaken by the students includes restoring and painting the elementary

schools in the area as well as providing other types of service such as literacy projects. The school supports all community events and also organ-
izes weekly cultural performances for area residents. Dance, music, and
estudiantina (traditional student music recital) groups perform where required and are recognized and appreciated by the community. Furthermore,
the field placements undertaken by student teachers in elementary schools
are supposed to include some type of community service activity.

The motto by which most of these types of educational establishments
appear to operate is "serving the community through the school." New
teacher training programs have eliminated courses with the following activities, but in rural teacher-training colleges, dance, music, workshops, and
banda de guerra (drum and bugle corps) are regarded as essential tools for
connecting with and serving the community and thus continue to play an
important role in the training of future teachers. Students regard these activities as an indispensable part of their training for their future work as
educators in areas where, as they put it, "a teacher has to be able to do
everything."

EDUCATION POLICY IN THE TRAINING OF TEACHERS AND CURRENT TRAINING PROCEDURES—PATHS THAT DO NOT CONVERGE?

The preliminary and partial conclusions from the research presented here
lead us to reflect upon the opening theme of this chapter: the link between
ethnographic research and education policy, and in this particular case,
education policy as it affects the basic training of teachers in Mexico.

We are currently entering a period of change that, under the banner of
globalization, is being revealed in a wave of reform affecting the educational systems of several countries, in compliance with the argument that
schools need to reestablish their role as a key factor for economic development. Teachers are being given a central role in this transformation, since
their committed participation is regarded as essential to put new educational proposals into effect in a productive manner. Additionally, current
social, political, and technological innovations mean that teachers have to
face an entirely new series of problems in their work, and they need to be
prepared to respond to these challenges in the most efficient manner possible. Thus, teachers currently in active service, as well as those in training,
are an indispensable part of the proposals regarding education being issued
by educational organizations or international funders (Banco Mundial,
1992; CEPAL-UNESCO, 1992; UNESCO, 1997). The main concerns being
expressed, with varying nuances and emphases, are, among others: the
change in attitudes, the continual formation of attitudes, the level of professional education necessary for actually teaching, and the training being
focused on the practice of teaching.

This is the context in which changes to the curriculum and courses of education provided in teacher-training colleges, which were first initiated in Mexico in 1997, are being made. However, it has become clear that rural teacher-training colleges have different needs from the principles outlined in the new courses proposed for the training of teachers in Mexico. In these courses, emphasis is placed on "learning to teach," and this essentially eradicates the idea of the teacher as a promoter of social change and as an educator-researcher.[10] Of course, rural teacher-training college courses also emphasize instruction in how to teach, but they espouse a broader doctrine that centers around the politics of education, the need for change, a link with the community, social interaction, and the collective interests of the communities they serve.

Occasionally, it seems as if time in these educational establishments has stood still in the era of post-revolutionary Mexico. In reality, though, and given that the processes of modernization are intertwined with traditions that have been long established in rural teacher-training colleges, we must recognize the breaks and disjunctures that result in a hybridization of conceptions regarding the type of teacher these schools aim to train. Despite reinstating certain aspects of the teacher profile currently being proposed, such hybridized conceptions have their own particularities.

FINAL THOUGHTS: THE RELATIONSHIP BETWEEN ETHNOGRAPHIC RESEARCH AND POTENTIAL CHANGES IN EDUCATION POLICY

Ethnographic research promotes familiarity with these current educational processes, which will "allow for understanding of current and future changes to be made in schools. . . . It lends a political significance to this task, the opportunity to blaze a trail toward possible change, to identify possible alternative codes out of aspects of daily school life from both the present and the past which, combined, define a viable prospect for future societies" (Rockwell, 1995).

The existing relationship between ethnography and education policy can be identified on several different levels. One of these is at the personal level. As ethnographers we identify with the methodological option because our interest lies primarily in social change. Public education, an environment in which the most disadvantaged sectors of society congregate, becomes a battleground for political struggle in an effort to promote change to favor the most needy sectors of society. Our precise role is to uncover gaps where new educational perspectives, which will be accepted and promoted by the subjects participating in the daily development of education, may be introduced.

However, creating a link between ethnography and education policy is not as simple as it sounds, if we define the latter as an environment for decision making on educational issues. We are therefore referring to two different goals: (1) to promote familiarity with the current educational climate, with a sufficiently critical outlook that will allow us to define those characteristics that will benefit from change; and (2) to make decisions on which aspects of education need to be changed, and the proposed method to follow. This trail still remains unblazed.

NOTES

1. The research in progress at the Universidad Pedagógica Nacional, with the support of CONACYT, is entitled "The Basic Training of Elementary School Teachers in Mexico: A Comparative Study." The researchers are Etelvina Sandoval (academic director), Gisela Salinas, and Patricia Medina.

2. By "basic," we refer to the standards employed by teacher-training colleges for the training of teachers. By the use of this term, we are thus establishing a difference from in-service professional development (for trained instructors who are already teaching), which is another institutional concern.

3. The precursors to teacher-training colleges were the *Academias de Instrucción Primaria* (Primary Education Academies), created in 1879 for teachers who already possessed a certain amount of training, in order to give them access to "modern methods of instruction." The idea was to establish a single teaching program for elementary teachers and to ensure "the uniformity of systems and methods" in elementary education (Meneses, 1986, p. 281).

4. This is a very general description of the different teacher-training colleges that exist in Mexico, although there are also several subdivisions, such as the Regional Centers for Teacher Training (CREN) or the experimental teacher-training colleges.

5. General Law of Education, chapter II, article 12, paragraph I.

6. CONALTE (1984), p. 36.

7. I refer to the 1930–1936 presidential term of General Lázaro Cárdenas, during which important educational changes were made, with the aim of establishing a socialist education system in Mexico.

8. Editors' note: A multi-grade school refers to remote, single-room rural schools in which children of rather different ages are taught by the same teacher.

9. Teacher-training colleges are sites for constant student protests that take the form of strikes or temporary work stoppages; this has led to authorities questioning their purpose. The magazine Proceso, in issue 1227 of February 27, 2000, reported the existence of a document from the SEP and the Ministry of the Interior entitled "Analysis of Rural Teacher-Training Colleges," which warned of the potential "instability" that these educational establishments posed to the educational system, "given that they are scaled-down versions of Marxist-Leninist political organizations, which are incompatible with the process of modernization expressed in the training of new teachers" (p. 27).

10. These conceptions of the teacher and teacher training were emphasized in Mexico in 1984, when a teaching degree was elevated to the university equivalent of a bachelor's degree.

REFERENCES

Banco Mundial (World Bank). (1992). *Educación primaria. Documento de política del Banco Mundial.* Washington, DC: World Bank.

CEPAL-UNESCO. (1992). *Educación y conocimiento: Eje de la transformación productiva con equidad.* Santiago de Chile: CEPAL (Comisión Económica para América Latina)–UNESCO.

CONALTE. (1984). *150 años en la formación de maestros en México.* Mexico City: Secretaría de Educación Pública.

Delors, Jacques. (1996). *La educación encierra un tesoro.* Mexico City: Correo de la UNESCO.

Meneses, Ernesto. (1986). *Tendencias educativas oficiales en México, 1911–1934.* Mexico City: Centro de Estudios Educativos.

Poder Ejecutivo. (1993). Ley General de Educación, Mexico City.

Rockwell, Elsie. (1995). De huellas, bardas y veredas: Una historia cotidiana en la escuela. In E. Rockwell (Coord.), *La escuela cotidiana.* Mexico City: Fondo de Cultura Económica.

Rosaldo, Renato. (1991). *Cultura y verdad. Nueva propuesta de análisis social.* Colección Los noventa, Conaculta-Grijalbo, Mexico.

Sandoval, Etelvina. (1998). La formación inicial de maestros de primaria en México: Un estudio comparativo. Proyecto de investigación UPN-CONACYT.

SEP. (1997). *Plan de estudios. Licenciatura en Educación Primaria,* Mexico. Mexico City: Secretaría de Educación Pública.

UNESCO. (1997). Recomendaciones de la 45° Conferencia Internacional de Educación. *Cuadernos biblioteca para la actualización del maestro,* Mexico. Mexico City: UNESCO.

Chapter 8

Education Policy and Ethnography: Problems, Prospects, and New Directions

Patricia Medina Melgarejo

Everyone knows that yesterday, don Quijote de la Mancha received order from the cavalry, and today put an end to the extensive torture and abuse generated by its injustice and cruelty.

He came to a road that split into four, and thought of the crossroads where knights errant would stop and ponder upon which one to take . . .

Miguel De Cervantes (1975, p. 69)

One of the focal objectives of educational ethnographic research is the study of schools and the classroom environment, which have been examined from several different perspectives, resulting in the development of tools and strategies for the interpretation of school practices. In the last decade, educational policies concerning the social process of schooling have had important repercussions. Ethnography and ethnographers, through their conceptual outlook and as a result of their position in institutional structures within the educational environment, fulfill varying roles. This situation influences the results, contributions, and application and goals of their research.

This chapter aims to present a conceptual and analytical discussion outlining suggestions for the sociocultural interpretation of educational policies and their impact on school spaces. It is important to take into consideration educational transformations and the opinions of relevant methodologists and theoreticians in the field of ethnography as well as problems that exist in the relationship between current ethnographic research and established policies for this sector.

OUTLINE OF A PERSPECTIVE FOR SOCIOCULTURAL INTERPRETATION OF EDUCATIONAL POLICIES: THE PROBLEM WITH ETHNOGRAPHIC OBJECTIVES

The historical and political importance of the school system resides within the cultural configurations for the learning of specific content material, which are in turn defined by the proficiency and skills that society expects of its citizens. Thus, school life revolves around multiple dimensions and layers of interaction consisting of the actions of everyday subjects who operate within its environment, the content of the school curricula, and the mediation of different objectives and projects that continually redefine the meaning of the processes that comprise the interweaving of institutional relationships.

Educational discourse as evidenced in content and practice results in proposals of collective representation from both private and social sectors, establishing parameters for the definition of the concept of reality. Two processes have emerged. On the one hand, identity is configured as a method of location within a world of shared experiences. On the other, individuals are defined in relation to their formation as subjects with rights and obligations, possessing a sense of inclusion through their ability to interact and make decisions on projects of collective action, and by the role they fulfill as subject actors (Bárcena, 1997; Giroux, 1992).

Due to their nature as realms of negotiation and confrontation, school spaces have long been the objects of deep scrutiny and, having been defined as places of social struggle, have thus evolved as targets for policy-making. In this sense, intervention diagnostics and strategies for subjects within the school system have been identified as practices and guidelines for the social regulation of the school system (Popkewitz, 1994). Modernizing measures mimic the effect of ideological computers that duplicate certain identities, where each individual is given a particular role. It is from this computerized framework that the structure of the subjects' social world is defined.

Current educational policies in Latin America support their discourse with a basic theory: "the educational model is exhausted" (Tedesco, 1992, p. 7). This criticism of the "exhausted style of education," rather than suggesting and acknowledging, through the active participation of its actors, a socioeducational solution within the field of pedagogical innovation, has contradictorily given rise to:

• The centralization of content in basic education, while promoting "flexibility" in the curricula for professional studies, accompanied by restrictions in enrollment of students and the hiring of teachers.[1] The range of final abilities of the student body is upgraded via the implementation of examinations whose purpose is to "assess the general abilities and basic knowledge of young persons" (SEP, 1999,

p. 72), which in turn leads to the solidification of the school networks and to "a rapid increase in the number of quality evaluation agencies world-wide" (Schugurensky, 1998, p. 139).

- Methods of control established for the tasks entrusted to teachers, as well as for salary adjustments, by means of procedures designed to stimulate productivity, whose core principle is the notion of "productivity and efficiency," linked to the fulfillment of current educational policies and their corresponding standards. Thus, a pyramid structure of maximum salary ranges develops, resulting in the shattering of the collective ties that unite professional associations, giving rise to teachers demanding, and often receiving, individually calculated and competitive remuneration.[2]

The "exhausted" style of education encountered in the above-mentioned international organizations, rather than strengthening public education systems, in fact leads to their demise and to the destruction of the relationships they have built with their ties to social issues.

A CHANGING SOCIETY, A TRANSFORMED SCHOOL: POLICIES AND POLITICS

In the case of Latin America, particularly Mexico, it has become essential to analyze social and educational changes and their cultural implications; that is, to interpret cultural transformations and their effect on socioeducational changes before focusing on the importance of introducing First World training opportunities.[3] The dynamic issue of society and culture is inextricably intertwined with historical tradition, which gives rise to practices heavily influenced by political climate.

My definition of politics and policies espouses the notion that they are two dimensions of this dynamic movement (i.e., of the awareness of historical authenticity, which manifests itself in the perception of our existence and consequent exercise of intersocial relationships within the world). The latter may manifest itself in various levels of reality, including within private daily lives and in the sharing of practices on wider levels of the social horizon.

Policies are the "construction process of projects within the context of social contradictions," while politics are described as "the dynamic course of action established between subjects, social practices and projects, whose specific content is intended to influence and determine a particular goal within a framework of viable options" (Zemelman, 1990, p. 13). The importance of policies and politics is based on their dependence on the social construction of projects in order to instill meaning and directionality in the practices of the subjects involved. This leads to the reaffirmation of the importance of educational and school processes, given that they establish an outline for definition of the private and social lives of the subjects.

In today's current stage of transition, it is hard to understand how discourses of freedom and equality could have broken down and, at the same time, comprehend the significant impetus of domination by capitalism and the business world. Our confusion is further fueled by the urgency of struggles by extremists, religious messianists and even ethnicists. Marc Auge (1993) defines this stage as "supermodernity" (and/or globalization), conceived as extremes of rationalization and technological development, which has a profound effect on cultural spaces. This state of affairs introduces the need to make sense of the present in order to understand the past, as a form of

salvation in the face of the over-abundance of occurrences that correspond to what we may term "supermodernity" in order to perceive its fundamental character: excess. . . . It can be said that supermodernity is the head of the coin for which postmodernism reveals only the tail: the positive of a negative. (Auge, 1993, p. 36)

If the parameters that define cultural practices—space and time, collectivity and individuality—are permanently altered and questioned by the supermodern quality of excess, different ways of acknowledging temporality are created due to an acceleration effect in history originating from "the over-abundance of occurrences in the contemporary world" (Auge, 1993, p. 36). Other spatial perceptions are established as a result of "shortcuts" promoted by the use of electronic media, transportation, and communication in such a way that territorial limits and boundaries are recreated and disrupted in accordance with the new parameters established. Individualization of reference points and, therefore, the exacerbation of differences encourage subjects to live—paradoxically—in large urban concentrations, to be involved in constant migratory relocation, and to experience a reproduction of homogenizing spaces. This increases polarization of the individual and creates the perspective of an individual destiny, as opposed to undifferentiated human nuclei. As indicated by Portal:

Thus, both individuals and groups focus their energies on establishing subjectivity, from which they pose the question, who am I? They find the answer from within from ever-shrinking micro-worlds immersed in macro-social spaces, constructed and facilitated by overwhelming technological development. (Portal, 1995, p. 30)

The real questions are: "From within what framework are those new transitional identities being formed?" and "From what point and from which elements is the subject recreating his/her culture and the meaning that has sustained the notion of the private and socio-historical world?" However, it is essential "before concerning oneself with new social forms . . . to focus on the changes that have affected the wide categories through which men have established their identity and reciprocal relationships"

(Auge, 1993, p. 46). The categories suggested by Auge may include education, schooling, and the spheres of knowledge we define as professions.

For the last two decades, transformations in the interactions of subjects have emerged in different methods of evaluating the world as perceived by adults, youths, and children. This has led to the establishment of family practices, networks of friendship, and ways of life that may result in generational clashes. The relationship between teachers and students, whose standards and rituals are fast losing their institutional and social significance, is one example of such a generational void. The excessive quantities of information contained within the programmed content of instruction, the overuse of technology applied in accessing them, and the use of authenticated tools for the development of intellectual learning (the reading of unabridged texts, rhetoric and the discussion of ideas, reading of original sources, and the production of manuscript texts), have resulted in a loss of teacher and student interest. In many cases, these social actors underrate such practices and undermine the importance of the curricula and methods of learning and instruction. Paradoxically, content is excessively abundant, rituality is confused with automated discipline, and school goals are also individualized, creating a fundamental breach in methods of collective relation and in the appropriation of conceptions of the social world. By concentrating their energies on mastering content, schools stagnate in their normative methods, which have thus undergone very little change. The tension between hardened practice, the wide chasms in discourse among subjects, the excess of information, and the growing social conservatism toward the "lack of future collectives" and "individualized evaluations" in schools (denominated as preschool up to the university level) have given rise to a context of uncertainty and the polarized action of educational projects and social actors.

CONSENSUS? THE ROLE OF ETHNOGRAPHIC DISCOURSE

The outline presented here aims to reveal the profile features of current education policy and its impact on public education. Its intention is to reflect on the character of these policies, which, by their all-inclusive nature, aim to provide directionality, not only in the definition of education in our countries but also with the goal of implementing direct change in practices and among social actors within the schools. The latter indicates strong contradictions in the situation and demands of social contexts and in the abilities and needs of the subjects and school institutions themselves.

Another key point that must be analyzed is reflection on the necessary consensus for the development of educational projects, which is a fundamental condition if an education policy is to be viable and have any kind of impact. Thus, we need to focus on the actions of the subjects involved, as it would be naive to presume that these policies have been introduced to the school environment in an impositional manner alone. We need to take stock and carefully consider the purpose, in addition to the intended social impact, of such policies: Why did many participants believe (and many continue to believe) in the viability of "a change in the school institution" outlined by the discursive parameters defined by the goals of those policies? Were they resigned to acceptance? Or rather, were they led to believe that the method suggested was the only existing solution? As Puig-grós states:

Consensus is essential to the process of educating oneself and others. Pedagogical neo-liberalism has entrenched itself in the precise discursive location where cracks in the traditional educational system are felt, for which other solutions are still needed. (Puiggrós, 1998, p. 50)

The perspectives that have questioned the educational systems and school environments are not homogenous in their paradigms of interpretation. Lamentably, however, the pivotal element behind the criticism of schools has been adopted as an axis for so-called neo-liberal policies. This has led to concurrence within the environment, although the content and direction of the changes to be implemented has not been shared among the social actors themselves.

Several different ethnographic studies coincide in their recognition of the need for change in schools, and have frequently detailed, in a critical manner, the principal problems of the objects of their study. On the other hand, there may be other approaches that classify themselves as qualitative and even ethnographic studies, serving more as a diagnostic of elements that have been previously characterized as "dysfunctional" to "the sound institutional organization." However, the relevant terminology has unfortunately been used, and even abused, in one situation or another. Operating with an element of legitimacy, such ethnography or qualitative research is thus lent an air of "verisimilitude," "truth," "approximation to educational reality," and "immediacy to the problems suffered by both teachers and students."

The link between ethnography and politics is a central issue worthy of urgent discussion. Given the current situation, we must thoroughly dissect the various reference points that constitute our research practices and the theoretical-political stances that sustain our interpretive vision. It is a matter of grave concern that:

1. Our critically oriented research often serves as a basis for school policies which, when implemented directly without any mediation, become incompatible with the beliefs of the influential theoreticians who undertook the research in the first place. This situation undoubtedly affects the subjects studied, as certain elements

that have significant impact on both teachers and students are gleaned from the course of ethnographic research and that, upon being reworked and applied in policy formation, become weapons of control.

2. Access to the conclusions of ethnographic research is predominantly awarded to political organizations, whose evaluators frequently are not experienced enough or do not possess the necessary training to be familiar with different school contexts. The primary audience for these types of studies should be the subjects within the school environments themselves and certain key figures within the decision levels of the policies to be developed.

3. Our research does not explicitly specify the nature of the contributions necessary for the development of new political projects, taking into consideration the transformation of existing educational practices, which must be grounded in the future prospects of the subjects themselves—students and teachers alike. We urgently need to develop intervention strategies through dialogue with the different social representatives—that is to say, governmental institutions, new political actors, and nongovernmental organizations—widening the spectrum of the notion of public participation.

4. Due to the need to carry out extensive research (i.e., developing spheres of knowledge, and taking into consideration the time frame needed as well as the space and subjects involved), direct intervention is based purely on diagnostics. Thus, we need to support the research process in developing intervention strategies and establish the necessary links with the participation of the subjects involved.

The problems indicated in this section are not merely a reflection of the researcher's personal opinion but also contain a theoretical and political perspective—that is, a definition of the conditions for change in historical reality, particularly the notion of change, continuity, and breach in educational and social practices.

INTERPRETIVE REDUCTIONISM IN ETHNOGRAPHIC STUDIES: THE INCLUSION AND TRANSFORMATION OF CRITICAL VIEWPOINTS IN OUR RESEARCH

One critical perspective of the reference framework in which we situate ourselves in ethnographic practice involves recognition of the multiple constructions of historical meaning and the discussion from various different stances that dichotomize social and educational reality. In this section I will attempt to outline three points of view that I have termed "reductionisms." Given the nature of their stance, their analysis is limited to certain key elements, leading to a loss of understanding in the necessary conceptual approach to sociocultural dynamics in the school space.

The first point of view maintains that daily routine goes on independently of wider structural and political changes. I denote this point of view "reductionism at the day-to-day level." The second approach represents an angle of interpretation that defines the object of study as being the result of a kind of trickle-down effect from the macro-political sphere. Thus, the day-to-day routine appears as a simple reflection of the "rational" action of such measures. I call this concept "political reductionism," given that it does not generate methods of understanding "politics" at different levels of reality. The third point of view is that which interprets purposeful processes in all actions by the subjects by means of the implementation of an open resistance to policy. Reducing all processes of collective action to some kind of resistance also clouds other perspectives and other angles of analysis that might enable us to understand the subject—a fragmented subject, to be sure, but a subject nonetheless in today's current social context.

In order to overcome the examples of reductionism indicated above, we need to profile theoretical-methodological proposals in our approach to notions of social, cultural, and historical reality. This chapter considers opting for reconstruction methods focusing around processes on different scales of reality, recreating the idea of different cultural and historical meanings, placing them in immediate and personal social settings, and from there dissecting the structural nuclei of the social sphere on a wider scale, from a deeper concept of historicity and policy.

In view of the analytical approaches for dealing with sociopolitical contexts from a cultural perspective, either by following these educational policies or clashing with them, and the recognition of their impact in the reconfiguration of school processes, I propose we work toward the following ethnographic goals:

- A contextual analysis of sociocultural practices in schools by means of pivotal issues of continuity and change in order to recognize historicity and the moments at which the gestational processes of perspectives within a framework of social tensions are expressed (i.e., politics). Furthermore, we must take into account the dynamic actions of the subjects and their practices and projects, whose purpose is to influence the definition of the conditions that characterize their lives, their work, and their education (i.e., policies).

- A reconstruction of cultural processes in schools that will permit ethnographic readiness in order to understand the transition between the daily actions of the different educational actors and the elements of influx in the conditions of their daily lives by means of proposals for intervention by the political discourse of education—that is to say, the prior establishment of options and the construction of projects with a particular purposefulness on the part of the social actors themselves.

The thoughts outlined throughout this chapter seek to convey the need to construct theoretical and political options within ethnographic practices in the field of education. At the same time, we need to understand that ethnographers are not merely "naïve" subjects, but critically thinking individuals. Our role and connection to projects of transformation in schools are infused with both logic and contradictions. It is impossible to consider the urgent need to debate "the change," with the intention that this bear repercussions on specific subjects, without hearing the voice and intellectual authority of those involved. I repeat: we must not blindly instigate educational change merely for the sake of doing so. It must be done with the full participation of the subjects in the construction of options for their private and social worlds.

Esteemed colleagues, it seems we are in a situation similar to that of Quijote:

> He came to a road that split into four, and thought of the crossroads where knights errant would stop and ponder upon which one to take . . .

Which path shall we take as a community project at the crossroads of the current educational situation?

NOTES

1. It is also worth reflecting upon the growing number of backup programs that have been introduced as methods of extra educational consideration for those social sectors that are regarded as "disadvantaged" or "backward." This branch of current educational politics is referred to as "equity and relevance." Contributions from the field of ethnography are reinforced in these programs; however, the issue under discussion relates to their pedagogical objectives and the political goals that such programs embrace, which frequently, within their framework, confuse poverty with cultural processes. That is, that establish the opposite relationship, attempting to sustain themselves on qualitative methodology.

2. See the work of Rueda and Landesmann (1999).

3. The contributions of Barbero (1991), Bonfil (1992, 1993), Brunner (1992), García Canclini (1989), Puiggrós (1995), Quijano (1988) and Rowe and Schelling (1993), among others, regarding reflections on the processes of modernization in Latin America and the permanent tension between modernization and tradition, advocate the recognition of new processes and new cultural identities. This situation is of interest to educators who conduct research on the sociocultural interpretations of educational processes.

REFERENCES

Auge, Marc. (1993). *Los no lugares: Una antropología de la sobremodernidad Barcelona*. Madrid: Gedisa.

Barbero, Jesús. (1991). *De los medios a las mediaciones: Comunicación, cultura y hegemonía*. Barcelona: Gustavo Gili.

Bárcena, Fernando. (1997). *El oficio de la ciudadanía: Introducción a la educación política*. Papeles de Pedagogía No. 33. Madrid: Paidós.

Bonfil, Guillermo. (1992). *Pensar nuestra cultura*. Mexico City: Alianza.

Bonfil, Guillermo. (1993). *Nuevas identidades culturales en México*. Mexico City: CNCA.

Brunner, José Joaquín. (1992). *América Latina: Cultura y modernidad*. Mexico City: CNCA/Grijalbo.

Buenfil, Rosa Nidia. (1993). *Análisis del discurso y educación*. Mexico City: Departamento de Investigaciones Educativas (DIE), CINVESTAV-IPN.

De Cervantes, Miguel. (1975). *Don Quijote de la Mancha*. Barcelona: Nauta.

García Canclini, Néstor. (1989). *Culturas híbridas: Estrategias para entrar y salir de la modernidad*. Mexico City: CNCA/Grijalbo.

Giroux, Henry. (1992). *Teoría y resistencia en educación*. Mexico City: Siglo XXI.

Popkewitz, S. Thomas. (1994). *A political sociology of educational reform: Power/ knowledge in teaching, teacher education, and research*. Barcelona: Moratta.

Portal, María Ana (1995). *Religiosidad popular e identidad urbana: El caso de San Andrés Totoltepec, Tlalpan, D.F.* Tesis-Doctorado. Mexico City: Facultad de Filosofía y Letras/Instituto de Investigaciones Antropológicas, Universidad Nacional Autonóma de México.

Puiggrós, Adriana. (1995). *Volver a educar: El desafío de la enseñanza argentina a finales del siglo XX*. Buenos Aires: Ariel.

Puiggrós, Adriana. (1998). Educación neoliberal y alternativas. In A. Alcántara, R. Pozas, and C. Torres (Coords.), *Educación, democracia y desarrollo en el fin de siglo*. Mexico City: Siglo XXI, pp. 46–56.

Quijano, Aníbal. (1988). Modernidad, identidad y utopía en América Latina. In *Imágenes desconocidas: La modernidad, una encrucijada posmoderna*. Mexico City: FLACSO, pp. 7–24.

Rowe, William, and Schelling, Vivian. (1993). *Memory and modernity: Popular culture in Latin America*. Mexico City: CNCA/Grijalbo.

Rueda, Mario, and Landesmann, Monique. (1999). ¿Hacia una nueva cultura de evaluación de los académicos? Mexico City: Centro de Estudios Sobre la Universidad, Universidad Nacional Autónoma de México.

Schugurensky, Daniel. (1998). La reestructuración de la educación superior en la era de la globalización: ¿Hacia un modelo heterónomo? In A. Alcántara, R. Pozas, and C. Torres (Coords.), *Educación, democracia y desarrollo en el fin de siglo*. Mexico City: Siglo XXI, pp. 118–149.

Secretaría de Educación Pública (SEP). (1999). *Perfil de la educación en México*. Mexico City: Subsecretaría de Planeación y Coordinación—Subsecretaría de Educación Básica y Normal.

Tedesco, Juan. (1992). Nuevas estrategias de cambio educativo en América Latina. In *Proyecto Principal de Educación en América Latina y el Caribe*. Boletín 28, Agosto. Santiago de Chile: UNESCO/OREALC, pp. 7–24.

Zemelman, Hugo. (1990). *De la historia a la política: La experiencia en América Latina*. Mexico City: Siglo XXI.

Zemelman, Hugo. (1998). Crítica, epistemología y educación. *Revista de Tecnología Educativa* 13(2), 119–131. Santiago, Chile: Organización de los Estados Americanos (OEA), Departamento de Asuntos Educativos.

Chapter 9

Perspective-Taking in the Practice-Research Gap: Using Ethnography to Help Schools See Themselves

Peter Demerath

This chapter discusses the importance of perspective-taking in doing ethnographic research to inform school improvement efforts. It assumes that one of the reasons academic research has not fulfilled its potential to impact policy is that practitioners and policymakers have not been historically thought of as central "constituencies" for researchers (Tierney, 2000, p. 188). The chapter argues, therefore, that impacting policy and practice involves a two-part exercise in perspective-taking: (1) understanding how policymakers and practitioners know the world, and thereby seeing problems and viable solutions from their perspective; and (2) understanding how policymakers and practitioners see academics and our work, so that we can gain the reflexive awareness required to make us valuable partners in policy dialogues. The chapter emphasizes that ethnographers are well suited to impact policy because we are explicitly trained in understanding local points of view and often have to adopt new ways of being in relation to our participants. After constructing a rationale for this approach, the chapter discusses issues involved in negotiating relationships with policymakers and practitioners in my own ethnographic projects in suburban and urban settings in a large midwestern U.S. city.

CONVERGING RATIONALES FOR POLICY-RELEVANT RESEARCH

Current calls for "actionable knowledge" (Sutton and Levinson, 2001) are congruent with the efforts of many U.S. universities to become "engaged" with the communities around them and become large-scale social change agents (Boyer, 1994). The rationales for such efforts are morally compelling (Harkavy, 1998), and several initiatives hold great promise. Nevertheless, these activities often proceed outside of the academic reward structure and, within academic departments, are often treated as "service" rather than scholarship (see Tierney, 2000).

While there is a long tradition of policy-relevant ethnographic research, particularly in applied anthropology (see Fetterman, 1993), it has been noted that the area is still conceptually underdeveloped (Sutton and Levinson, 2001). Current trends in social science and education, however, suggest a new thrust toward work informed by a sociocultural perspective that can inform policy and practice. Portes (2000) hailed such approaches in sociology for being able to examine the "unrecognized, unintended, and emergent consequences of goal-oriented activity," and for being able to take into account the "definitions of the situation of relevant actors" (p. 1). Moreover, the emerging area of "public anthropology" directs researchers to "address broad critical concerns" in ways others beyond the discipline can understand and value (Borofsky, 2000, p. 9). Some of the adherents of this movement have coined the term "public or perish," to reflect the urgency they feel to make their work relevant (Peacock, 1998).

In addition, there have been recent calls among educational researchers to move beyond the "paradigm wars" and orient empirical work more explicitly around public policy. Bryke (1999) has pointed out that because policymakers usually have to use multiple criteria to make judgments, ideally their decisions ought to emerge from a competition of ideas, informed by research. Thus, research in a public policy field ought to foreground the purposes of inquiry over the different epistemologies that may frame them (Donmoyer, 2001). While researchers will, of course, have their own perspectives and research agendas that will shape their studies, what this means is that (in classic anthropological fashion) we need to privilege concerns that are foremost in our participants' minds—in essence, that we do "use-inspired basic research" (Schoenfeld, 1999; Stokes, 1997).

Implicit in doing such research is narrowing what is commonly referred to in U.S. educational research as the "research-practice" gap: the perceived lack of connection between research and practice (see Kennedy, 1997). Vivian Robinson recently illuminated some of the causes of this gap by arguing that research is often ignored because it bypasses the problem-solving processes that sustain the practices that researchers seek to alter (1998). Her "problem-based methodology" understands practices and policies as activities that people develop to solve problems in particular situations. This kind of theory of local problems helps us to understand what it is to solve one and how research can be involved in the solution. In this sense, the research-practice gap comes about when the theories of the researcher don't articulate with the theories of the practitioner. Researchers' culpability for the gap is well illustrated by the story (not my own) of the "incurable academic." The incurable academic is given a tour of a highly effective school and is shown bustling classrooms where students are engaged in creative and challenging projects and seem to be clearly learning. At the end of the day the incurable academic turns to the school guide and says, "Well, that's all very good, but does it work in theory?"

USING ETHNOGRAPHY TO PLAY THE POLICY "GAME"

Ethnography has great potential to close this gap because it is a way of "seeing" (Wolcott, 1999) that can help policymakers and practitioners interpret lived experiences and local practices. More specifically, where school improvement efforts involve changing the culture of the school (i.e., the constructed meanings of students, teachers, parents, and administrators that shape the ways in which they approach schooling), ethnography can help by exploring people's reasoning, assumptions, and actions to discover how they, as active agents, formulate problems and their responses to them. Such efforts build "contextual understanding" that can enlighten policy and practice (Rist, 2000, p. 1003; see also Gibson, 1985).

Accordingly, Michele Foster (1998) has suggested that we might see the product of our ethnographic work as a kind of mirror that reflects an image back to our participants. She stresses that the surface of a mirror can be altered to show different things—reflecting our interpretations and representations of who our participants (and ourselves) are and what they (and we) do. However, the ends that research findings ought to serve are less clear: whether researchers have a moral responsibility to serve as advocates if their findings merit it (Fetterman, 1993); how researchers can identify ways in which findings or principles from a study may be disseminated to a broader audience so that they may impact policy; and how findings may be rendered into a usable form for practitioners (see Tierney, 2000).

Indeed, "playing the [policy] game" (Fetterman, 1993, p. 243) involves the significant tension of making forceful recommendations while preserving the anthropological contingencies and complexities of our findings. In the remainder of the chapter I argue that making this tension productive—maximizing our contributions to policy and practice, and advancing our own scholarly understandings—requires negotiating a relationship and dialogue with policymakers and practitioners that facilitates the sharing of perspectives. In short, ethnographers need to: (1) understand policymaker and practitioner epistemology and needs; (2) explicitly solicit policymaker and practitioner views of academics and academic research so that we may gain more reflexive awareness of ourselves; and (3) while remaining true to our disciplinary roots and mission, be willing and able to adopt other ways of being in relation to our research participants—from the research questions and the purposes we ascribe to our work, to roles we take on to ensure the "public utility" of the research (Tierney, 2000).

CONTINGENT CONSTRUCTIONS OF ETHNOGRAPHY

I now turn to local policymakers' and practitioners' perceptions of research in general, and ethnography in particular, to show how these shape their willingness to participate in research projects and to use findings generated from them. I draw here on my experiences over the last 18 months in planning, negotiating access, and beginning data collection for a comparative study of student culture and academic engagement in a suburban and urban high school and an urban middle school in the city in which I work.[1] The key research questions concerned the cultural production of advantage and disadvantage, and the research team investigated how students determine what "goods" are worth pursuing in life. Yet in each school my research assistants and I also solicited and sought to investigate research questions suggested by teachers and administrators. Accordingly, the work had multiple purposes, informed by multiple frameworks. The different experiences we have had illuminate how local policymakers' and practitioner's perceptions of the uses of the research were shaped by their school's nested historical and social contexts as well as their own experiences with research.

The first school is a resource-rich U.S. Blue Ribbon high school in suburban Columbus, Ohio that consciously uses research to better its practices and programs. The principal, a European-American woman and the state's 1999–2000 Principal of the Year, provides her faculty with a reading list every year of recently published books on education-related topics and conducts a series of informal fireside chats with them during the school year. Unlike the middle-class and upper-middle class schools described by Emihovich (1999) that, conscious of their reputations as "good" schools, were not amenable to suggestions from ethnographers to become "critically conscious" of their practice, the principal (who has degrees in anthropology and counseling) welcomed my proposed longitudinal research. She said that it would be much better suited to helping them understand whether they were achieving their intended goals than short-term (read quantitative) research, and proposed a four-year study. This principal seemed to be valuing the "mirroring" quality of ethnographic research described by Foster above.

At a meeting after the first year of the study, I shared with her some of the study's preliminary findings, including some of the effects of the culture of competition in the school, the increasing authority of students' selves, the compression of adolescence, and how students in the school experience others and "otherness." Some of the findings prompted her to describe one of the central dilemmas she faced as a principal: knowing when and how to treat high school students as children and when to treat them as adults. She said, "How do you give kids space so that they can make mistakes without loading the school down with punitive measures?" The dialogue we had between researcher and practitioner perspectives is illustrated more specifically by an exchange concerning the sharing of a particular research finding. The finding concerned a trend my assistants and I had seen in the school where individual students were regularly given rewards for prosocial behavior. The catch phrase for one such student-sponsored program was "You got caught showing respect." I told her we had coded such instances as "incentivized morality" in our notes, and thought that they posed the risk of making prosocial behavior the exception rather than the norm in the school. She said she had thought from the outset that some of these programs were "wrong," but couldn't "put her finger" on why. She said that in light of our discussion she was going to reconsider a national citizenship advocacy group's proposed program that used similar means. At the end of the meeting the principal said, "Thank you for helping us see ourselves."

The second and third schools were located in an economically disadvantaged region of the city. The city school district of which they were a part had recently been designated as under "academic emergency" by the state Department of Education due to consistent poor performances on state-mandated proficiency tests. The urban high school had been reconstituted for the 1999–2000 school year (a process that involved a turnover of 60 percent of its faculty), and the local press had written extensively about the "deficits" of the school and community. The new African-American principal of the school hesitated to support the research on such a potentially sensitive topic in his first year; most likely he was weary of the critical ways his and similarly disadvantaged schools had been portrayed in the media and by researchers. Moreover, he said that student culture was a "sensitive issue," as people "didn't always know" why they did particular things. Most important, the principal was extremely wary of the possibility of being taken advantage of by researchers with their own agendas: he said that, as a rule, he would not "pimp" the reform process he was initiating to outsiders (I interpret this phrase to mean that he would not allow someone else to benefit from this process to the detriment of the efforts themselves). Indeed, in July 1999 a prominent member of the high school community partners group told me that the university at which I work "hadn't done a damn thing" to help the school or the people of his community.

The principal suggested that we postpone the research to the 2000–2001 school year and that in the meantime we establish a relationship with one another. He also suggested that I participate in the school's community partners group (a relational approach that resonates with much Afrocentric epistemology). During the last year, he appointed me to a "College Partnership Committee" and proposed that we work to "hold the university accountable to schools in its backyard." Our exchange resulted in the articulation of a goal of demanding that area universities use their resources to create a "learning culture" (the principal pointedly commented to me that we were working on an issue concerning culture) in the university district by fostering enriched educational opportunities and ensuring better educational futures for young people.

The urban middle school had nearly been closed three times in the early 1990s for poor performance. During the 1999–2000 school year it had among the lowest proficiency test scores in the city. The principal of the school, a European-American woman, agreed to the study primarily because it was linked to the university's partnership efforts. She and several teachers in the school expressed pointed frustration at much of the prior research that had been carried out at the school—a considerable amount, as this was the closest middle school to the campus: "We're just sitting here," said one teacher. These teachers were all critical on several points: the lack of consistency with which local universities and colleges were engaged with the school, the poor quality of the research, and the nondissemination of research results. One teacher said, "Rarely was it presented to us that this is why we're doing it [research] and this is the benefit to you." One teacher summed up many of her colleagues' attitudes regarding university personnel when she said, "You keep asking us questions and nothing happens."

Establishing a relationship with the staff and students of this school seemed to turn on our ability to demonstrate that we respected their work, struggles, and needs. The school's poor proficiency test scores, poor public image, and tumultuous relationship with the District Central Office seemed to have galvanized its staff around the mission of teaching and caring for disadvantaged students. In the middle of the school year, a teacher and the principal told us that they were increasingly saying "no" to external programs and requests that were not clearly aligned with this mission. Part of this resolve seemed related to the ways in which the school had been mistreated (and disrespected) by university researchers. The teacher summarized their present position on research by saying, "Basically, if it's not going to help us, then it won't happen here."[2]

Most recently, however, while the administrators and many teachers in both the urban high school and middle school have indicated that they welcome the increased understanding of educational processes that research could bring, what they really need, in the words of the high school's director of guidance, is "Less talk, and more action." She elaborated, "If teachers just see more meetings and planning and research that is going to be someone's paper or dissertation, they're going to say, 'What's the use?' " These people hoped the university would be able to help them enrich their programs by providing a significant number of classroom interns and mentors. Consequently, my colleagues and I who are working on these partnership efforts are finding ourselves adopting new roles within our own institution related to the advocacy of underresourced local schools and generating recommendations for policies and practices that can assist them.

CONCLUSIONS

This chapter has argued that doing policy- and practice-relevant research requires ethnographers to negotiate a relationship with policymakers and practitioners that focuses on understanding their epistemology, local needs, and perceptions of the utility of research. Such perspective-taking enables ethnographers to gain greater reflexive awareness and be in a better position to help schools with contextual understanding—to "see" themselves.

The chapter gave brief examples of how policymakers' and practitioners' immediate needs and perceptions of inquiry shaped their willingness to engage in a relationship with a university researcher. The principal of the resource-rich suburban high school, with a background in anthropology as well as counseling, was concerned about meeting students' needs in a rapidly changing time: she was particularly worried that increasing numbers of them were becoming "morally bankrupt." Through a long-term exchange of views, the researcher-policymaker dialogue in this case centered in part on ways of conceptualizing and addressing moral issues in the education of high school students.

The ways in which many of the personnel in the urban schools reacted to the research seemed related to the highly stressed and underresourced environments in which they worked as well as to the historically problematic relationships with university researchers. In addition to providing them with data that could be used in their school improvement efforts, these school actors called for my university colleagues and me to take on new roles as advocates for them in the university policy arena. As anthropologists we ought to be willing and able to take on such new roles because our fieldwork, carried out as it is in the stream of daily life and anchored in the notion of *participation*, constantly requires us to adopt new ways of being in relation to our participants—including being entailed with them. For example, because the village in Papua New Guinea where I work is one in which Margaret Mead began doing research 70 years ago, I am considered "Lain bilong Margrit Mid" there, and have inherited dozens of preordained relationships and entailments.[3]

Fostering such kinds of entailed relationships may be characteristic of the process of give and take that researchers must engage in if they wish to affect policy and practice. Accordingly, one way in which ethnographers may "play the [policy] game" is by doing multifocal research, wherein selected research questions are either aligned with local concerns or come directly from local policymakers or practitioners. This is not to say that our scholarly missions or theoretical frameworks must be jettisoned in such undertakings; indeed, for us to retain our unique points of view, they should be always present. However, the negotiation of the tensions inherent in our relationships with policymakers and practitioners may require us to background some of these concerns as we seek to employ ethnography's focus on context and particular description to contribute findings to local dialogues. In this sense, doing use-inspired research ought to strive toward a more symbiotic arrangement wherein local practitioners and policymakers contribute to our research foci and the ways we conceptualize a setting or problem and we contribute new ways of seeing as well as possible solutions to their practices and policies.

NOTES

1. The urban projects were also part of a "contexts of learning" study intended to identify specific ways in which the university at which I work can better partner with local schools to help them achieve their improvement goals.

2. The extent to which the project will help remains to be seen. At the time of writing, data analysis was nearing completion, and a presentation to school, district, and university personnel was scheduled for mid-October 2000.

3. For example, an old woman named Siska Niapin was born in 1928, the year Mead first got there. Her mother had taken ill after her birth, and Mead had fed her taro and papaya. By feeding her, Mead had become a mother to her, and had placed all of her descendants into a relationship of reciprocal indebtedness with Siska and her line.

REFERENCES

Borofsky, R. (2000). Public anthropology: Where to? What next? *Anthropology News* 41(5), 9–10.

Boyer, E. (1994). Creating the new American college. *Chronicle of Higher Education*, March 9, p. A48.

Bryke, A. (1999). Invited remarks. In J. Greeno (Chair), Contributing to school change and the advancement of scientific knowledge: New patterns of partnership of research and practice. Paper presented at the Annual Meeting of the American Educational Research Association, Montreal.

Donmoyer, R. (2001). Paradigm talk reconsidered. In V. Richardson (Ed.), *Handbook of research on teaching* (4th ed.). Washington, DC: AERA.

Emihovich, C. (1999). Studying schools, studying ourselves: Ethnographic perspectives on educational reform. *Anthropology and Education Quarterly* 30(4), 477–483.

Fetterman, D. (1993). Ethnography and policy: A catalytic combination for change. In E. Jacob and C. Jordan (Eds.), *Minority education: Anthropological perspectives*. Norwood, NJ: Ablex, pp. 235–252.

Foster, M. (1998). Critical race theory and the "translation" of ethnographic knowledge for empowerment. In B. Levinson (Chair), Whose voice? What commitment? Debating anthropological approaches to research and educational change. Paper presented at the Annual Meeting of the American Anthropological Association, Philadelphia.

Gibson, M.A. (1985). Collaborative educational ethnography: Problems and profits. *Anthropology and Education Quarterly* 16(2), 124–148.

Harkavy, I. (1998). Organizational innovation and the creation of the new American University. In L.A.K. Simon (Ed.), *University-community collaborations for the twenty-first century.* New York: Garland.

Kennedy, M. (1997). The connection between research and practice. *Educational Researcher* 26(7), 4–12.

Peacock, J. (1998). Public or perish? In P. Sanday (Chair), Defining a public interest anthropology. Paper presented at the Annual Meeting of the American Anthropological Association, Philadelphia.

Portes, A. (2000). The hidden abode: Sociology as the analysis of the unexpected. *American Sociological Review* 65 (February), 1–18.

Rist, R.C. (2000). Influencing the policy process with qualitative research. In N.K. Denzin and Y.S. Lincoln (Eds.), *Handbook of qualitative research* (2nd ed.). Thousand Oaks, CA: Sage, pp. 1001–1017.

Robinson, V. (1998). Methodology and the research-practice gap. *Educational Researcher* 27(1), 17–26.

Schoenfeld, A.H. (1999). Looking toward the 21st century: Challenges of educational theory and practice. *Educational Researcher* 28(7), 4–14.

Stokes, D.E. (1997). *Pasteur's quadrant: Basic science and technological innovation.* Washington, DC: Brookings Institution Press.

Sutton, M., and Levinson, B.A.U. (Eds.). (2001). *Policy as practice: Toward a comparative sociocultural analysis of educational policy.* Westport, CT: Ablex.

Tierney, W.G. (2000). On translation: From research findings to public utility. *Theory into Practice* 39(3), 185–190.

Wolcott, H. (1999). *Ethnography: A way of seeing.* Thousand Oaks, CA: Sage.

Chapter 10

Workshop Discussion: Ethnography and Policy—The State of the Art

Participants in the Eighth Interamerican Symposium

Peg Sutton: Whenever a term like "use-inspired" comes up, it scares me. Working as I do, focusing especially on international assistance agencies and how they formulate policy questions and policy research, it's such a powerfully utilitarian approach to policy. I always come back to Habermas' three types of knowledge constitutive interests. Clearly, in this type of policy research the goal is utilitarian and there's no room even for voice from elsewhere. And I always think in that context, of the difficulty of opening up policy research not only to interpretive but particularly to critical and dialogical modes of research, which is extremely difficult in that perspective. There's a long history of academic reflection on the use of research in policymaking—the knowledge utilization brand of sociology in particular. And it always tends to ultimately come back to this fairly utilitarian perspective. So my question is, how do we as ethnographers work in a use-inspired way, which is legitimate and appropriate, without losing the ability to reformulate questions, to ask questions in ways that don't serve the audience. You know, you can take a contract or not take a contract, but how can we work against a very narrow-minded view of "use" in research?

Peter Demerath: I think it's a real challenge, and I think it's a tension that many people have been talking about at this symposium from the beginning—the tensions between doing utilitarian research and being true to some of our own scholarly interests and traditions as well. And I think it's quite difficult, but one of the more promising areas that I've heard about is trying to perhaps work toward a convergence between researcher and practitioner epistemology and goals as well.

Juan Fidel Zorrilla: Well, I'm on the other side of the fence now. The project I'm in charge of is called precisely "for a relevant education." So when people say, "What do you mean by relevant?" and I say, "Useful," and they say, "What do you mean by useful?" I say, "Well, it is very simple." I believe that, say, in the last 150 to 200 years the world learned to transform reading, writing, and arithmetic from being an elite type of knowledge into being a universal type of knowledge. So we have to do the next step, that is to say, what is beyond reading, writing, and arithmetic—the patrimony of everyone—because reading, writing, and arithmetic are very useful. So, it's a new way of understanding "useful." That doesn't mean it is only useful in the productive sense, but it is useful for leisure, for education, for everyday life—for everything. So, maybe we could start thinking of new ways of understanding "useful" instead of *avoiding* being "useful," which probably is the direction of some of the comments that are usually made.

Patricia Medina (original in Spanish; translation by Bradley Levinson): I'd like at this point to place a small stone in the path we've been traveling. I'm always one of the very first to defend teachers, to call attention to the difficult conditions in which they work in the schools, and so forth. But it also worries me that educational policies always seem to look bad or misguided in relation to the "poor teachers," no? I would like to suggest some things for us to consider. Any policy, even if it's formulated at the macro level, needs a kind of consensus to be successfully introduced into the school. The teachers often accept such policies from their position within the school. There are moments, as I've discovered in the research I'm conducting—and it's even painful to recognize it—that this happens. But we have to ask why this happens, how and why it is that teachers accept and interact with such policies, even though one can anticipate ethnographically that three or four years down the road the teachers will reject the policy that they're now accepting because they'll have seen its ill effects and so on.

So I would put forth a proposal for us to begin studying, in a parallel manner, the two levels of policy—this is in relation to the third question we were asked to consider, about how to study education policy ethnographically. One would be about beginning to conscientiously follow through with an investigation of the effects of policy in the schools—how does the policy get enacted in schools, how is it received there, and so forth, no? The parallel project would be to keep in focus the subjective relations that ethnography has always studied so well—processes of knowledge construction, the relationship between teachers and students, and the like. What we need to do is put these two levels directly and intentionally in relation to one another, to begin contextualizing one with the other to enable a better understanding of how they interrelate.

[. . .]

Elsie Rockwell: I'd like to pick up on a couple of the points made in several of the position papers, which have to do with history. Also, I'll toss in the issue of scale, which is one thing that we experience particularly in Latin America because reforms come from very centralized federal governments. So preoccupations always come back to matters of scale. We know we can make changes at the level of individual schools, we can do a good job at that. But what happens with the larger picture? And I want to take issue with something that Fred [Erickson] said today. I think I heard you right. You said that in this counterhegemonic struggle, we're going "against the weight of history." The first thing I want to say is that some of that history comes from the other side, the side of struggles, you know? We have got to start understanding how to take advantage of that part of history that is on our side, no?

[Sounds of approbation by several participants]

Now I'd like to explain how I got into doing historical research after doing ethnography. Way back in 1975 we started doing some ethnographic research, and it was unheard of. People would say, "What is this ethnographic work?" It sounded exotic and was considered research done only about ethnic groups. And then the Ministry [of Education] started hearing about this kind of research. One day I was called in by someone from the undersecretary [of education]. He asked to know what we were finding out about the schools we were studying. He asked: "What are the deviations from the norm?" [Laughter] "Norm," of course, meant the law and the programs and regulations that all teachers were supposed to follow. Later I found out that the undersecretary of education had asked him, in writing, to find out what the researchers at the DIE [Departamento de Investigaciones Educativas—Rockwell's academic unit] knew about the "hidden curriculum." [Laughter] Teachers were supposed to follow the new "official" curriculum, so all this talk of a hidden curriculum was evidently bothering them. [More laughter]

This kind of question coming from policymakers has an impact on research and theory. And that's something that we're not looking at, we're always looking the other way. For us, in the first place, we saw that we had to do some thinking about some of these theoretical concepts. First of all, we had to rethink institutions completely because this Durkheimian idea of an institution as norm-regulated, with an associated notion of pathology as deviation from the norm, didn't work at all for what we were observing and studying. We had to toss out "hidden curriculum" as well because who is it hidden from? It's obviously hidden from the people "up there," the policymakers, but it was very much visible to the people who lived in schools every day, though much of it was implicit. So it was this "meeting" with policymakers, plus the textbook reform of those years that some of us were also involved in, that provided some starting points for the analysis of our ethnographic fieldnotes. The experience with reforms also made me think about doing historical research, at a later date. One result of these reforms was a generalized frustration summed up in: "Schools don't change"; "Teachers don't change"; "We've done all these great things, and changed the policies, the programs, the textbooks, and everything, but schools just don't change." So I decided to look to history to see whether and how schools change. And I believe they do change.

[. . .]

Elsie Rockwell [after a brief discussion by several participants about wanting to make their research more "policy-relevant"]: If we want to impact policy, do we really know what policy is and how it's made and who makes it and where it's made? Do we have to understand that ethnographically in order to have a way of talking to policymakers, for example?

Fred Erickson: It struck me in this morning's discussion that I wasn't very clear about how policy was made and who the policy people were. And there was talk about the practitioner-policy gap. And I thought of something else that I don't know very much about and that is the policy researchers, who I've tended to avoid, who supposedly are more hooked into the scene than ethnography is. I mean, there are journals of policy research. . . . And I don't know anything ethnographically about them either. And as I think about the problem of how to address policy people, I realize that I also don't know how to address these policy researchers who appear to be, I mean, I may be a little paranoid, but they always appear to me to be brokers. They certainly seem to have a symbiotic relationship with policymakers, and they act as if they know how to talk to policy people. And maybe they do, but I realize I don't know anything about them, either. And in fact, one way of approaching the study of policy— and this would make an interesting project—would be to go find some traditional policy researchers doing a project and see how they operate between the world of practice and the world of policy, and that might be illuminating. I think that in fact educational anthropologists, and in general qualitative researchers, have been pretty naive about who these people are, or whether or not they are people. [laughter] I was thinking of Jan's [Nespor] point, that it's not just people and words, it's material artifacts and processes and buildings and all kinds of things that are part of all this. But I don't know. So I think a conversation about this would be very helpful. It also might be a necessary prelude to trying to theorize because we don't seem to have articulated much of a notion of what this phenomenon of policy "stuff" is.

Juan Fidel Zorrilla: It struck me when you were talking about this, that most, or probably all, descriptions of policy are always personal references to documents, to laws, bylaws, regulations, but never to the type of description we are acquainted with in ethnographic work. We never get any description of negotiations, of the processes that lead to the issue of a given policy. But they appear to be given, you know, something that is just there. They are not produced, not a product of anything, not the result of anything. And then the gap is filled with interpretations—very classical inter-pretations of filling in the gap and saying, "This policy corresponds to this type of interests." But we really don't have access to any type of ethno-graphic data on the process. So that's one thing that's not very clear. Most descriptions of policy have this impersonal, unidimensional sort of char-acteristic. That's the first problem. And the second one is, in actor's terms, policy can refer to anything to do with authority, anything that has to do with the rule, tradition, or even inertia. People say, "That's a matter of education policy." No one seems to see that there are any actors behind policy. And I think that links to what Graciela [Batallán] said, and it's very striking in Mexico, which is that power is always looked upon as if power is linked to elite political power and never to social power or to subjects' ability to do things. And so maybe we have a problem there. You always look at power and policy from the outside, and there doesn't seem to be any participation in policy or in power.

Geoffrey Walford: But I think there are studies like that. I think there are actually studies that look at the way in which laws, in particular, have been generated, how they've gradually grown, how there are various dif-ferent bodies that have put forward one idea and others have put forward other ideas, and now you've got a variety of competing discourses. And they study the way those discourses then become lodged in a document. Now of course, they're not ethnographic. I agree with you there entirely. Because it's actually quite difficult to do an ethnography of what is actually a whole wide body of different people and groups and discourses. That's absolutely right. But you know I see policymakers as not just being those people who are making the laws at the top, but I see policymakers as also being those who actually act to interpret, because they are actually doing policy. And there are ethnographic studies of that.

[. . .]

Juan Fidel Zorilla [after recounting a research project in which various interviewees characterized policy as a set of existing constraints on their own action]: What I'm saying is that policy has to be considered also in terms of the use actors make of what policy is all about. I'm not giving a true description of what policy is. I'm giving a description of the use policy is made of by all of these categories of people. And there is a common strain from the minister of education to, say, the teacher, whereby every-body talks about policy in a sense that it is external to them, and it is something that limits their own action.

Amy Stambach: I think that there are analogies, if not complete homol-ogies, between the concept of policy and culture. And the way that you have just presented your policymakers objectifying their policies as the "set-ting of limits"—the thing that sets the limits—is quite similar to the way that people talk about their culture in an objectified and reified manner, as though, "It's my tradition, it's what I'm bound to do." It seems to me that as cultural analysts we should be able to think through our ethnographies and through our ethnographic writing and thinking about the way that people use policy as a vehicle for making arguments.

[. . .]

Elsie Rockwell: I'd like to clarify the way *"la política"* and *"lo político"* are being translated. In Spanish, we don't have separate words for politics and policy. They are both *política*. The use of *la* and *lo* gives a little bit of that idea. So *la política educativa* is meant a little more like education policy. *Lo político* is a bit more abstract, referring to the process of politics. Or sometimes people will say *"la política política"* to refer to political processes, movements and such.

Olga Vasquez: So Elsie, maybe you could continue the discussion of what policy and politics mean in English. Do they sort of correlate with *la política* and *lo político*? Every time I think about policy I have to call my friend who is a political scientist, and she makes a major distinction between politics and policy. The point about politics is that that's the laws that are made. And then policy is how you implement those laws. So how do you bring about change in response to the politics? And I'm not sure that this is what I understood here. But this is from a political scientist's perspective. And so am I getting the wrong training?

Peg Sutton: I think that is a particular political science perspective— highly functionalist, for example! It's very hard to imagine—I mean we distinguish in English and in the North American context between policy formation and implementation, right? And even so we manage to talk about policy formation as an apolitical process. I think that it is very North American to act as if it is not politics. But policy is the formulation of a political position, however, and wherever it takes place, it's a political position.

Juan Fidel Zorrilla: Policy has to do with the struggle for power.

Olga Vasquez: Yes, right. But can policy be a way to resolve that?

Juan Fidel Zorrilla: It's what you do when you accede to power.

Jan Nespor: You could also look at policy as a way of generating scale, of defining institutional relationships, across scale of time and space. It is a way of institutionalizing power. It's probably a euphemism, in a way, to talk about the policy and make that distinction. I did want to respond very briefly and just raise a question to some of the earlier discussion about how we could, either by studying policymakers or by learning how to communicate the findings of our ethnographic research to policymakers, somehow influence the policy process. I just raise the question of whether or not we are looking at policy as a much too rationalistic, linear process, as opposed to a much more fragmented power process where a lot of retrospective sense-making is employed to make things look better. This is the problem I have with trajectory studies or even studying up. I think it is fairly easy to reconstruct some sort of linear, rational policy trajectory, whereas, in fact, looked at from the other side it may have been an incredibly contingent and messy process.

Geoffrey Walford: You can do that, too. In fact you can study up and find that it was an incredibly messy, contingent activity. And there are studies that have done exactly that.

Jan Nespor: You can. I've read some of them. The point is that if you understand it that way, then what does that say for the possibility of using ethnography, or ethnographic knowledge, to inform the process?

[. . .]

Aurolyn Luykx [after introduction to make a position statement]: Well, some of the points I wanted to talk about have already been mentioned, so I'll just try to jump off from there and refer a little bit to my current research without going into a big description of what that's all about.

Mainly I'm concerned these days with the fact that the bulk of our ethnographic study of educational policies is so often directed at implementation and seldom at the point of elaboration and development of policies—and that's, you know, for obvious reasons, the difficulty that some people mentioned of studying up and that sort of thing. I think there's a common conception. We talked a little bit this morning about how our ethnographic studies and the results of those studies can filter through to teachers and how they're appropriated in schools. I think these days most teachers are quite aware that schooling is full of cultural factors and that learning processes are cultural processes, and that sort of thing. But I think among teachers there's also a common perception that all the cultural stuff stops when you get above a certain institutional level, and above that it's all political stuff—that in the classroom it's cultural stuff, but the higher-ups are so internationally savvy that they're not cultural anymore. [Laughter]

And working in Bolivia with indigenous education, it's so much in my face all the time of how much these *are* cultural processes, the processes of policy formation, and not just because it's indigenous education. Just to mention a couple of examples, one of the things that sparked my current research: Bolivia's in the midst of a nationwide educational reform. It was decreed in 1994, and it's in the fifth year of a very difficult implementation process, with lots of opposition from different fronts. This involves, among many other things, the development of primary school materials in different indigenous languages. These were developed by teams of indigenous-language-speaking educators. And yet, some of these materials, you look at them, it's very clear that they were developed in Spanish and then translated, which was not what was supposed to happen. And I thought, "Why should this happen?" When they form teams of indigenous professionals, to develop the materials from an indigenous perspective, the whole idea was to avoid, you know, imposing a very Spanish view of the world and then just translating it. And yet it looks like that's exactly what's happened. If the policy was otherwise, why did this happen? And talking to some of those people, if you ask them, you know, in a rather delicate way, or if you have a good relationship, I found that they would eventually admit that yes, all of the work was done in Spanish. The planning of the materials was done in Spanish, when they would get together and talk about it, it was usually in Spanish, and so it's not surprising that the materials would reflect that. And so one of my basic questions was why did that happen, and looking at various sociolinguistic constraints that cause that to happen. Those constraints are very much rooted in a certain sort of institutional culture in which these people were working. Constraints in terms of their own linguistic competence were not operating; these were people who are fully bilingual. But the question of unspoken limitations on where and when and for what functions they can use the indigenous language was operating very strongly.

Another example from the reform that made me think about these questions of institutional culture: a centerpiece of the reform is that it's all going bilingual and intercultural. And there's been much criticism of the reform partly on that front and much public discourse about how the World Bank is imposing this bilingual model. Recently I read a paper presented by the vice minister of [Primary and Secondary] education—that she presented at Harvard, interestingly enough; she did not present it in Bolivia—talking about all the negotiations that went on between the Bolivian government and the World Bank around the reform and how the whole bilingual part of it barely got through. Apparently, according to how she tells it, people like her within the government really had to argue and argue and negotiate with the World Bank to make that a part of the reform, and it almost did not even get through. Which is so different from the public perception of how the reform happened. And in her description of it, it's much more a description of cultural negotiation between these different actors than it is a description of "policy elaboration" per se, in a more formal way, if we might think that way.

So, it seems to me that, since the gaps between policy and practice are often what frustrate us, that we need to try to look much more at the cultural processes that happen around educational policies before they filter down. And especially between different countries, I think this is often very big. If we think of just the institutional cultural differences in different anthropology departments we've known in the United States, for example, in the way that conflict gets handled, and the way that social relationships are handled, those differences can be huge, just between one academic department and another. So when we're talking about different countries, obviously it has a much greater chance of being much bigger. The program

I'm working in involves five countries—well, it's five in terms of the target countries, which are Bolivia, Ecuador, Peru, Colombia, and Chile. But then we also are dealing with, well—most of the money for the project comes from Germany, some of it is from Belgium; Japan gave us computers—and so, there are a lot of actors involved here. The director of the program is a very skilled administrator, to my mind, and I think part of his great skill is that he's culturally sensitive to how he needs to deal with all these functionaries from all these different countries. I've seen other people in related projects in Bolivia lose their jobs because they didn't have that cultural sensitivity and created some terrible *faux pas* that resulted in them losing their jobs.

Among our students, many of them are people who have worked in ministries of education in their own countries, where there has not been a lot of formal training in bilingual-intercultural education available; so they're now studying in this program, basically to go back and do their same job, but to do it with a better foundation. And it's very noticeable, the differences in institutional culture that they bring to the program. As I mentioned, we have students from Bolivia, Peru, Ecuador, Colombia, and Chile, and the differences, when we talk about, say, *gestión educativa*, what the Colombians understand by that and what the Chileans understand by it is often quite different. And so, too, are the ways that they deal with each other in the classroom. Next year, Argentina has asked to come into the program, and we're all sort of [mock nervous shudder] "What's gonna happen when the Argentinians arrive?" because there's a whole *different* institutional culture working *there*.

Something we were talking about during the break is that often the terminology that we use diffuses among all our countries. Any national level education policy at this point has a lot of contact with what's going on in the entire region and often all over the world. So, we often use a lot of the same terminology to talk about these things, but I think those terms often represent a reality that is totally different. The categories seem to be universal, but what they are referring to is really something very different in each case. And not realizing that can get us into a lot of confusion. Just to mention sort of a superficial example, but just to give us an idea of how this can lead to confusion, a complaint that I always hear from teachers in Bolivia, and frequently from educators in the United States also, is that education is too "political" and that keeps us from working the way we want to. And usually I find that what that means in the United States is that politically controversial issues are getting into the classroom in a way that they shouldn't. And, my first year or so in Bolivia, I thought that that was what people meant when they said education was getting too political. It wasn't what they meant at all. They meant that positions of authority in the educational system, from school directors or principals on up, were determined by political party affiliations, which is a totally different concept! And yet they used the same terms to talk about it. And so when we talk about politics and policy and *lo político* and *la política* and *las políticas*, I don't know if it's necessary to make sure that we're all talking about the same thing, but if we're not talking about the same thing, we need to be clear on what we're talking about, in each one of those countries that we're in, because I think it could be something quite different.

And also, the relation between law, policies, and practice in education in all these countries—we have, I think, the idea that the ideal situation would be that there'd be a total coherence between all those things. You know, the law is a general statement, the policy works out the details, and the practice does what the policy says. [Laughter] And yet, in many countries, that's often obviously not the case, and in the program I'm working in, often it kind of happens the other way around. You know, we'll have a situation that's come up a few times, we see how we've dealt with it at different times, we sit down and talk about what would be the best way to deal with it, and "Okay, why don't we write a policy that describes what we're already doing, so that it's written down somewhere." In terms of trying to study these processes ethnographically, obviously there is the whole barrier to studying up and the fact that policymakers are less accessible to this kind of study than students and teachers, who, in terms of power relations, have always been more accessible to university academics than have policymakers. I'm in a rather privileged position right now in that this study that I'm doing is focused on policymakers, but right now those policymakers happen to be my students. So, at the same time, there was a whole consent and debate process that we went through to [be able to] do the investigation. But still, I have them all there in one place, you know. The logistics of it are all much easier because they happen to be my students. And the power relations, on the one hand, when we think of studying up and studying policymakers, it gives us the idea of flipping the [usual] power relations between researcher and researched. That's one thing that makes it so hard to do. And yet in this case, that's not really the situation in that I'm the white First World academic and my students are indigenous people, and even though they are the policymakers, all the different power relations cut across each other in somewhat contradictory ways. And another thing that I haven't studied but that I'm curious about is that the density and the levels of bureaucratization in the different countries are quite varied. Those are also cultural institutions. I've found that in a country like Bolivia, which is only about 6 million people, the number of people who are in the position to make policy is small enough that really you get a rather small group of academics, who are well-positioned, and just a very few people can actually be quite influential in national level education policy. It was surprising to me to find out, as a new Ph.D. who sort of just ended up there by accident, that I quickly fell into a position where my educational practice could directly affect what's happening, not directly but eventually affect education policy in all of these different countries just by the fact that these people are now my students and that what interaction they're having with me is going to, hopefully, affect their actions as policymakers and decision makers in their own countries. And I just intuitively feel that when we are dealing with small countries with a small population, the factors of institutional culture become that much more significant. But those who have worked more in education policy in the United States may tell me that I'm wrong about that, that the cultural factors have a much bigger influence in the United States than I'm aware of. It's more obvious to me in a country like Bolivia, where personal connections have such a clearly primary place in a lot of policy decisions, and I'm not saying that it's always in a negative way. So I think eventually it would be interesting to study that sort of thing in a country like the United States, where supposedly the whole policy process is more formalized and maybe more transparent. For the time being the context where I'm able to do it is in Bolivia. I guess I'll leave it at that.

Juan Fidel Zorrilla: I think this point just made is absolutely crucial because if one takes the category of law, or of the law, only as policymaking in different countries, they have very different meanings. You know, a very cynical friend of mine visited Mexico. He said, "In Mexico, the law is a mere suggestion." [Laughter] Which is very different from what happens in Britain, where you say, "the law of the land"—it's this huge ideological, political, historical concept. And in America when you say, "This is illegal," it has a very different meaning to what it has in Mexico. So, to begin from there, one has very different contexts. Then when you refer to national policy, you have other differences that come into play. In Mexico, national higher education policy is very important. In the States, there is no such thing as national higher education policy, to begin with. You know, the Department of Education is just a department that deals with very different matters from what the Secretaría de la Educación Pública does in Mexico—it's just this huge, very important historical, ideological and policy instrument for the national government and for all public universities throughout the land. And local policy in Mexico has a very different meaning from local politics in the States. And the same, for instance, at the school level. In Mexico, for instance, we don't have the local school districts. We are dealing, in Mexico, with a very authoritarian and non-accountable system of education. Education is not accountable to anybody in Mexico except within these huge structures, public structures of the Secretaría de la Educación Pública, etc. So, I think it is always useful to give a brief description of context, because otherwise we might be understanding each other by misunderstanding everything. (As the French say, probably the best way to understand each other is when everyone misunderstands everything.) So we have to be very careful about this. And the other thing is that concepts in Mexico, in Bolivia, Argentina, Chile, and in the States arise out of very different academic traditions. So the meaning of qualitative research in the States has a very different meaning from qualitative research in Mexico. You are coming out of a very scientific tradition of quantitative research. In Mexico we never had that tradition. We never had an over-whelming domination of that tradition. So qualitative research has a totally different meaning.

So, just a couple examples that can act as caveats for being careful when one discusses this. And so once one establishes those descriptions, maybe we can find some very interesting processes which can be studied compar-atively when one deals with policy. Because maybe you have to compare policy at the national level in one country with policy at the state level in another country. Or even policy at the local level in another country, de-pending on where the resources are, etc.

Aurolyn Luykx: If I can add a little bit. It's a fact that the institutions we think are parallel in different countries often are not. The Department of Education in the United States is not parallel to the Ministry of Edu-cation in Mexico. In many countries, I think one result is that the impor-tance of individuals in determining tacit policy often may vary. If there are areas that are sort of insulated, or if the structure of authority determines that it works this way, policy can be what the principal has decided is going to happen in a school. It may be very unrelated to what the state or national government has decided to do.

I remember yesterday Geoffrey [Walford] was talking about the govern-ment education policy [in Britain]. Well, there was no government educa-tion policy. It was just Margaret Thatcher's education policy. And I think that often it is true that the influence of one individual on a project can be very decisive. A brief example is, a big part of the Bolivian education reform has been the standardization of textbooks in different languages and re-ducing [indigenous] languages to writing so that school texts can be writ-ten. And this has been very debated and many of the materials have been rejected because the speakers of these languages are not happy with the standardization. And the criteria for the standardization of these languages were basically determined by one person. It was done by many teams of linguists and that sort of thing; but one linguist with a very forceful per-sonality and lots of academic prestige always seems to head up these teams. And basically the criteria he set and advocated are the ones that determined how the standardization was going to be done. As an academic he is quite influential. His influence resulted in the languages being standardized and written in a certain way, which happens to be a way that was over-whelmingly rejected by [most] speakers of those languages. The fact that that form of standardization was rejected meant that the materials were rejected and so it has all sorts of consequences that are snowballing from the influence of one person. In a country like Bolivia, where the pool of academics working on this kind of thing is quite small, this is not unusual. In the United States, perhaps, since there is no real centralized educational system, since it is more fragmented, maybe that happens more at the state level. In Bolivia it is very centralized. Of course, it is going toward decentralization under the reform, but the cultural practices that people are used to keep that decentralization from happening even though it's been decreed by law. So a small group of individuals does have a big impact on education.

[. . .]

Elsie Rockwell: I think that one of the things that might come out of these discussions is the need for the comparative study of education in anthropology, an ethnology of education. This was a point made by Dell Hymes 20 years ago, but we've never really done it. I would also like to say that I think at the center of ethnography there has to be the concept of culture. We could go on and on about which concept of culture, obviously, and that's a big question in itself. But I wondered as we've talked about how we can study policy and policymaking in institutions in terms of cultural processes and institutional cultures—how do you separate, analytically, a level of analysis of politics itself? That's not reducible to culture. It might come in the guise of culture—what words mean and how things are done, and how people construe and construct local realities, etc.—but there is also a dimension of politics and education policy, especially now with the World Bank and globalization processes and neo-liberal policies, that can't be reduced to culture, in that sense. So I think that we do need a level of analysis where we can study these political processes and the deep cultural changes that they are engendering in order to better grasp some of these forces that are affecting all of our countries in some ways—each one in different ways, perhaps, but I also think that's where the commonalities would come up in a comparative project and that is what would help form a collective political position as well. And this could help us to see if we can come to some agreement concerning the basic issues that are not separated by cultural differences. Although I fully agree with the need for contextualization of these political processes in cultural terms—that's what makes comparative study in anthropology so difficult, no?

[. . .]

Aurolyn Luykx: I just don't know if I ever want to separate those questions and say they are not cultural. Would you say that there is a level of politics or a level of educational practice that can't be reduced to culture? I'm not sure what that level would be. I try to think of a conception of culture that would have certain limits and then things beyond those limits are not cultural enough in the sense in which you're locating some of these practices, and I'm not sure.

Elsie Rockwell: But I wouldn't do it topically, that is, in different spheres or locations. When you see it happening, of course, it's all together—politics, policy, and practice all have cultural forms and meanings, or rather cultural dynamics. But analytically I think it's important to seek out the political within culture, as well as the cultural within politics and policies, because so often we hear things like, "Oh, that institution can't change because of its institutional culture." Yet certain key groups are benefited by maintaining policies and practices as they are. There's this use of culture as an explanation of or pretext for nonchange. I kind of think of politics as providing the *movement within culture*, as that which can explain and produce both change and nonchange at any level or scale, and in various directions of course.

Aurolyn Luykx: I kind of think, maybe because of the context I'm working in, of culture as changing rapidly, too. I think that my desire to recognize cultural practices was driven not by a relativist impulse in this case but rather the need to analyze culturally what was happening. Could be about the limitations of policy, could be about racial policies. For example, in Bolivia something that everyone complains about in terms of educational practice and policy is this grand category of "corruption," and the influence of this at every level of education. And it is not hard to identify different instances of what's called corruption as cultural practices governed by privileged relationships. Which doesn't mean taking a relativist position in relation to that. But it is also clear that the government's [anti-corruption] campaigns have not been very effective. And until you look at the cultural, historical, and economic roots of these practices, it is difficult to say. I'm still working on the idea of analytically trying to separate these two areas. I almost feel like they've been *over*separated, and that we need to try to integrate them and *then* try to separate them. The whole long tradition (well, not so long) of ethnography in the classroom has given us this tremendously powerful concept of the hidden curriculum and looking at things in the classroom that are not explicit. And I'd like to see similar studies at the "hidden policy" level, which I think is so influential in what is happening.

Someone mentioned this morning about teacher evaluations and how when a teacher is doing a bad job and the director wants to get rid of that teacher, then often they will put 100 because that gives that teacher more possibility of getting transferred somewhere else, whereas if we put a 51 no one would want that teacher. And I think that happens in a lot of contexts—teachers getting good evaluations so they will leave. Something similar that happens in Bolivia is teachers that have been accused of sexually abusing a student and the solution is to transfer them to another school. There is this hidden policy level. We were talking on the porch about "what is policy?" Is it what is written down, what we're actually doing, the tacit agreements about "this is the way things work"? The levels of conflict between the explicit policy and the hidden policy are parallel to the conflicts between the hidden curriculum and the explicit curriculum. I'd like to see more study of these areas. And I think, like Elsie, that there needs to be comparative study. Very useful. But I'm less convinced that it would be really useful to separate out the political realm and the cultural realm. Because I almost have a feeling that all our thinking has been on the political side to the exclusion of the cultural side. My tendency would be to pull it back in.

Amy Stambach: I think you're right onto something that we haven't developed, which is the language at the macro level for thinking about policy and the commonalities that we see despite the local differences. But to separate culture from policy/politics I feel would reproduce some of the inequalities that policies are already locating outside culture. You know, "Culture stops at a certain level and then it is policy above that." We need to be careful not to reproduce that. But at the same time what we haven't developed is a language for thinking about global culture. An anthropologist who has begun to think about this (and there are others), Arjun Appadurai, has been thinking about various forces at the global level—financial connections, ecological connections, ethnic or cultural connections—and how various forces intersect and play out in local context. It seems to me that in the anthropology of education we have a very fine language for describing the classroom culture. But yet we haven't connected that so clearly to a larger political culture that is articulated around policy.

NOTE

Most of the transcript is faithful to original statements. Certain selections by Rockwell and Luykx were expanded and/or edited by the authors and lightly edited by the editor. Ellipses between statements [. . .] indicate significant breaks in the conversational exchange.

Chapter 11

A Teacher in Transition: Coming to Terms with Prior Beliefs

Barbara Greybeck

One of the questions posed for discussion in this book is, "How can we best train teachers and policymakers to 'see' and 'think' ethnographically?" However, I would like to reframe the question, since in my work in teacher education and staff development in both the United States and in Mexico, my goal has not been so much that teachers see and think ethnographically, but rather that they *improve* in their teaching. My concern as a teacher trainer then focuses on how an ethnographic stance might facilitate the process of teacher development.

I have chosen the term *improvement* in my discussion of teaching practices with reference to both new and veteran teachers, since even university students with no classroom experience already have some idea of what teaching is all about. Because they have spent years in classrooms observing what teachers do, they most likely have developed some personal theory about teaching, even before being introduced to the more formalized theories and practices in teacher preparation programs. For both new and experienced teachers, these unstated ideas about teaching form the basis of a belief system that may either facilitate or hinder the learning process.

In working with new or experienced teachers, then, one of our tasks should be to enable them to identify their underlying belief patterns (which might also be referred to as prior knowledge about teaching) and to examine these beliefs in light of the new knowledge that is being presented. As ethnographers we recognize that we have some tools at our disposal that will help us in uncovering these implicit patterns: Treviño Vázquez (1998) has suggested in her "Etnografía de Nosotros" ("Ethnography of Ourselves") that as teachers we should study our own teaching practices through dialogues with ourselves as "subjects-researchers." I am also suggesting that we teach our students to use ethnographic tools for the purpose of reflecting on their own practices and coming to terms with their prior beliefs. In this way, I believe they will begin to see and think ethnographically simply because they will see the benefits of doing so through the study of what is probably the most interesting subject for all of us as human individuals, that is, the study of ourselves.

The idea of self-observation in staff development with teachers is not new and, in fact, has been much in vogue in the past few years under the guise of terms such as reflective teaching and reflective practice. Teachers have been asked to keep logs of what they do in the classroom and to reflect on how well they are meeting their stated objectives. They are asked to evaluate themselves and to propose goals for improvement.

As part of this process, Zeichner (1993) suggests that teachers should try to bring to consciousness what has become routine and natural in their actions and ideas, and he distinguishes between what is traditional and ordinary in teaching from what might be termed more reflective. He goes on to say that reflective practitioners make explicit their tacit understandings in order to critically examine their beliefs, expectations, and actions in the hope of improving their teaching practices.

Bringing to light what is implicit in our words and actions is the essence of reflective teaching, but more important, it is also the essence of the ethnographic approach to research. Such is particularly the case if we assume a more ethno-methodological stance through which we attempt to understand the point of view and the assumptions found in the talk and actions of those we are observing (Ogbu, 1992). We can liken this notion, then, to the goals of reflective teaching, since reflection also entails observation. But ethno-methodologically, we observe ourselves and analyze the implicit assumptions in our own talk and actions. The methods that we use in the classroom are not simple strategies presented in cookbook style to our students but are instead an interpretation of information, transformed by prior beliefs about human development, learning, and social interaction. The language we choose in the course of any particular learning event, because it is a reflection of these beliefs, influences not only the student's cognitive or academic development but his/her affective and social development as well. In a sense, we must take a position somewhere outside ourselves, trying to distance ourselves in order to understand *why* we say and do *what* we say and do in the classroom. In other words, the process of self-reflection, to be effective, implies that we take on an ethnographic stance, in the role of full-time participant and observer.

As evidence of how ethnography and self-reflection have common ground, I would like to present some conclusions from a study that I did some years ago while teaching basic reading at a community college. In this study, I initially attempted to describe the communicative patterns of face-to face interaction that I had with my students. In so doing, I came to see how my assumptions about my students in one particular remedial reading class translated into linguistic events, topic choices, and participant structure and, in turn, how these ways of arranging classroom discourse affected students' responses, motivation, and academic performance. Interestingly, I have been able to reexamine the data from this study, now several years later, and have found that rather than becoming outdated, they have provided me with further insights regarding my own personal development in teaching.

CONTEXT AND METHODOLOGY

The study took place while I was teaching a course designed for students who needed assistance in reading comprehension, decoding skills, and vocabulary. Counselors had referred most students for remedial assistance because they had been high school dropouts, had been diagnosed as dyslexic, or because English was their second language. There were 39 students in the classroom, ranging in age from 18 to 74 years.

I began with a somewhat simple objective: to examine why some of my students participated more than others in the classroom. One of my goals was to get the students actively involved in the class, but I had noticed that I was only meeting this goal with a core group of students. I hypothesized that topic choices and changes in participant structure may have been influencing the extent of some students' participation, and so I set about gathering data to find out more about the communicative events in my classroom. I was acutely aware of how language in the classroom reflects attitudes and assumptions and at the same time directs the course of learning events. I was influenced by Courtney Cazden's tripartite core of language functions (1988), that is, that language communicates information, establishes and maintains social relationships, and expresses identity and values (p. 3). I was aware that how I was speaking would affect not only the cognitive aspects of learning but the affective ones as well.

My observations spanned the entire 12-week quarter, although for the first eight weeks I kept only logs. During the ninth week, I began audiotaping class sessions, then writing extensive field notes immediately after I left the classroom. From these tape-recorded sessions, I transcribed nine segments in which students actively participated in discussions. Additionally, I interviewed five students (two men and three women) regarding their study habits, their opinions about the class, and their reasons for enrolling in this particular course. I chose two of the students because each contributed to class discussions when appropriate, while two others were chosen because they had not readily participated. The fifth student was chosen because she had been observed talking privately with peers during many of the class discussions. These interviews proved useful in determining these students' assumptions about studying, learning, and appropriate classroom behavior. The interview was unstructured, although I asked all the students how they prepared for the class, what they thought were the characteristics of a good student in terms of academic work and behavior, how they felt in class, and why they enrolled in the class. We also discussed their home life and school experiences.

During the semester I gathered a variety of work samples and test scores for each student in the class and at the end of the course, the students completed an evaluation form on which they rated the activities, my teaching, and the course in general.

In analyzing the data, I began by examining my transcripts and notes to identify points at which shifts in topic or participant structure occurred during the class discussions and found that frequent changes in events were marked by confusion on the part of some of the students. At this point, I decided to do a content analysis to determine the nature of the confusion and to examine how teacher-talk may have contributed to its resolution or continuation.

I analyzed the interviews, transcripts, and evaluations of the students to determine the students' perception about the value of class discussions and other learning activities as well as to ascertain their feelings about their participation within the structure of the classroom events. I reviewed the interviews and transcripts in order to find information about the students' prior experiences and their motivational level upon entering the class, since motivation had been one of my initial concerns. In other words, how effective had I actually been in motivating them? Finally, I looked at the work samples of the students to see if there had been gains in academic performance.

At the same time, I felt it necessary to examine my initial assumptions about my students in light of my observations of them in class, what students stated about themselves, and my evaluations of their written work.

CLASSROOM INTERACTION WITH THE BEST OF INTENTIONS

Through this analysis, what was not obvious when I was in the instructional arena became almost painfully clear to me when I reflected on the data. I heard myself using language not only to communicate information, but also to control behavior, to establish and maintain certain types of social relationships, and to express a belief system. I saw how my initial assumptions influenced how I arranged participant structure and how such changes may have at times negatively influenced student learning.

What was so important to me in these findings is that many of my initial assumptions were made not only with the best of intentions, but for me, they seemed rather commonplace in teaching. In fact, I had internalized these ideas through years of experience with second-language learners and remedial and special education students. For example, I assumed that in order for my students to be motivated, I would have to make the class interesting by providing group activities, games, videos, and graphic aids. After all, I had learned that ESL students should be grouped in different ways and that they should have a variety of activities during class (Crookes and Chaudron, 1991; Enright, 1991; Omaggio, 1986). However, in reviewing my transcripts, I found that I had so many activities that some students became confused because with each new activity they had to learn a new procedure. Students who are learning English as a second language also need to rely on familiar routines to enable them to understand the language that accompanies these routines. As Wong Fillmore points out (1991), second-language learners rely on their prior social knowledge to figure out what is being said in any given situation. Here was a tension that I had not resolved successfully.

Another common assumption, and one which I too held, was that students in a remedial reading program would have poor self-esteem. In fact, throughout the years, I had been instructed about the need to find ways to improve self-esteem in students with learning disabilities and reading problems by providing them with positive feedback. In reviewing my interactions with students, however, I realized that I manifested this assumption in a hesitancy to focus on the incorrect responses of students or to correct students in front of their peers when they answered incorrectly. Because I did not correct their responses, the instructional point of the lesson was often diverted from its intended goal. My assumptions about their self-esteem also led to an attempt to establish a casual, friendly atmosphere, leading to openness and joking or teasing. Although students reported to me that they enjoyed my class because of this open atmosphere, when I looked at specific classroom interaction patterns, I found that some students, particularly those who spoke English as a second language, did not always appear to understand my jokes. These students had been left out by my good intentions.

I found, as well, that my students' perceptions of themselves did not match my initial assumptions. Most of the students entered the course with a high level of motivation and maintained it throughout the quarter. Many students, especially the ESL students, had not failed in school previously and were accustomed to traditional school settings where hard work and discipline were required to succeed. Some of the students who had experienced failure were highly motivated because of outside factors in their lives, leading them to appreciate the importance of education. A low level of motivation was not necessarily due to boredom with the class routine but, at least in one case, to frustration with the level of difficulty of the work. Those students with good reading ability but low motivation did not change during the quarter and ended the class equally as unmotivated as when they had entered.

There were many ways in which my initial good intentions were played out in the classroom, but when I analyzed the results in terms of real learning, I understood that I had not really accomplished my instructional objectives. My students may have liked the class and, indeed, on their final evaluations some stated that they felt better about themselves. These were very positive results, and I wouldn't have wanted to change that, but on the other hand, based on honest reflection, I don't believe that I gave my students enough of the academic tools they would need to succeed in later classes. Would they have enough skills to stay motivated and confident? That was my concern.

EPILOGUE

Now a few years down the road and with semesters of teaching, studying, and reflection behind me, I can see more clearly what was really taking place in that classroom. It is even more obvious to me what I was doing wrong. Looking back, I understand that this study marked a break for me with the established models of teaching I had unconsciously assimilated through my years of experience with remedial students. This ethnomethodological reflection initiated a personal journey, a journey that would lead me to different paradigms, to further research on teaching, and to educational reform.

However, what was most important is that I began this journey, not because someone else showed me that I needed to do so, but because I myself discovered that my teaching did not yield the results I had hoped for in terms of student learning. I experienced a point of conflict, and it was this inner conflict that needed to be resolved.

In my work with inexperienced teachers, I see these points of conflict being played out again and again. Almost all of them have good intentions, and in some sense, these subtle good intentions seem to be a natural transition to newer ways of thinking. However, if teachers do not move beyond their initial beliefs, these may become just as insidious as the traditional assumptions that prevented teachers in the past from accepting individual differences or from loosening lines of authority.

My analysis lends support to Erickson's discussion (1986) of the role of teacher as researcher in the improvement of the status of the teaching profession. Teachers are faced with decisions moment to moment in the course of classroom instruction. How they respond, for the most part, is based upon what they believe to be true about their students, about instructional practices, and about themselves. They are asked to make rapid-fire choices that may not be the most appropriate but are, in fact, the best they can do under the circumstances. Unless time is taken to critically examine these choices in the context of the various social worlds being played out in the classroom, recurrent themes of instructional practice begin to take hold, and the teacher finds him/herself less and less able to evaluate them objectively.

Teachers must be fully aware that their own learning is never completed, that with each new group of students, they will have new challenges to master. Beyond this awareness, however, they must have the tools to be able to meet these challenges. As Erickson points out, teachers need to "hold themselves accountable for the depth of their insight into their actions as teachers" (1986, p. 157). From my point of view, if teaching is to attain the professional status it deserves, good intentions are simply not enough.

REFERENCES

Cazden, C. (1988). *Classroom discourse: The language of teaching and learning.* Portsmouth, NH: Heinemann.

Crookes, G., and Chaudron, C. (1991). Guidelines for classroom language teaching. In M. Celce-Murcia (Ed.), *Teaching English as a second or foreign language.* Boston: Heinle & Heinle Publishers, pp. 46–66.

Dressman, M. (1998). Teacher research for cultural action. In B. Calvo Pontón, G. Delgado Ballesteros, and M. Rueda Beltrán (Eds.), *Nuevos paradigmas, compromisos renovados.* Ciudad Juárez, Mexico: Universidad Autonoma de Ciudad Juárez, pp. 89–98.

Elliot, J. (1991). *El cambio educativo desde la investigación acción.* Madrid: Morata.

Enright, D.S. (1991). Supporting children's English language development in grade level and language classrooms. In M. Celce-Murcia (Ed.), *Teaching English as a second or foreign language.* Boston: Heinle & Heinle Publishers, pp. 386–401.

Erikson, F. (1986). Qualitative methods in teaching. In M.C. Wittrock (Ed.), *Handbook of research on teaching.* New York: Macmillan.

Greybeck, B. (1999). *A teacher in transition.* Paper presented at the Eighth Interamerican Symposium on Educational Ethnography, Bloomington, IN.

Greybeck Daniels, B., Moreno Bayardo, M.G., and Peredo Merlo, M.A. (1998). Reflexiones acerca de la formación de docentes. *Educar 5,* 15–22.

Gumperz, J. (1988). La sociolingüística interaccional en el estudio de la escolarización [Interactional sociolinguistics and the study of schooling] (R. Alonso, Trans.). In J. Cook-Gumperz (Ed.), *La construcción social de la alfabetización.* Madrid: Paídos, pp. 61–84. (Original work published in 1986.)

Ogbu, J. (1992). *What makes educational ethnography ethnographic?* Unpublished lecture outline, University of California at Berkeley.

Omaggio, A.C. (1986). *Teaching language in context: Proficiency oriented instruction.* Boston: Heinle & Heinle Publishers.

Page, R. (1987). Lower-track classes at a college preparatory high school: A caricature of educational encounters. In G. Spindler and L. Spindler (Eds.), *Interpretive ethnography of education: At home and abroad.* Hillsdale, NJ: Erlbaum.

Phillips, S.U. (1972). Participant structures and communicative competence: Warm Springs children in community and classroom. In C. Cazden, D. Hymes, and V. Johns (Eds.), *Functions of language in the classroom*. New York: Teachers College Press.

Treviño Vázquez, N.D. (1998). La etnografía del "nosotros": Reflexiones metodológicas sobre la etnografía en la investigación de la práctica docente. In B. Calvo Pontón, G. Delgado Ballesteros, and M. Rueda Beltrán (Eds.), *Nuevos paradigmas, compromisos renovados*. Ciudad Juárez, Mexico: Universidad Autonoma de Ciudad Juárez, pp. 99–110.

Wong Fillmore, L. (1991). Second language learning in children: A model of language learning in social context. In E. Bialystok (Ed.), *Language processing in bilingual children*. New York: Cambridge University Press, pp. 49–66.

Zeichner, K.M. (1993). El maestro como profesional reflexivo. *Cuadernos de Pedagogía* 220, 44–49.

Chapter 12

Teaching the Ethnographic Vision as a Way into Policy? A Brazilian Perspective on Ethnography as a Social Control Practice

Isabela Cabral Félix de Sousa

Editors' note: The author developed this position statement in response to one of the workshop themes of the Interamerican Symposium, "Teaching the Ethnographic Vision: A Way into Policy?" In the structure of the chapter, the author conserves the original questions that were posed.

HOW CAN WE BEST TRAIN TEACHERS AND POLICYMAKERS TO "SEE" AND THINK ETHNOGRAPHICALLY?

Ethnography can be a social control practice. It can be used as a device for understanding culture with the objective to exert social control and influence policy. Educators and policymakers need to be attentive not only to how culture influences and shapes their work, but how, through their cultural understanding, they can work toward establishing points of departure so that more democratic cultural meanings and practices can be created in societies.

I believe the best training for teachers and policymakers to see and think ethnographically involves several items of content that could be arranged in workshops, courses, and programmed visits. The contents are as follows:

1. *Provide cultural information that is relevant to the teachers' and policymakers' activities.* This can be done by teaching specialized topics related to social studies of how cultural markers such as class, race, and gender influence the education of a group. In terms of social class, curriculum tracking tends to reproduce social class division in the United States (Col-

clough and Beck, 1989). Further, Collins (1982) shows how American teachers treat groups according to race and class prejudice, which in turn affects groups' achievement and thus disadvantages those who are minority students. Stromquist (1992), analyzing the Latin American region, states that "the formal educational system is clearly segregated by class" (p. 21). Levy (1986) also explains the mechanisms some Latin American states undertake to favor the higher education of the middle and upper classes. In Brazil, having access to private high schools versus having access only to public high schools, or not having access at all, also leads to the same reproduction of class divisions. Soares (1997) explains how the Brazilian poor fail in schools because they do not have the same language and cultural apparatus of their middle-class counterparts and of their teachers. Likewise, Mehan (1987) concludes that U.S. American children suffer stratification through language. The response to these inadequacies is very striking when analyzed from the child's point of view. Vigil (1988) collected a revealing child's reply in the United States:

I did poorly in school because I couldn't speak English. We used to segregate ourselves at school, because that's what everybody did. I never went outside the *barrio* except to go to school. This didn't make me conscious of the injustice, because I took it as the order of things. (p. 58)

After studying special topics, professionals should try to observe their own cultural behaviors. As suggested by Kneller (1965):

The teacher must examine the influence of culture on his own behavior. Unless he knows the cultural signals that he himself is sending out, he gains little from perceiving the signals of his pupils. (p. 129).

2. *The provision of cultural information that is relevant includes not only specialized studies but also information about tradition and popular habits.* Thus, it is very important that educators and policymakers have opportunities to experience expressions of folk and traditional arts. They should visit street fairs, walk in less privileged neighborhoods, go to museums and operas. It is important to value both popular and elite expressions of culture and discuss the different status they share in formal education systems and in society at large. The teaching of widespread cultural habits can promote appreciation of popular culture. For example, in Brazil teaching about the famous *feijoada* country dish, which originated as a mix of food discarded by large landowners, teaches not only about the creativity of enslaved people but also its importance to cultural heritage. Likewise, teaching about the habit of valuing apartments and houses with "dependencies" (small annex rooms and bathrooms designed for ser-

vants), shows architecturally the tradition of the upper class being served by servants.

3. *In our increasingly pluralistic societies, it is important to train educators and policymakers about the importance of cultural backgrounds.* Learning about people's cultures can happen in indirect ways, such as watching foreign movies and TV programs, reading foreign books, or going to the typical festivals of a group. Learning can also occur directly by talking with people from different backgrounds, traveling, or meeting them in their settings.

It is of utmost importance to train professionals about the difficulties in encounters with cultural differences, which have been marked by both prejudice and discrimination. These concepts have been used, at times, interchangeably. According to Merton (1985), while prejudice is an attitude, discrimination is a behavior. There is some controversy about the causes of prejudice and discrimination. Goldstein (1980/1983) explains that, on the one hand, prejudice and discrimination are caused mainly by cultural, historical, economical, political, and social factors; on the other hand, other researchers have testified that prejudice and discrimination do not always abate when such factors are modified. McDavid and Harari (1974/1980) claim that humans use stereotypes and prejudices as a natural process of the organization of perception, which helps them deal more securely with the continuous change of the world. Another important factor that is seen as leading to prejudice is humanity's need to create categories in order to deal with the transforming world. According to the psychological social theory explained by McDavid and Harari (1974/1980), humans have the inclination to classify their experiences and organize them in conceptual systems. However, McDavid and Harari say that most of the time people lack all the information necessary. Therefore, they advocate that the new experiences be classified in conceptual categories following the previous experiences. These authors emphasize that prejudice emerges precisely from conceptual generalizations based on limited knowledge. Taking into account the important value of this process, it seems desirable to provide people with more resources so that information can be increased.

Merton (1985) also mentions that prejudice and discrimination are often considered a result of mere ignorance. Yet this author argues that there is no evidence supporting the idea that ethnic and racial discrimination are not as common in those people who have a higher education than in the ones who do not have it. Merton's view seems inspired by a functionalist approach to educational systems rather than a conflict approach. According to Colclough and Beck (1986), Ballantine (1989), and Hurn (1985), while the functionalist approach would lead one to expect the development of a fairer society with decreasing levels of discrimination toward race, sex, and social origins, the conflict approach sees educational systems as leading people to have values that will not dismantle the status quo. Schools propagate values that are full of prejudice and will lead to discriminatory behaviors.

Other aspects that are important are the emotions involved in prejudice and discrimination. Goldstein (1980/1983) states that classification usually involves an emotional linkage. This idea makes it easier to understand Alport's (1958) concept, referred to by Yetman (1985), that prejudice is an attitudinal event often involving an intense emotional response. Goldstein (1980/1983) also affirms that an important feature of prejudice is that it is a negative attitude toward members of a group or a group itself, based on the unique condition of belonging to that particular group.

An interesting aspect that has been attributed to discriminatory practices is the psychological defense mechanism of projection. Goldstein (1980/1983) reviews some authors who believe that the development of discrimination against minorities happens like the scapegoat hypothesis, in which the aggression is transferred from the original source of frustration to members of a group with which one is unfamiliar. Still another interesting psychological aspect that has been linked to discrimination is the need for self-esteem. Some authors propose that intergroup discrimination is stimulated by individuals' and groups' will to attain and keep self-esteem. Thus, the needs groups have to compete are not always material but may involve anything that can assure their self-definition. In this way, discriminatory practices can be seen as both symbolic and material devices to maintain superiority.

Yetman (1985) also provides interesting definitions of discrimination that can be of two kinds: the attitudinal and the institutional. The first one can be further divided into individual—relating to acts induced by personal prejudice—and adaptive—originating in the individual's conformation to a group. Finally, the second kind proposed by the author corresponds to the results of inequalities promoted by the social policies and practices of institutional structures. A good example of discriminatory practice promoted by educational institutions benefiting the majority is the allocation of educational credentials. According to Bock (1982): "The dominant status groups in society define who will be permitted to obtain what kinds of educational certification" (p. 88). I believe it is important that educators and policymakers study all these aforementioned theories so that they can discuss them in light of their personal and professional experiences.

Furthermore, it is very important to teach educators and policymakers the educational strategies that have proven effective in reducing both prejudice and discrimination. Goldstein (1980/1983) provides a thorough understanding of strategies being used to reduce prejudice and discrimination in the field of social psychology. The first of these strategies is quite simply contact between conflicting groups. The second strategy described by Goldstein (1980/1983) is called "cultural assimilator." The technique's aim is to help a group to see the world with the eyes of the other group before any contact is made. The approach assumes that such perspective-taking increases understanding and cooperation. The third strategy mentioned by Goldstein (1980/1983) has been used with some good results in the political domain and it is named "work group for the intergroup conflict situation." It consists of a neutral group assisting communication and understanding among the conflicting groups. Goldstein (1980/1983) concludes that all these strategies are effective to the extent that they can change the subjects' group reference. Since group affiliations avoid stereotyping, effective teaching should stimulate membership in various groups.

It is also important to develop the skill to see through unconventional lenses the apparently conventional social world. Thus, relevant teaching looks for the logic in what wrongly seems in conformity versus what deceptively appears in opposition. For instance, in Brazil, at the same time that public institutions are used by a bureaucratic culture in order to assure legitimacy, the need for personal exchange of favors to get through the bureaucratic system and get work done quickly is also part of the culture. While these systems seem to be in conflict, they end up reinforcing one another. The bureaucratic cultural system exists to prevent the personal exchange of favors, and it increases whenever procedures are questioned for not being professionally or ethically based. However, the bureaucratic cultural system is often seen as slow, antidemocratic, and incongruent. Thus, many individuals end up resorting to, and positively valuing, the personal exchange of favors, since it is the way that they believe work gets accomplished faster and in a natural manner.

HOW CAN SCHOOLS STUDY THEMSELVES ETHNOGRAPHICALLY? WHAT ARE THE PROMISES AND PERILS OF ENCOURAGING SUCH STUDY?

Schools can study themselves by availing themselves of all pieces of information. Schools can look for readily available information such as written history that appears on television and radio announcements, recorded tapes, community newspapers, pages on the Internet, and folders. However, it should be kept in mind that many schools do not have documents about their activities, and when they do, these are not always produced on a regular basis (Lükde and André, 1986). Schools can also study themselves through interviews with present and former students, faculty, and staff. The study of schools should include the cultural meanings and functions of specific moments; glory and sorrow; rituals of entrance, graduation, and prizes; continuous success and repeated failure of students; staff promotion; and lack of promotion. Schools need to study themselves when there are different patterns of contracts for hiring and firing personnel and of accepting students, since this diversity may unfold into hierarchical relations of power and unequal distribution of benefits and treatment. Schools can further study themselves by promoting theme workshops relevant to their members. Finally, schools can study themselves by verifying the extent to which it is possible to integrate the views of all who interact with schools directly (teachers from all subject matters, coordinators, staff in all hierarchical positions, students and parents) and indirectly (family and community members and invited or curious outsiders).

Before designing an ethnographic study, it is necessary to recognize the power conflicts inherent in settings where educational policies unfold. Schools are sites that reproduce one of the possible mediations among social classes (Miranda, 1988). Thus, the peril of conducting studies in formal settings where educational policies are more structured and enjoy more status is that it is more difficult to see and think the unconventional. Everybody has their role previously defined through models that precede those who work in the institution. This does not imply that in all instances teachers, coordinators, students, and researchers cannot question, create, and subvert these models. Schools and other institutions are sites where conflicts of ideas and practices are experienced. Thus, the promise of this kind of study is reporting how social actors organize the social world. While some may be more active in promoting cultural change, others will take more actions to maintain the status quo. It is important to note that social actors cannot be seen as part of homogenous groups. In short, they may take both emancipatory and conservative actions.

On the other hand, doing ethnographic research in settings where educational policies are less structured and enjoy less status may be more promising because roles are being established. In this fashion, it is possible to create new ways of organization. However, these settings will not always provide more room for a democratic endeavor among the social actors. Although social actors may attempt new educational frameworks, caution should be exercised, since the bargaining power may be even smaller than in formal settings. It should not be overlooked that in order for actors to construe different enterprises, they need power to negotiate with other institutions, which means knowing how to deal with aristocratic and authoritarian models.

SHOULD EVERYONE BECOME AN ETHNOGRAPHER OF HIS/HER OWN INSTITUTION? WHY OR WHY NOT?

Ethnography demands looking for partners in social and cultural spheres. This challenge requires capturing the unfamiliar in the familiar scene. While some authors argue that to best capture the unfamiliar, strangers and foreigners best do this work, other authors argue that strangers will never represent all the nuances of the familiar.

Everyone would benefit by becoming an ethnographer of his or her own institution. There are always lenses that an insider has that an outsider does not, and vice versa. However, it is not always possible to do ethnographic research in one's own institution. Such research implies criticisms, and not every institution is ready to be evaluated and criticized. Further, in the present capitalist social order, where employees' contracts are becoming increasingly frail and without rights, not all have the opportunity to evince critical thinking or the political commitment to try to change the order of things. Although institutions can benefit from this kind of enterprise, they may resist it. It seems that outsiders with fewer strings attached to the institution are in a unique position to do ethnographic research.

Nevertheless, one can always look for negotiable instances when doing research in one's own institution is possible. In my case, I began researching formal school settings where educational policies are more structured. Nowadays, my research relates to nonformal settings where educational policies are less structured. Whereas before I was not part of the institutions I researched, today most of my fieldwork concentrates on the institution where I work. My work moved in this direction because it was easier to overcome bureaucracies and because of the amount of time I needed to share between being at the institution and conducting the fieldwork. Despite the fact that as it was initially proposed this research would be done in other settings, the unintended change toward my own setting evolved into more accurate research data. I have more information about those actors whom I interviewed through other social networks. Thus, I am always revalidating the data. While a few social actors interviewed have expressed concern about the research results, I see this concern as the development of confidence to express themselves as subjects—to say that they also own the research process and are therefore as entitled as anyone to exert social control.

NOTE

I am very grateful to the support received from the editors of this book. I thank Bradley Levinson and Ana Patricia Elvir for their invaluable work of organizing and supporting participation at the Eighth Interamerican Symposium on Ethnographic Educational Research. I thank Sandra Cade for being a great discussant during this symposium, and I thank Ana Padawer for taking so mindfully the supervising role of editing this chapter.

REFERENCES

Allport, G.W. (1958). *The nature of prejudice*. Garden City, NY: Doubleday.
Ballantine, J.H. (Ed.). (1989). *Schools and society: A unified reader*. Mountain View, CA: Mayfield.
Bock, J.C. (1982). Education and development: A conflict of meaning. In P.G. Altbach, R.F. Arnove, and G.P. Kelly (Eds.), *Comparative education*. New York: Advent Books, pp. 78–101.

Colclough, G., and Beck, E.M. (1989). The American educational structure and the reproduction of social class. In J.H. Ballantine (Ed.), *Schools and society: A unified reader*. Mountain View, CA: Mayfield, pp. 319–332.

Collins, J. (1982). Discourse style, classroom interaction and differential treatment. *Journal of Reading Behavior* 14(4), 429–437.

Goldstein, J.H. (1983). *Psicologia social* [Social psychology] (J.L. Meurer, Trans.). Rio de Janeiro: Guanabara Dois. (Original work published in 1980.)

Hurn, C.J. (1985). *The limits and possibilities of schooling: An introduction to the sociology of education*. Boston: Allyn & Bacon.

Kneller, G. (1965). Education and cultural values. In *Educational anthropology*. New York: John Wiley and Sons, pp. 115–131.

Levy, D.C. (1986). *Higher education and the state in Latin America: Private challenges to public dominance*. Chicago: University of Chicago Press.

Lüdke, M., and André, M. (1986). *Pesquisa em educação: Abordagens qualitativas* [Research in education: Qualitative approaches]. São Paulo: Pedagógica e Universitária.

McDavid, J.W., and Harari, H. (1980). *Psicologia e comportamento social* [Psychology and social behavior] (F.R. Guimarães & H.R. Krüger, Trans.). Rio de Janeiro: Interciência. (Original work published in 1974.)

Mehan, H. (1987). Language and schooling. In G. Spindler and L. Spindler (Eds.), *Interpretive ethnography of education: At home and abroad*. Hillsdale, NJ: Erlbaum, pp. 109–136.

Merton, R. (1985). Discrimination and the American creed. In N.R. Yetman (Ed.), *Majority and minority: The dynamics of race and ethnicity in American life*. Newton, MA: Allyn & Bacon, pp. 40–53.

Miranda, M.G. (1988). O processo da socialização na escola: A evolução da condição social da criança [The socialization process in school: The social evolution of children]. In S.T.M. Lane and W. Codo (Eds.), *Psicologia social: O homem em movimento* [Social psychology: The men in movement] (6th ed.). São Paulo: Brasiliense, pp. 125–135.

Soares, M. (1997). *Linguagem e escola. Uma perspectiva social* [Language and schools. A social perspective] (15th ed.). São Paulo: Ática.

Stromquist, N.P. (1992). Women and literacy in Latin America. In N.P. Stromquist (Ed.), *Women and education in Latin America: Knowledge, power and change*. Boulder, CO: Lynne Rienner, pp. 1–32.

Vigil, J.D. (1988). *Barrio gangs: Street life and identity in Southern California*. Austin: University of Texas Press.

Yetman, N.R. (1985). *Majority and minority: The dynamics of race and ethnicity in American life* (4th ed.). Boston: Allyn & Bacon.

Ethnography and Education Policy: A Commentary

Frederick Erickson

In introductory remarks at the beginning of the conference from which these chapters came, I addressed some implications of the etymology of the term "ethnography" for our understanding of its uses in contemporary educational research. After reviewing the chapters in this volume, that place still seems an appropriate site from which to begin a brief concluding commentary. Accordingly, I will consider the Greek terms underlying our words "ethnography" and "policy." These are *ethnekos* (*ethnoi, ethne*), *graphein* (*graphos*), and *politeia* (*polis*).

Ethnekos refers to those people who were not Greeks—the "others" such as Persians, Medes, Egyptians, Thracians, Etruscans. *Graphein* is the verb "to write." *Politeia* (from *polis*, city-state) is a constitution or polity, a commonwealth.

By combining *ethnekos* with *graphein*, "ethnography" quite literally means "writing about other people"—those who are not us. There is an exquisite irony in this, a paradox, in the invention of this term in the late nineteenth century to refer to professionally analytic narrative accounts of the lifeways of those who were not part of the cosmopolitan Euro-American mainstream—"primitive" peoples in small-scale societies and working-class people who lived in the slums of large cities such as London and New York. This irony of etymology is intensified by the Malinowskian definition of ethnography as an interpretive enterprise—writing about the lifeways of others in such a way as to portray and analyze with validity and accuracy the meaning-perspectives of the social actors whose actions were being reported. Ethnography should make contact with the "native's point of view." It is description informed by an observer's empathy rather than by negative prejudice.

Yet in the original Greek there is a pejorative tone to the term *ethnekos*. The contrast term for *ethnoi* was *'ellenoi*—those who lived in such city-states as Athens and Sparta. To be "Hellenic" was a self-congratulatory term with an edge of chauvinism. To be called "ethnic" by a Greek was implicitly—and explicitly—denigrating of the other. Indeed, in the Septuagint, the Greek translation of the Hebrew Scriptures, the contrast pair *'ellenoi-ethnoi* was used to translate the Hebrew contrast pair *am-goy* (us-them). The "goyim," in ancient and modern Hebrew usage, were not only "others" but were those considered inferior to "us"—the goyim were and are the "peoples," the Gentiles.

How then can one do "ethnography" successfully—write about others' everyday actions in a way that fairly represents their points of view? Can one, in writing about "others," ever avoid the bias that comes with "othering," as that process is identified by postmodern critics of the claims to realism and accuracy that were made by previous generations of professional ethnographers since Malinowski? The aim of Malinowskian realist ethnography appears to be an ultimate *hubris* inherent in an ultimate modernist project. I think we need to take very seriously the criticism of realist ethnography. The classic work of exotic ethnography—an outsider going to some very unfamiliar setting and then after long-term participant observation and reflection writing an account that "makes the strange familiar and intelligible" to an audience of fellow outsiders to the setting described—is far more difficult to do than Malinowski was willing to admit. And attempts to remedy this by substituting domestic for exotic ethnography—changing the observer's and audience's standpoints from that of outsider to insider—have their own distinctive problems. The very sensitivity to nuance, and possession of tacit background understanding, which the insider brings to ethnographic fieldwork, carries with it problems of transparency and myopia—a difficulty in "making the familiar strange" because of lack of analytic and experiential distance. I think that as outsiders and insiders we still need to attempt description that makes contact with the native's point of view, even as we realize that we will never be fully successful in that attempt. Never will we get it exactly right, whether we start on the study of everyday life perspectivally from the outside in or from the inside out. This is a time when humility in ethnographic attempts seems especially appropriate.

How also can we do ethnographic reporting and analysis of policy? In considering this we can reflect on a term for the enterprise of ethnography that might have been used rather than *ethnekos*. The nineteenth-century inventors of the term "ethnography" could have used *paganos* rather than *ethnekos*, but they didn't. *Paganos* refers to those who live in the countryside—in wilderness or small villages. It contrasts with *politeia*, which concerns the situation of city-dwellers, the "civilized." In anthropology's attempt to differentiate itself from sociology, anthropological exotic ethnography was treated as if it were "paganography"—the study not only of "others," but the study of those "others" in the countryside by those who live in the city.

Fortunately for our attempts to use ethnography in modern societies, whether it was done intentionally or not, the choice of *ethnekos* by various of our founders as the root for ethnography gives etymological warrant for a breadth of reach in research today, for a focus on *ethnekos* entails the study of both large-scale and small-scale social aggregates—in both "non-civilized" and "civilized" circumstances. The *ethnoi* were not only country people—barbarians like the Thracians. They were also people living in even larger social groupings than the *'ellenoi*—Persians, Egyptians. These were "others" who were just as sophisticated as were the Hellenes in technology, architecture, military organization, and literature (although the Greeks might not have wanted to admit it to the last).

Today, as I usually say in my introductory lecture in anthropology of education, *anthropos* (humanity) lives right down the street, on the same block as we do, even next door. And the *ethnoi* are all around us. Indeed, they are us. For example, in the United States, Episcopalians of English descent are in fact just as "ethnic" as are Salvadoran or Vietnamese immigrants, even though the Episcopalians may not be so usually constructed as "ethnic" by their fellow Americans. The same is true of the elites who live in the most prestigious neighborhoods of Rio de Janeiro and the poor who live immediately up the hill from them in geographically contiguous *favelas*. Both are *ethnoi* relative to one another.

Having ruminated briefly on the implications of *paganos* and *ethnekos*, now let us consider *politeia*. Our term "policy" derives from this. As defined in the *Oxford English Dictionary*, "policy" in its archaic senses, refers to citizenship, government, constitution, and commonwealth. Indeed "polity" is listed as a synonym. "Policy" was also used to mean political sagacity or cunning, action that was prudent or expedient. Only after these senses of the term were listed, appearing in fifth place comes a definition that fits our modern, utilitarian sense of the word "policy": "a course of action adopted and pursued by a government, party, ruler, statesman, etc." Implied in that sense is the presence of alternative courses of action potentially available as options. When we say "making policy," we mean making choices from among a set of options. The simplest of these is a binary choice set—(1) keep on doing what we are doing now or (2) do something else.

If we were doing "paganography" rather than "ethnography" it would seem that we couldn't study "policy" at all. That is because of the conceptions of society and culture held by anthropology still as late as the 1960s, when I was a graduate student. The so-called "traditional" societies studied by anthropology (the division of academic labor having assigned the study of modern societies to sociology, political science, and history) were still seen as, in their (ideally) "untouched" state, very slowly changing. "Culture" was so integrated, so internally consistent, and social life was so homeostatic a process that change might not occur at all between generations. And that was a *good thing*. Not only because it left "pure" cases for anthropologists to study (I am of the same academic generation as those who went in haste to the New Guinea Highlands and the Amazon River Delta in search of the "last" primitives) but also because interference through contact with "moderns" usually had disastrous consequences for traditional societies. Look at the cargo cults in Melanesia and the Ghost Dance in the American Southwest. "Just stay as beautiful as you are" was the plea. Such were the consequences of too loosely construed cultural relativism, synchronic ethnography, and structural-functional social theory. Not 100% wrong, but at least only half right.

The intellectual terrain and its horizons look quite different today, and I think that is not just because of increasing cultural diffusion since World War II, the growth of mass media and new information technology, and economic "globalization." It appears now that even in small-scale nonliterate societies there was more social change (and reflective awareness) going on than met the early-twentieth-century anthropologist's eye. Then it was possible to think that "policy" choices were never made outside modern societies—in a traditional community people were culturally uniform, shared the same power interests, and conducted daily life on automatic pilot, as directed by implicit and explicit culture, which changed little from generation to generation. Even the simplest binary policy choice set (do it the same or do it differently) would seem to be beyond the ken of such people. Like the Energizer Bunny they just kept on keeping on. "If it ain't broke, don't fix it."

Now we realize that view did not account adequately for the social processes at work in traditional societies, let alone so-called "modern" ones. With our eyes now focused on everybody's borderlands and hybridity, we can see that relatively "traditional" people are (and in the past must also have been) more tactically pragmatic, more driven by political interests, and more innovative than conventional exotic ethnography gave them credit for. We also see that "modern" people are more "tribal" in their formal and informal decision making than they may appear to be at first glance. The limits of rational choice theory become increasingly apparent empirically, in the wake of what has been happening in the Balkans, in worldwide migration movements and capital flows, and in the wake of the events of September 11, 2001. Ethnicity, religion, mother tongue, gender, and age-group interests, working in combination with social class but not simply reducible to class interests, all visibly relate to differences in the allocation of power within society in complex ways within processes of social reproduction involving a continual interplay between continuity and change. Social transformation, finally, should be of as much theoretical interest to anthropology today as social stasis used to be.

I wish that I could say that anthropology of education was the first sub-field to move anthropology more generally to confront directly a total contemporary world in which *anthropos* lives and works everywhere, even in high-rise apartment buildings and on the floors of stock exchanges. I don't think that's the way it happened. Even though the anthropology of education got to the modern world first, the rest of social and cultural anthropology wasn't paying attention then. But for whatever reasons, some anthropologists can now see why it makes sense to study what people think of as deliberate attempts at policy choice making, as those attempts are taking place continually in every society and local community in the world.

Given the anthropological imagination's most fundamental "gift"—that of an ethnological, cross-cultural comparative awareness which leads us not to take first glances literally and surface appearances for granted—we can consider and portray "policy" in its articulation and implementation as not only rational but (formally speaking) irrational, not only deliberate but nondeliberate, not only a matter of social engineering but also of opportunistic social bricolage, not only working from top down but from bottom up and midway between. Policy decisions are about options within choice sets that are themselves socioculturally framed and that on some days are tipped one way rather than another by technical information, on other days are tipped by brute power interests, and yet on other days by quasi-religious or literally religious leaps of faith or by whiffs (and more than whiffs) of race, ethnicity, language, and gender. There is as much folk ontology underpinning the jockeyings for influence that go on in a local school faculty or central government educational ministry (and in the uncritical commitment to "high stakes" accountability testing manifested in current public discourse on educational reform in the United States) as there is in the witchcraft-avoidance strategies of a community of Evans-Pritchard's Azande. "Policy" is something done by urban and rural villagers and disestablished nomads out on the periphery, in circumstances of rural and urban poverty and of societal invisibility and stigma—in other words, by various kinds of *paganoi*—as well as it is being done by cosmopolitan elites whose knowledge and *habitus* are valorized and who reside at the core of the *polis* with their hands on the levers of modern state power or on those of multinational corporate entities. And all policy decision and action, whether done locally or globally, is done from some "native's point of view." Except in very extreme cases, groups of people don't deliberately make self-destructive policy decisions, even though that may be the unintended consequence of their decisions.

Thus policy processes, as crucial and ubiquitous arenas of human choice and action, would seem ripe for study by means of ethnography. And using education policy decisions as a lens through which contemporary social and cultural processes within and across societies are concentrated and within which social and cultural interests and assumptions are contested, would seem to be a fruitful place to situate ethnographic fieldwork as the study of *anthropos*. It could also improve the design and conduct of educational efforts, formal and informal. Ethnographic fieldwork is inveterately local, always considering the doings and meaning-perspectives of a particular set of social actors. But in today's world, in every place, just as the personal is also political so the local also extends to the global and back again.

The scope of topics across the chapters in this volume seems to confirm what I just said about the appropriateness of ethnography for the study of education policymaking and the relevance of such a substantive focus for anthropological inquiry and positive change in educational practices. Whether one is considering the social construction of cultural notions of difference, similarity, and civility, or the conduct of professional performance evaluation, or attempts to implement nongraded schools, or attempts at national-scale implementation of centrally mandated educational policies (now not only an issue in Latin America but in Anglophone North America), or the use of anthropological perspectives by local educational practitioners in action research—ethnography as inquiry process rather than as report—we can see that the critical study of education policy by means of ethnographic perspectives and methods is both possible and informative. We can also see that the promise of ethnographic research in formal education policy formation may lie more in the ways such research can help policymakers break out of self-defeating and short-sighted utilitarian frameworks than in the use of ethnography as "realist snapshots" while staying within the conventional cultural assumptions of simple cost-benefit analysis and means-ends rationality that underlie the professional world of elite policymakers and their "wonk" specialists and lobbyists. We can also see how ethnography as action research can help those "street level" policymakers who are educational practitioners (and potentially also those who are parents and other local educational stakeholders) make decisions more wisely.

What remains is for anthropologically oriented ethnographers of education policy processes to develop a rhetoric that will persuade elite policymakers and the professional policy community (who in their daily practices create and maintain the conventional policy worldview) that what their kind of ethnography has to offer will be of benefit for policy formation and the improvement of education, rather than making things worse for policymakers and educators. That's a tall order—how to do that without selling out and blunting the critical edge that ethnography can bring to education policy deliberation? I don't presume to advise on how to achieve that aim. But I expect that progress toward it will be made by the authors whose work has been presented here as well as by those who read this work and find it inspiring. They are undertaking a long march, but one which seems to have been well worth beginning.

Index

About the Contributors

RAFAEL ÁVILA PEÑAGOS is professor and researcher at the Universidad Pedagógica Nacional (UPN) in Bogotá, Colombia. He earned his master's degree in university management from the Universidad de los Andes, Bogotá, and his doctorate in sociology from the Catholic University of Louvaine, Belgium. His professorship is in the specialty of social research theories, methods, and techniques (ICFES-UPN). He is also a research project evaluator at COLCIENCIAS and an advisor for ALUNA (Abraham Lincoln School Research Project), both in Bogotá, Colombia. His latest books include *Organization and Management in Research at the University* (1998) and *The Utopia of the Institutional Educational Projects in the School Labyrinth* (1999).

GRACIELA BATALLÁN is full professor and researcher at the Department and Institute of Anthropological Sciences, School of Philosophy and Letters, University of Buenos Aires, Argentina, where she is also a doctoral candidate. She was instrumental in establishing anthropology of education as a formal field of study in Argentina, and has published widely in books and journals such *Cuadernos de Antropología Social*, *El Niño y la Escuela*, and *Educational Qualitative Research in Latin America*.

ISABELA CABRAL FÉLIX DE SOUSA earned her bachelor's and professional degrees in psychology at the State University of Rio de Janeiro, Brazil, and her doctoral degree in international education at the University of Southern California. She has been working since 1996 as a research fellow of CNP at LEAS-IOC, Oswaldo Cruz Foundation, Rio de Janeiro. Her research interests are in health education, women's education, and social development.

SANDRA L. CADE currently teaches at Olivet College in Michigan. Before that, she was senior research associate at the David C. Anchin Center, University of South Florida–Tampa, where she was engaged in an NSF-sponsored team evaluation of the Urban Systems Initiative reform of mathematics and science education in Chicago, El Paso, Memphis, and Miami. A doctoral candidate in educational leadership and policy studies and curriculum studies at Indiana University–Bloomington, her research focuses on immigrant education, professional development, and the role of mothers in home-school relations.

MARINA CAMARGO ABELLO is a psychologist at the Universidad Javeriana in Bogotá, Colombia. She earned her master's degree in educational and social development from CINDE, a unit of the Universidad Pedagógica Nacional (UPN). She is currently a doctoral candidate at the CINDE–Universidad de Manizales, and works for Bogotá's ministry of education on developing policy for the improvement of primary and secondary education. She has 22 years of experience in education working as a teacher, advisor, and researcher. She has published several books, including *The Utopia of the Institutional Educational Projects in the School Labyrinth* and *Innovation and Social Change* (co-author in both cases).

MARGARET CONTRERAS, since returning from years in Colombia, has served as a bilingual educator and advisor to international students for about a decade. She has worked at several secondary schools, both public and private, and she has worked with students from around the world. She specializes in culturally relevant pedagogy, and she particularly enjoys working with adolescents.

PETER DEMERATH has an M.A. in cultural anthropology from the University of Pennsylvania and an Ed.D. in educational research from the University of Massachusetts at Amherst. He is assistant professor of education in the School of Educational Policy and Leadership at the Ohio State University. His research interests include the comparative study of student class cultures, school-university partnerships, and urban education. His publications have appeared in *Comparative Education Review* and the *American Journal of Education*.

ANA PATRICIA ELVIR is a doctoral student at the Harvard Graduate School of Education. She holds a master's degree in international and comparative education from Indiana University. Her research interests include educational reform in Central America from a nongovernmental perspective, the role of universities in basic education teacher training in Central America, and pedagogies that can help economically and socially disadvantaged children to learn in an effective way.

FREDERICK ERICKSON is George Kneller Professor of Anthropology of Education in the Graduate School of Education and Information Studies, University of California at Los Angeles (UCLA). He has been a fellow at the Center for Advanced Study in the Behavioral Sciences in Stanford, California, and received the George and Louise Spindler Award for Outstanding Scholarly Contributions to Educational Anthropology. He has published widely in numerous journals and books, including *Human Development*, the *Encyclopedia of Educational Research*, and the *Handbook of Research on Teaching*.

BARBARA GREYBECK has been a professor in the Department of Educational Studies at the University of Guadalajara and the coordinator of graduate programs in education at the ITESM (Monterrey Institute of Technology), Campus Guadalajara, since 1996. She is currently an associate professor at Texas A&M International University in the College of Education and is an active member of the Texas A&M University System's Academy for Educator Development. She has been involved with research on such diverse topics as biliteracy in elementary school children, teacher preparation, and the development of critical thinking in university students.

BRADLEY A.U. LEVINSON is associate professor of education in the Department of Educational Leadership and Policy Studies, School of Education, Indiana University, where he also holds an adjunct appointment in the Department of Anthropology. He is editor of *Policy as Practice* (with Margaret Sutton), *The Cultural Production of the Educated Person* (with Douglas E. Foley and Dorothy C. Holland), and *Schooling the Symbolic Animal*, and author of *We Are All Equal: Student Culture and Identity at a Mexican Secondary School, 1988–1998*. His articles have appeared in *Anthropology and Education Quarterly*, *Comparative Education Review*, *American Anthropologist*, and the *Journal of Contemporary Ethnography*. Most recently he has turned his attention to developing an ethnographic approach to the study of public policy and public spheres, especially in relation to new immigrants in Indiana schools and communities and to the study of civic education reform in Mexico.

PATRICIA MEDINA MELGAREJO is a researcher at the Universidad Pedagógica Nacional de Mexico (UPN) and a professor at the Universidad Nacional Autónoma de México (School of Philosophy and Literature, Department of Pedagogy), both in Mexico City. She obtained her master's degree in social sciences, specializing in education, from the Departamento de Investigaciones Educativas (CINVESTAV-IPN) in Mexico City. She has published widely on teaching and ethnographic research.

ANA PADAWER has her professional degree in anthropological sciences and is a doctoral candidate in anthropology in the School of Philosophy and Letters at the Universidad de Buenos Aires, Argentina. She currently serves as an instructor and researcher at the aforementioned school as well as in the Ministry of Education of the city of Buenos Aires. The topics of her recent research include social inequality and alternative educational proposals for primary school, school government and democracy, gender perspectives on power and authority in primary schools, public policies for at-risk youth, and the functions of school supervision. She has published in the book *Estado y Sociedad: Las Nuevas Reglas del Juego* and the journal *Cuadernos de Antropología Social*.

ELSIE ROCKWELL is titular professor in the Departamento de Investigaciones Educativas of the Center for Research and Advanced Studies in Mexico City, from which she holds a doctorate in educational research. She also holds a master's degree in history from the University of Chicago and studied anthropology at the National University in Mexico. One of the founders of the field of educational ethnography in Latin America, she has published widely, in both Spanish and English, in journals such as *Human Development, Educational Foundations, Anthropology and Education Quarterly, Infancia y Aprendizaje*, and *Cultural Dynamics*, and books such as *The Cultural Production of the Educated Person* and *Language, Literacy and Power*. She has also edited or written books such as *Escuela y Clases Populares, La Escuela, Lugar del Trabajo Docente*, and *La Escuela Cotidiana*.

ETELVINA SANDOVAL FLORES is a researcher at the Universidad Pedagógica Nacional de México (UPN). She obtained her master's degree in social sciences, specializing in education, from the Departamento de Investigaciones Educativas (CINVESTAV-IPN) in Mexico City, and a doctorate in pedagogy from the National Autonomous University of Mexico (UNAM). The subjects of her ethnographic research include elementary education, methods of instruction, the school institution, the working conditions of teachers, gender and education, secondary schools, and teacher training. Her most recent publication is entitled *La Trama de la Escuela Secundaria; Institución, Relaciones y Saberes* (2000).

GEOFFREY WALFORD is professor of education policy at Oxford University. His research interests include faith-based schooling, private education, education policy, and research methodology. His most recent books include *Policy and Politics in Education* (2000), *Doing Qualitative Educational Research* (2001), and two edited collections on Emile Durkheim.

STANTON WORTHAM teaches in the Educational Leadership Division at the University of Pennsylvania Graduate School of Education, with a specialization in education, culture, and society. He earned his doctorate from the Committee on Human Development at the University of Chicago. He is a linguistic anthropologist of education whose work explores how the sociocultural aspects of language use can facilitate learning and identity development in educational settings. He has also developed analytic methods of discourse for studying the interactional functions of language use. All of his work explores how speech both represents content and establishes interactional positions for speakers, and how these two functions interrelate.